CHINA'S FOREIGN ECONOMIC LEGISLATION

Vol. IV

中国对外经济法规汇编

第 四 辑

FOREIGN LANGUAGES PRESS BEIJING

First edition   1991

ISBN 0-8351-2410-X
ISBN 7-119-01263-0

Copyright 1991 by Foreign Languages Press, Beijing, China

Published by Foreign Languages Press
24 Baiwanzhuang Road, Beijing 100037, China

Printed by Beijing Foreign Languages Printing House
19 Chegongzhuang Xilu, Beijing 100044, China

Distributed by China International Book Trading Corporation
21 Chegongzhuang Xilu, Beijing 100044, China
P.O. Box 399, Beijing, China

Printed in the People's Republic of China

PUBLISHER'S NOTE

Volume IV of this book contains twenty-six laws and regulations promulgated between January 1985 and April 1987. In application, any discrepancy between the English translation and the original Chinese text shall be resolved in favour of the Chinese edition issued by the Chinese government, as for previous volumes.

CONTENTS
目　　录

RULES FOR IMPLEMENTATION OF THE PATENT LAW OF THE PEOPLE'S REPUBLIC OF CHINA

(Approved by the State Council and Promulgated by the Patent Office of the People's Republic of China on January 19, 1985)

CHAPTER I GENERAL PROVISIONS

Article 1   These Implementing Rules are drawn up in compliance with the Provisions of Article 68 of the Patent Law of the People's Republic of China (hereinafter referred to as "the Patent Law").

Article 2   "Invention" mentioned in the Patent Law means any new technical solution relating to a product or a process of the improvement thereof.

"Utility model" mentioned in the Patent Law means any new technical solution relating to the shape or the structure, or their combination, of a product fit for practical use.

"Industrial design" mentioned in the Patent Law means any new design of the shape, pattern or colour, or their combination, of a product that creates an aesthetic feeling and is fit for industrial application.

Article 3   Any proceedings provided for by the Patent Law and these Implementing Rules shall be conducted in written form.

Article 4   Any document submitted under the Pa-

1

tent Law and these Implementing Rules shall be in Chinese. The standard scientific and technical terms shall be used if there are such prescribed by the State. Where there is no generally accepted translation in Chinese for a foreign name or scientific or technical term, the original language shall be attached.

Where any certificate or certified document submitted in accordance with the Patent Law or these Implementing Rules is in a foreign language, the Patent Office may request a Chinese translation be submitted within a specified time.

Article 5 For any document sent by mail by the Patent Office to an addressee residing in any municipality under the people's governments of provinces, autonomous regions, or the Central Government, the eighth day from the date of mailing shall be presumed to be the receiving date. For an addressee residing in any other place in China, the receiving date shall be the sixteenth day from the date of mailing.

For any document by mail sent to the Patent Office by an applicant in China, the mailing date indicated by the postmark shall be the filing date. If the postmark on the envelope is not legible, the date on which the Patent Office receives the document shall be presumed to be the filing date, except where the mailing date is proved by the applicant.

Article 6 The first day of any time limit prescribed in the Patent Law or these Implementing Rules shall not be counted. Where a time limit is counted by year or by month, it shall expire on the corresponding day of the last month; if there is no corresponding day in that month, the time limit shall expire on the last day of that month.

If the time limit falls on an official holiday, it shall expire on the first working day after that official holiday.

Article 7 Where a time limit prescribed in the Patent Law or these Implementing Rules or specified by the Patent Office is not met because of force majeure or any other justified reason, the applicant, the patentee or any other interested party may, within one month from the day on which the impediment is removed, state the reasons and request an extension of the time limit, with the exception of time limits prescribed in Article 24, Article 29, the first sentence of Article 41, Article 45 and Article 61 of the Patent Law.

Before the expiration of any time limit specified by the Patent Office an applicant who, for justified reasons, wishes to have the time limit extended may, with relevant proof, so request the Patent Office.

Article 8 Where the invention or creation is for the national defence system and relates to national security, the application for a patent shall be filed with the patent organization set up by the competent department of science and technology of national defence. The Patent Office shall base its decision on examination of the application presented by the said patent organization.

Article 9 Except as provided in the preceeding article, the Patent Office, after receiving a patent application relating to national security, shall send it to the department concerned of the State Council for examination. The said department shall, within four months from receipt of the application, send a report on the results of the examination to the Patent Office. Where the invention or creation for which a patent is applied for is required to be kept secret, the Patent Office shall handle it as an application for patent relating to national security and notify the applicant accordingly.

Article 10 "A job-related invention or creation made in the course of performing the tasks of the unit concerned," mentioned in Article 6 of the Patent Law, refers to any invention or creation made:

(1) In the course of performing one's own duty;

(2) In the execution of any task, other than one's own duty, entrusted to one by the unit to which one belongs;

(3) Within one year from one's resignation, retirement or change of work, where the invention or creation relates to one's own duty or other task entrusted to one by the unit to which one previously belonged.

"Material means of such unit," mentioned in Article 6 of the Patent law, refers to the unit's money, equipment, spare parts, raw materials, or technical data that are not to be disclosed to the public.

Article 11 "Inventor" or "designer," mentioned in the Patent Law, refers to any person who has made a creative contribution to the substantive features of the invention or creation. Any person who, during the course of accomplishing the invention or creation, is responsible only for organization work, offers facilities for making use of material means, or takes part in other auxiliary functions shall not be considered as an inventor or designer.

Article 12 Two or more applicants who apply separately on the same day for a patent for an identical invention or creation shall as provided for in Article 9 of the Patent Law, after receiving notification from the

Patent Office, decide through mutual consultation who shall be entitled to file the application.

Article 13 A patentee who has concluded contract for exploitation of the patent with a unit or individual shall, within three months from the entry into force of the contract, submit the contract to the Patent Office for record.

Article 14. "The patent agency," mentioned in Article 19, Section 1, and Article 20 of the Patent Law, refers to the China Council for the Promotion of International Trade, the Shanghai Patent Agency, the China Patent Agent Ltd. and other patent agencies designated by the State Council.

Article 15 Any applicant that appoints a patent agency for filing an application for a patent with the Patent Office or for dealing with other patent matters shall submit a power of attorney indicating the scope of the power entrusted.

CHAPTER II APPLICATIONS FOR PATENTS

Article 16 Anyone who applies for a patent shall submit to the Patent Office application documents in duplicate.

Article 17 "Other items," mentioned in Article 26, Section 2, of the Patent Law, refer to:

(1) The nationality of the applicant;

(2) Where the applicant is an enterprise or other organization, the name of the country in which the applicant has its principal business office;

(3) Where the applicant has appointed a patent agency, the name and address of the patent agency and

the name of the patent agent;

(4) Where the applicant is a unit, the name of its representative;

(5) Where the priority of an earlier application is claimed, the relevant matters that should be indicated;

(6) The signature or the seal of the applicant;

(7) A list of the documents constituting the application;

(8) A list of the documents appending the application.

Where there are two or more applicants and they have not appointed a patent agency, they shall designate a common representative; if no common representative is designate, the applicant first named in the request shall be considered as the common representative.

Where a patent application for an industrial design is filed, the request shall, when necessary, also contain a brief description of the design.

Article 18 Except where the nature of the invention or utility model calls for a different type and order of presentation, the description in a patent application of an invention or utility model shall, in the following order:

(1) State the title of the invention or utility model as it appears in the request;

(2) Specify the technical field to which the invention or utility model relates;

(3) Indicate existing technology that, so far as is known to the applicant, can be regarded a useful for understanding, inspecting and examining the invention or utility model and cite the documents reflecting such technology;

(4) Specify the task the invention or utility model is designed to fulfil;

(5) Describe the invention or utility model in a manner sufficiently clear and complete as to enable a person having ordinary skill in the art to construct it;

(6) State the merits or effective results of the invention or utility model as compared with existing technology;

(7) Briefly describe the figures in the drawings, if any;

(8) Describe in detail the best method contemplated by the applicant for carrying out the invention or utility model with reference to the drawings, if any.

The description of the invention or utility model may contain chemical or mathematical formulae but no commercial advertising.

Article 19 The same sheet of drawings may contain several figures of the invention or utility model. The figures shall be numbered consecutively in Arabic numerals and arranged in numerical order.

The scale and the distinctness of the drawings shall be such that a reproduction with a linear reduction in size to two thirds would still enable all details to be distinguished clearly.

Reference signs used in the drawings of an application shall be consistent throughout. Reference signs not appearing in the description of the invention or utility model shall not appear in the drawings.

The drawings shall contain only indispensable explanatory notes.

Article 20 The written patent claim shall define clearly and concisely the matter for which protection is sought in terms of the technical features of the invention or utility model.

If several claims are included in one written patent claim, they shall be numbered consecutively in Arabic numerals.

The technical terminology used in the claims shall be consistent with that used in the description. The claims may contain chemical or mathematical formulae but no drawings. They shall not, except where absolutely necessary, contain such references to the description or drawings "as described in part. . . of the description," or "as illustrated in figure. . . of the drawings."

Article 21 Patent claims may be independent or dependent.

An independent patent claim shall outline the essential technical contents of an invention or utility model and describe the indispensable technical features constituting the invention or utility model.

A dependent claim, relying on reference to one or more other claims, shall refer only to the preceding claim or claims.

Article 22 Except where the nature of the invention or utility model calls for other forms of expression, an independent claim shall be presented in the following form:

(1) A preamble portion, indicating the technical fields to which the invention or utility model pertains and the technical features of the existing technology that relate closely to the subject matter of the invention or utility model;

(2) A characterizing portion, stating, in such words as "the invention (or utility model) is characterized by

. . ." or similarly concise expressions, the technical features of the invention or utility model, which, in combination with features stated in the preamble portion, constitute the technical features calling for protection.

Each invention or utility model shall be allowed only one inlependent claim, which shall precede all the dependent claims relating to the same invention or untility model.

Article 23 Except where the nature of the invention or utility model calls for other forms of position, a dependent claim shall be presented in the following form:

(1) A reference portion, indicating the serial number(s) of the patent claims referred to. Where possible, the reference to the serial number shall be placed at the beginning of the claim(s).

(2) A characterizing portion, which, by stating the additional technical features of the invention or utility model, further defines the technical features cited in the reference portion.

Dependent claims referring to more than two other claims shall not serve as basis for any other multiple dependent claims.

Article 24 The abstract shall indicate the technical field to which the invention or utility model belongs, the technical problems to be solved, the essential technical features and the use or uses of the invention or utility model. The abstract may, where applicable, contain the chemical formula or the figure that best characterizes the invention or utility model. The complete text of the abstract shall contain preferably not more than 200 words.

Article 25 Where patent application is for an in-

vention that involves a microbiological process or product
and the use of a microorganism not available to the
public, the applicant shall, in addition to the other requirements provided for in the Patent Law and these
Implementing Rules.

(1) Deposit a sample of the microorganism with a
depository institution designated by the Patent Office
before the date of filing or, at the latest, on the date of
filing;

(2) Include in the application document relevant
information about the characteristics of the microorganism;

(3) Indicate in the Request the scientific name
(with its Latin name) of the microorganism, the name of
the depository institution, the date on which the sample
of the microorganism was deposited and the file number
of•the deposit and submit a receipt of deposit from that
institution.

Article 26 After the publication of a patent application for an invention relating to a microorganism,
any unit or individual intending to use the said microorganism for the purpose of experiment shall make a request
to the Patent Office containing the following:

(1) The name and address of the unit or individual
making the request;

(2) A pledge by the requesting unit or individual
not to make the microorganism available to any other
party;

(3) A pledge to use the microorganism for experi-
mental purposes only before grant of the patent right.

Article 27 The size of drawings or photographs
of an industrial design submitted in accordance with the

provisions of Article 27 of the Patent Law shall not be smaller than 3 cm×8 cm. or larger than 19 cm× 27 cm.

The applicant may submit for each design one or more drawings or photographs from different angles, sides or positions so as to clearly show the object for which protection is sought. The applicant shall indicate on each drawing or photograph the angle, side or position and mark on the top left and right of the back of the drawing or photograph its consecutive number and the name of the applicant respectively.

Article 28 Where a patent application for an industrial design seeking protection of colours is filed, a drawing or photograph in colour and a drawing or photograph in black and white shall be submitted, and a statement of the colours for which protection is sought shall be made on the drawing or photograph in black and white.

Article 29 Where the Patent Office finds it necessary, it may require the applicant for a patent for an industrial design to submit a sample or model of the product incorporating the design. The volume of the sample or model submitted shall not exceed 30 cm × 30 cm × 30 cm, and its weight shall not surpass 15 kilogrammes. Perishable, fragile or dangerous articles may not be submitted as samples or models.

Article 30 Academic or technological conferences mentioned in item (2) of Article 24 of the Patent Law mean any academic or technological conference or conference organized or called by a competent department of the State Council or by a national academic or technological association.

Article 31 Where a patent application falls under

the provisions of item (1) or item (2) of Artcile 24 of
the Patent Law, the applicant shall, upon filing the application, make a declaration and, within two months
from the date of filing, submit a certificate issued by the
unit that organized the international exhibition or academic or technological conference, stating that the invention
or creation was in fact exhibited or disclosed there and
also the date of its exhibition or disclosure.

Where a patent application falls under the provision
of item (3) of Article 24 of the Patent Law, the Patent
Office may, when necessary, require the applicant to submit relevant proof.

Article 32 Where the applicant for a patent for
an invention claims a right of priority, it or he shall,
within 15 months from the date on which the application was first filed in a foreign country, submit the filing
number accorded by that country.

Article 33 Where two or more priorities are claimed for a patent application, the earliest priority date shall
prevail.

Article 34 Where a patent application is filed
by a foreigner, foreign enterprise or other foreign organization having no habitual residence or business office in China, the Patent Office may, in case of doubt,
require the applicant to submit the following documents:

(1) A certificate concerning the nationality of the
applicant;

(2) A certificate concerning the site of the headquarters of a foreign enterprise or other foreign organization;

(3) A testimonial showing that the country to which
the foreigner, foreign enterprise or other foreign organiza-

tion belongs recognizes that Chinese citizens or units are, under the same conditions applied to its nationals, entitled to patent rights and other related rights in that country.

Article 35 According to the provisions of Article 31, Section 1, of the Patent Law, the patent claims in a patent application for an invention or utility model may be any of the following:

(1) Two or more independent claims for the same category of product or process that cannot be included in one claim;

(2) Independent claims for a product and for a process adapted especially for the manufacture of the product;

(3) Independent claims for a product and for the use of the product;

(4) Independent claims for a product, for a process adapted especially for the manufacture of the product, and for the use of the product;

(5) Independent claims for a product, for a process adapted especially for the manufacture of the product, and for an apparatus designed especially for carrying out the process;

(6) Independent claims for a process and for an apparatus designed especially for carrying out the process;

(7) Independent claims for a process and for a product directly manufactured by carrying out the process.

Article 36 Where a patent application for an industrial design contains two or more designs in accordance with the provisions of Article 31, Section 2, of the Patent Law, the designs shall be numbered consecutively and the products incorporating the designs shall be indicated in the written request of the application. The consecutive numbers shall be marked on the bottom left of the back of the drawings or photographs of the design.

Article 37 To withdraw a patent application the applicant shall submit to the Patent Office a declaration stating the title of the invention or creation, the filing number and the date of filing.

Where a declaration to withdraw a patent application is submitted after preparation for publication of the application documents has been completed by the Patent Office, the application shall be published as scheduled.

CHAPTER III EXAMINATION AND APPROVAL OF PATENT APPLICATION

Article 38 In any of the following situations an examiner or a member of the Patent Re-examination Board shall, on his own initiative or upon the request of the applicant or any other interested party, be excluded from exercising his function:

(1) Where he is a close relative of the applicant or the patent agent;

(2) Where he has an interest in the application for patent;

(3) Where he has other relations with the applicant or the patent agent that might influence the impartial examination of the application.

Where a member of the Patent Re-examination Board has taken part in the examination of the application, the provisions of the preceding paragraph shall apply.

Article 39 Upon the receipt of a request, a description (a drawing being indispensable for a utility model) and one or more claims in a patent application for an invention or utility model, or a request and one or more drawings or photographs showing the industrial design in an application for a patent for an industrial design, the Patent Office shall record the filing date and filing number and notify the applicant thereof.

Article 40 If the application documents do not contain a request, description or patent claims, or if they are not in conformity with the provisions of Article 27 of the Patent Law, the Patent Office shall declare the application unacceptable and notify the applicant accordingly.

Article 41 Where the description of an invention mentions that it contains "explanatory notes to the drawing" but the drawings are missing, the applicant shall, within the time limit specified by the Patent Office, either furnish the drawings or make a declaration for deletion of "explanatory notes to the drawings." If the drawings are submitted later, the date of their delivery or mailing to the Patent Office shall be the filing date of the application; if the mention of "explanatory notes to the drawings" is to be deleted, the initial date of filing shall be the filing date of the application.

Article 42 Where a patent application contains two or more inventions, utility models or industrial designs, the applicant may at any time before announcement of the application under Article 39 or Article 40 of the Patent Law or after the said announcement, if the Patent Office considers the filing of separate applications justified, submit the Patent Office a request for division of the application and divide it on its or his own initiative into several applications.

If the Patent Office finds that a patent application

is not in comformity with the provisions of Article 31 of
the Patent Law and Article 35 of these Implementing
Rules, it shall request the applicant to divide the application within a specified time limit. If, without any justified
reason, the applicant fails to make any response within
the time limit, the application shall be deemed to have
been withdrawn.

Article 43 Divided applications filed in accordance with Article 42 of these Implementing Rules
may enjoy the filing date of the initial application, provided they do not go beyond the scope of the initial description.

Article 44 Where, upon preliminary examination,
the Patent Office finds that a patent application obviously
falls under Article 5 or Article 25 of the Patent Law or
is obviously not in conformity with Article 18 or Article
19 of the Patent Law or Article 2 of these Implementing
Rules, it shall request the applicant to present its or his
observations within a specified time limit. If the applicant, without any justified reason, fails to meet the
time limit for presenting observations, the application
shall be deemed to have been withdrawn.

Where, after the applicant has made the observations,
the Patent Office still finds that the application is obviously not in conformity with the provisions of the articles
cited in the preceding paragraph, the application shall be
rejected.

Article 45 Where the patent application has any
of the following deficiencies, the applicant shall, within
the time limit specified by the Patent Office, correct them:

(1) The request is not presented in the prescribed
form or the indications therein are not in conformity with

the requirements.

(2) The description and its drawings or the patent claims of the invention or utility model are not in conformity with the relevant provisions.

(3) The patent application for an invention or utility model does not contain an abstract.

(4) The drawings or photographs contained in a patent application for an industrial design are not in conformity with the relevant provisions.

(5) Where a patent agency is appointed, no power of attorney is submitted.

(6) The application contains other deficiencies calling for correction.

If the applicant, without justified reason, fails to meet the time limit for correcting the deficiencies, the application shall be deemed to have been withdrawn. If, after correction, the application is still not in conformity with the relevant provisions of the Patent Law or these Implementing Rules, it shall be rejected.

Article 45 If the applicant desires early publication of its or his application for patent for invention, request shall be made to the Patent Office. The Patent Office shall, after preliminary examination of the application, publish it immediately unless it is to be rejected.

Article 47 When indicating, in accordance with Article 27 of the Patent Law, the product incorporating the industrial design and the class to which that product belongs, the applicant shall refer to the classification of products for industrial designs published by the Patent Office. Where no indication or an incorrect indication of the class to which the product incorporating the industrial design belongs is made, the Patent Office may supply the indication or correct it.

Article 48 From the date of publication of a patent application for invention until the date of announcement of preliminary approval after examination as to substance, any person may submit to the Patent Office arguments, with the reasons thereof, as to the application's nonconformity with the provisions of the Patent Law.

Article 49 Where the applicant for a patent for invention cannot furnish, for justified reason, the documents concerning any investigation or the results of any examination under Article 36 of the Patent Law, it or he shall make a statement to that effect and submit the said documents when the results are available.

Article 50 When proceeding on its own initiative to examine a patent application for invention in accordance with the provisions of Article 35, Section 2, of the Patent Law, the Patent Office shall notify the applicant accordingly.

Article 51 Within a period of 15 months from the filing date, or when a request for examination as to substance is made, or in response to an objection, the applicant for a patent for invention may amend the description and the patent claims on its or his own initiative.

When an amendment of the description and the patent claims in a patent application for invention or utility model is made, a replacement sheet in prescribed form shall be submitted, unless the amendment concerns only the alteration, insertion or deletion of a few words.

Article 52 Within the period from the filing date until the date of announcement of the application for a patent, or when an objection is responded to, the patent applicant for a utility model or industrial design may amend the application on its or his own initiative. When an amendment is made, it shall not change the essential elements of the industrial design.

Article 53 As prescribed by the Patent Law, the conditions whereby a patent application shall be rejected by the Patent Office include the following:

(1) Where the application does not comply with the provisions of Article 3 of the Patent Law and Article 2 of these Implementing Rules;

(2) Where the application falls under the provisions of Article 5 or Article 25 of the Patent Law, or it does not comply with the provisions of Article 22 or Article 23 of the Patent Law;

(3) Where the applicant has no right to apply for patent according to the provisions of Article 6, Article 8 or Article 18 of the Patent Law, or cannot obtain a patent right according to the provisions of Article 9 of the Patent Law;

(4) Where the application does not comply with the provisions of Article 26, Section 3 or Section 4, or Article 31 of the Patent Law;

(5) Where the amendments to the application or the divided applications go beyond the scope of the initial description.

Article 54 The conditions whereby an objection may be filed under Article 41 of the Patent Law with regard to a patent application for an invention or utility model announced by the Patent Office include the following:

(1) Where the invention does not comply with the provisions of Article 3 of the Patent Law and Article 2,

Section 1, of these Implementing Rules or the utility model does not comply with the provisions of Article 3 of the Patent Law and Article 2, Section 2, of these Implementing Rules;

(2) Where the application falls under the provisions of Aritcle 5 or Article 25 of the Patent Law or it does not comply with the provisions of Article 22 of the Patent Law;

(3) Where the applicant has no right to apply for a patent according to Article 6, 8 or 18 of the Patent Law or the essential elements of an application have been taken from the descriptions, drawings, models, equipment, etc., of another person or from a process used by another person without his consent;

(4) Where the application does not comply with provisions of Article 26, Section 3 or Section 4, of the Patent Law;

(5) Where the amendments to the application or the divided applications go beyond the scope of the initial description.

Article 55   The conditions whereby objection may be filed under Article 41 of the Patent Law with regard to a patent application for an industrial design announced by the Patent Office include the following:

(1) Where the industrial design does not comply with the provisions of Article 3 of the Patent Law and Article 2, Section 3, of these Implementing Rules;

(2) Where the industrial design falls under the provisions of Article 5 of the Patent Law or does not comply with the provisions of Article 23 of the Patent Law;

(3) Where the applicant has no right to apply for a patent according to Article 6, 8 or 18 of the Patent Law

or cannot obtain a patent right according to Article 9 of the Patent Law, or the essential elements of the industrial design have been taken from the designs, drawings, photographs, articles or models of another person without his consent;

(4) Where amendments to the application have changed the essential elements of the industrial design.

Article 56   Anyone who files an objection in accordance with the provisions of Article 41 of the Patent Law shall submit the objection, with the reasons thereof, in duplicate to the Patent Office.

Article 57   Upon receipt of an objection the Patent Office shall examine it. Where an objection does not conform to prescribed requirements, the Patent Office shall notify the filer to rectify it within a specified time. If the objector fails to rectify the objection within the specified time the objection shall be deemed not to have been filed.

Where the reasons for objection are not stated or do not conform to the provisions of Article 54 or 55 of these Implementing Rules, the objection shall be declared unacceptable.

Article 58   The Patent Re-examination Board shall consist of experienced technical and legal experts designated by the Patent Office. The Director General of the Patent Office shall be the Director of the Board.

Article 59   If the applicant wishes re-examination by the Patent Re-examination Board in accordance with the provisions of Article 43, Section 1, of the Patent Law, it or he shall file a request for re-examination and state the reasons thereof, supported by relevant documents. The request and the supporting documents shall be in duplicate.

The applicant may amend the patent application when requesting re-examination, but the amendment shall be limited to that part of the application related to the decision for rejection.

Article 60 Where the request for re-examination does not comply with the prescribed form, the requester shall rectify it within the time limit fixed by the Patent Re-examination Board. If rectification is not made within the time limit, the request for re-examination shall be deemed to have been withdrawn.

Article 61 The Patent Re-examination Board shall send a request for re-examination to the original examiner for consideration. The Patent Re-examination Board shall decide as to the request's validity and notify the applicant accordingly.

Article 62 Where the Patent Re-examination Board finds after re-examination that the request does not comply with the provisions of the Patent Law, it shall invite the person who has made the request for re-examination to submit his arguments within a specified time. If, without justified reason, that person fails to meet the time limit, the request for re-examination shall be deemed to have been withdrawn.

Article 63 At any time before the Patent Re-examination Board makes known its decision on a request for re-examination, the requester may withdraw it.

Article 64 After deciding to grant a patent right, the Patent Office shall notify the applicant to pay the fee for a patent certificate and claim it within two months. Where the applicant fails to pay the fee within the time limit, it or he shall be deemed to have abandoned the right to obtain a patent.

CHAPTER IV   DECLARATION OF INVALIDATION OF PATENT RIGHT

Article 65   Anyone making a request for declaration of invalidation or part invalidation of a patent right, according to the provisions of Article 48 of the Patent Law, shall submit the request, with the reasons thereof, to the Patent Re-examination Board. Where necessary, relevant documents shall be submitted. The request and the relevant documents shall be in duplicate.

Article 66   Where the request for a declaration of invalidation of the patent right does not comply with the prescribed form, the requester shall rectify it within the time limit fixed by the Patent Re-examination Board. If rectification is not made within the time limit, the request for declaration of invalidation shall be deemed to have been withdrawn.

The provisions of Article 54 or 55 of these Implementing Rules shall be applied so far as reasons for declaration of invalidation of the patent right are concerned.

Where no reasons have been stated in the request for declaration of invalidation or where the reasons stated do not comply with the provisions of Article 54 or 55 of these Implementing Rules, the request shall be declared unacceptable.

Article 67   The Patent Re-examination Board shall send a copy of the request for declaration of invalidation of the patent right and a copy of the relevant documents to the patentee and invite it or him to present objections within a specified time. If the patentee, without justified reason, does not respond within the time limit, it or he shall be deemed to have no objection.

CHAPTER V COMPULSORY LICENSING TO UTILIZE A PATENT

Article 68 Any unit requesting, in accordance with the provisions of Article 52 of the Patent Law, or any patentee requesting, under Article 53 of the Patent Law, a compulsory license to utilize a patent for an invention or utility model shall submit to the Patent Office a request for a compulsory license, including supporting documents proving the failure of the party concerned to conclude a licensing contract with the patentee on reasonable terms. The request and the supporting documents shall be in duplicate.

Any unit requesting, in accordance with the provisions of Article 52 of the Patent Law, a compulsory license to utilize a patent for an invention or utility model shall at the same time furnish documents in duplicate to show that it is in a position to utilize the patent.

The Patent Office shall, upon receipt of the request for a compulsory license, invite the patentee concerned to present its or his opinion within a specified time; if the patentee, without justified reason, does not respond within the time limit, it or he shall be deemed to have no objection.

The Patent Office shall, after having examined the request for a compulsory license and the opinion of the patentee, make its decision and notify the unit or individual making the request and the patentee concerned.

Article 69 Any unit or individual, or any patentee,

requesting, in accordance with the provisions of Article 57 of the Patent Law, the Patent Office to adjudicate user fees shall submit a request for adjudication and furnish documents showing that the parties have not been able to conclude an agreement as to the amount of the fees. The patent office shall, after receipt of the request, make an adjudiction within three months and notify the parties accordingly.

CHAPTER VI REWARDS TO INVENTOR OR DESIGNER OF JOB-RELATED INVENTION AND CREATION

Article 70 "Rewards" mentioned in Article 16 of the Patent Law include monetary prizes and remuneration awarded to inventors and designers.

Article 71 Any unit holding a patent right shall, after the grant of the patent right, award to inventors or designers of a job-related invention or creation a sum of money as a prize. The prize money for a patent for invention shall not be less than 200 yuan; the prize for a patent for utility model or industrial design shall not be less than 50 yuan.

Where an invention or creation was made on the basis of an inventor's or designer's proposal adopted by the unit to which he belongs, after grant of the patent right, the unit holding it shall award him a liberal monetary prize.

Any enterprise holding a patent right may include the prize money in its production cost; any institution holding a patent right may disburse the prize money out of its operating expenses.

Article 72   After utilizing the patent within the duration of the patent right, any unit holding a patent right shall each year reward the inventor or designer with 0.5-2 percent of the increased after-tax profits for utilizing an invention or utility model or 0.05-0.2 percent of the increased after-tax profits for utilizing an industrial design, or the unit shall, referring to the said percentages, reward the inventor or designer with a lump sum of money.

Article 73   Where any unit holding a patent right for invention or creation authorizes other units or individuals to utilize its patent, it shall reward the inventor or designer with 5-10 percent of the after-tax user fees.

Article 74   The rewards provided for in this chapter shall all be disbursed out of the profits derived from the making of patented products or the use of a patented process or out of the fees obtained for utilization of patents. The rewards shall not be included in the normal bonus fund of the unit or be subject to the bonus tax, the inventor or designer shall pay tax for his income.

Article 75   Units under collective ownership and other enterprises may refer to the provisions in this chapter in giving prize money and rewards.

CHAPTER VII PATENT ADMINISTRATION AUTHORITY

Article 76   "The patent administration authority" in Article 60 of the Patent Law and in these Implementing Rules refers to the patent administration authority set up by the departments concerned of the State Council, the people's governments of the provinces, autonomous regions, municipalities directly under the Central Government, open cities and special economic zones.

Article 77 If, after publication of a patent application for invention and before the grant of the patent right, any unit or individual utilizes the invention without paying appropriate fees, the patentee may, after the grant of the patent right, request the patent administration authority to handle the matter or may directly bring suit in the people's court. The patent administration authority handling the matter shall have the power to decide whether the unit or individual shall pay appropriate fees within a specified time. Where any of the parties concerned is not satisfied with the decision of the said authority, it or he may bring suit in the people's court.

The provisions of the preceding paragraph shall apply mutatis mutandis with respect to a patent application for a utility model or industrial design.

Article 78 Where any dispute arises between an inventor or designer and the unit to which he belongs as to whether an invention or creation is a job-related invention or creation or whether a patent application is to be filed in terms of a job-related invention or creation, the inventor or designer may request the competent department at a higher level or the patent administration authority of the region in which the unit is located to handle the matter.

Article 79 Where parties to any transdepartmental or transregional infringement dispute request the patent administration authority to handle the matter, the said dispute shall be handled by the patent administration authority of the region in which the infringement has arisen or by the patent administration authority of the higher competent department of the infringing unit.

CHAPTER VIII   PATENT REGISTER AND
PATENT GAZETTE

Article 80   The Patent Office shall maintain a Patent Register in which shall be recorded the following matters relating to any patent right:

(1) Any grant of the patent right;

(2) Any assignment of the patent right;

(3) Any renewals of the term of the patent right;

(4) Any termination and invalidation of the patent right.

(5) Any compulsory license for utilization of the patent;

(6) Any changes in the name, nationality and address of the patentee.

Article 81   The Patent Office shall publish the Patent Gazette at regular intervals, publishing or announcing the following:

(1) Data contained in the request for a patent application;

(2) Abstract of the description of an invention or utility model;

(3)   Any request for examination as to substance of a patent application for invention and any decision made by the Patent Office to proceed on its own initiative to examine as to substance of a patent application for invention;

(4) Preliminary approval after examination of a patent application for invention and announcement of a patent for invention and announcement of a patent application for a utility model or design;

(5) Any rejection of a patent application;

(6) Any decision concerning an objection and any

amendment in a patent application;

(7) Any grant of a patent right;

(8) Any termination of a patent right;

(9) Any invalidation of a patent right;

(10) Any assignment of a patent right;

(11) Any grant of compulsory license for utilization of a patent;

(12) Any renewal of the term of a patent;

(13 Any withdrawal of a patent application and a patent application deemed to have been withdrawn or abandoned;

(14) Any change in the name or address of a patentee;

(15) Any notification of an applicant whose address is not known;

(16) Any other related matters.

The description, drawings and patent claims of a patent application for an invention or utility model and the drawings or photographs of a patent application for an industrial design shall be published together.

CHAPTER IX   FEES

Article 82   The fees to be paid when a patent application is filed with the Patent Office or for other procedures in the Patent Office are as follows:

(1) Application fee and application-sustaining fee;

(2) Examination fee, re-examination fee and objection fee;

(3) Annual fee;

(4) Handling fee for transacting other patent matters: renewal fee for a patent, fee for a change in the data,

patent certificate fee, fee for proof of priority, fee for a
request for declaration of invalidation, fee for a request for
a compulsory license, and fee for a request for adjudication on the user fee of a compulsory license.

The amount of the fees listed above shall be prescribed by the Patent Office separately.

Article 83 Fees provided for in the Patent Law
and in these Implementing Rules may be paid to the Patent
Office by bank or postal remittance. They may also be
paid directly to the Patent Office.

Where fees are paid by bank or postal remittance, the
applicant or the patentee shall indicate on the money order
the kind of fee, the title of the invention or creation, and
the filing number or the patent number. If no filing number or patent number has yet been accorded to the invention or creation, the date of application shall be indicated.

Where fees are paid by bank or postal remittance, the
date on which the remittance is made shall be the date of
payment.

Article 84 Where the application fee is not paid
at the time of filing or if the fee paid falls short of the
amount required, the Patent Office shall notify the applicant to pay the fee or make up the deficiency within one
month from the date of filing the application. If the fee is
not paid or the deficiency is not made up within the time
limit, the application shall be deemed to have been withdrawn.

Article 85 Where the prescribed fees are not paid
when the applicant requests examination as to substance
or re-examination or any person files an objection or requests an invalidation of a patent right, it or he may pay
the fees within 15 days from the date on which the request

is made or the objection filed but the date of payment may not exceed the time limit the Patent Law prescribes for the request for examination as to substance or re-examination or for an objection to be filed. If the payment is not made within the time limit, the request is deemed not to have been filed.

Article 86 Where the applicant for a patent for invention has not been granted a patent right within two years from the date of filing, the applicant shall pay a fee from the third year for sustaining the application. The first sustaining fee shall be paid within the first month of the third year. The subsequent sustaining fees shall be paid in advance within the month before expiration of the preceding year.

Article 87 The first annual fee shall be paid when the patent certificate is issued. Where the application's sustaining fee for the year has already been paid at the time of granting patent right, the patentee shall make up the difference between the two fees of that year. Subsequent annual fees shall be paid in advance within the month before expiration of the preceding year.

Article 88 Where the application's sustaining fee or the annual fee is not paid in due time by the applicant or the patentee, or the sustaining fee or the annual fee paid is insufficient, the Patent Office shall notify the applicant or the patentee to pay the fee or make up the deficiency within six months from expiration of the time limit within which the sustaining fee or the annual fee is to be paid. The applicant or the patentee shall at the same time pay a surcharge amounting to 25 percent of the sustaining fee or the annual fee. If the fees are not paid within the six months, the application shall be deemed to have been withdrawn or the patent right shall be deemed to have lapsed from expiration of the time limit within which the sustaining fee or the annual fee is to be paid.

Article 89 Where in accordance with the provisions of Article 45, Section 2, of the Patent Law the patentee requests renewal of the term of the patent for a utility model or industrial design, it or he shall make the request within six months before the term expires and at the same time pay the renewal fee. If at the expiration of the said period the patentee fails to pay the renewal fee, the request shall be deemed not to have been made.

Article 90 Any individual who files an application for a patent or has other matters to attend to and has difficulties in paying the various fees prescribed by Article 82 of these Implementing Rules may submit a request, according to prescriptions, to the Patent Office for a reduction or postponement of payment.

The conditions for reduction or postponement of payment shall be prescribed by the Patent Office.

CHAPTER X SUPPLEMENTARY PROVISIONS

Article 91 Anyone may, upon approval by the Patent Office, inspect or copy the files of the published or announced patent applications, the Patent Register and any relevant supporting documents.

Article 92 Any communication with the Patent Office shall be made in the form prescribed gy the Patent Office. It shall be signed or sealed by the applicant or its or his patent agent.

Article 93 Where documents or objects relating to a patent application or patent right are submitted to the

Patent Office, the number of the application or the patent and the title of the invention or creation shall be indicated. Documents or objects sent to the Patent Office by post must be registered.

Article 94 Any sheets constituting the patent application shall be typed or printed. All the characters shall be neat and clear, and they shall be free from any alterations. Only one side of the paper shall be used.

Drawings shall be in black ink and made with the aid of a drafting instrument. All lines in the drawings shall be uniformly thick and clear.

Article 95 The Patent Office shall be responsible for the interpretation of these Implementing Rules.

Article 96 These Implementing Rules shall enter into force as of April 1, 1985.

PATENT FEES

(unit: RMB¥)

1. Application fee for
   (1) Patent for invention   150
   (2) Patent for utility model   100
   (3) Patent for industrial design   80
2. Sustaining fee for patent application for invention, per year   100
3. Examination fee for a patent application for invention   400
4. Re-examination fee for
   (1) Patent application for invention   200
   (2) Patent application for utility model   100
   (3) Patent application for industrial design 80
5. Objection fee for

     (1) Patent for invention   30

     (2) Patent for utility model   20

     (3) Patent application for industrial design   20

6. Renewal fee for the term of a patent for a utility model or industrial design   100

7. Handling fee for making changes in data 10

8. Patent certificate fee for

     (1) Patent for invention   100

     (2) Patent for utility model   50

     (3) Patent for industrial design   50

9. Fee for proof of priority   20

10. Fee for a request for declaration of invalidation of

     (1) Patent for invention   300

     (2) Patent for utility model   200

     (3) Patent for industrial design   150

11. Fee for a request for a compulsory license for utilization of a

     (1) Patent for invention   300

     (2) Patent for utility model   200

12. Fee for a request for adjudication on user fee of a compulsory license   100

13. Annual fee for

     (1) Patent for invention

         From the 1st year to the 3rd year, per year   200

         From the 4th year to the 6th year, per year   300

         From the 7th year to the 9th year, per year   600

         From the 10th year to the 12th year, per year 1,200

         From the 13th year to the 15th year, per year 2,400

     (2) Patent for utility model

         From the 1st year to the 3rd year, per year   100

      From the 4th year to the 5th year, per year   200
      From the 6th year to the 8th year, per year   300
  (3) Patent for industrial design
      From the 1st year to the 3rd year, per year   50
      From the 4th year to the 5th year, per year   100
      From the 6th year to the 8th year, per year   200

Notes:

1.   Where the applicant or the patentee is a foreigner, any of the above-listed fees shall be paid in foreign currency according to the exchange rate at the time of payment.
2.   The ordinal number of years listed in Item 13 shall be counted from the filing date. The annual fee shall, beginning with the year in which the patent right was granted, be paid according to the amount prescribed for that year.

中华人民共和国专利法实施细则

（一九八五年一月十九日国务院批准，
一九八五年一月十九日中国专利局公布）

第一章　总　　则

第一条　根据《中华人民共和国专利法》（以下简称专利法）第六十八条的规定，制定本细则。

第二条　专利法所称的发明是指对产品、方法或者其改进所提出的新的技术方案。

专利法所称的实用新型是指对产品的形状、构造或者其结合所提出的适于实用的新的技术方案。

专利法所称的外观设计是指对产品的形状、图案、色彩或者其结合所作出的富有美感并适于工业上应用的新设计。

第三条　专利法和本细则规定的各种手续，应当以书面形式办理。

第四条　依照专利法和本细则规定提交的各种文件应当使用中文。对于国家有统一规定的科技术语，应当采用规范词。外国人名、地名和科技术语无统一中文译文的，应当注明原文。

依照专利法和本细则规定提交的各种证件和证明文件是外文的，专利局可以要求在指定期间内附送中文译本。

第五条　专利局邮寄的各种文件，送达地是省和自治区辖市以上城市的，自文件发出之日起满七日，其他地区满十五日，推定为收件人收到文件之日。

申请人向专利局邮寄的各种文件，以寄出的邮戳日为递交日。如信封上寄出的邮戳日不清晰，除申请人能提出证明外，以专利局收到日为递交日。

第六条　专利法和本细则规定的各种期限的第一日不计算在期限内。期限以年或者月计算的，以其最后一月的相应日为期限届满日；该月无相应日的，以该月最后一日为期限届满日。

期限届满日是法定节假日的，以节假日后的第一个工作日为期限届满日。

第七条　申请人、专利权人或者其他利害关系人因不可抗拒的事由或者其他正当理由而耽误专利法或者本细则规定的期限，或者专利局指定的期限的，在障碍消除后一个月内，可以说明理由，请求顺延期限。但专利法第二十四条、第二十九条、第四十一条第一句、第四十五条和第六十一条规定的期限除外。

在专利局指定的期限届满前，申请人因有正当理由要求延长期限的，应当向专利局提出请求，并附具有关的证明。

第八条　国防系统各单位申请专利的发明创造，涉及国家安全需要保密的，其专利申请由国防科技主管部门设立的专利机构受理，专利局应当根据该机构的审查意见作出决定。

第九条　除前条规定外，专利局受理专利申请后，应当将需要进行保密审查的申请转送国务院有关主管部门审查；有关主管部门应当在收到之日起四个月内，将审查结果通知专利局；申请专利的发明创造需要保密的，专利局按保密专利申请处理，并且通知申请人。

第十条　专利法第六条所称执行本单位的任务所完成的职务发明创造是指：

（一）在本职工作中作出的发明创造；

（二）履行本单位交付的本职工作之外的任务所作出的发明创造；

（三）退职、退休或者调动工作后一年内作出的，与其在原单位承担的本职工作或者分配的任务有关的发明创造。

专利法第六条所称的本单位的物质条件是指本单位的资金、设备、零部件、原材料或者不向外公开的技术资料等。

第十一条 专利法所称的发明人或者设计人是指对发明创造的实质性特点作出了创造性贡献的人。在完成发明创造过程中，只负责组织工作的人、为物质条件的利用提供方便的人或者从事其他辅助工作的人，不应当被认为是发明人或者设计人。

第十二条 专利法第九条规定的两个以上的申请人在同一日期分别就同样的发明创造申请专利的，应当在收到专利局的通知后自行协商确定申请人。

第十三条 专利权人应当将其与他人签订的实施专利许可合同，在合同生效后二个月内向专利局备案。

第十四条 专利法第十九条第一款和第二十条所称的专利代理机构是指中国国际贸易促进委员会、上海专利事务所和中国专利代理有限公司以及国务院指定的其他专利代理机构。

第十五条 申请人委托专利代理机构向专利局申请专利和办理其他专利事务的，应当同时提交委托书，写明委托权限。

第二章　专利的申请

第十六条　申请专利应当向专利局提交申请文件一式两份。

第十七条　专利法第二十六条第二款所称的请求书中的其他事项是指：

（一）申请人的国籍；

（二）申请人是企业或者其他组织的，其总部所在的国家；

（三）申请人委托专利代理机构的，专利代理机构的名称、地址和专利代理人的姓名；

（四）申请人是单位的，代表人的姓名；

（五）要求优先权的，应当注明的有关事项；

（六）申请人的签字或者盖章；

（七）申请文件清单；

（八）附加文件清单。

申请人有两个以上而未委托专利代理机构的，应当指定一人为代表人；未指定代表人的，以第一署名人为代表人。

申请外观设计专利的，必要时还应当写明对外观设计的简要说明。

第十八条 发明或者实用新型专利申请的说明书，除发明或者实用新型的性质需用其他方式和顺序说明的以外，应当按照下列顺序撰写：

（一）发明或者实用新型的名称，该名称应当与请求书中的名称一致；

（二）发明或者实用新型所属技术领域；

（三）就申请人所知，写明对发明或者实用新型的理解、检索、审查有参考作用的现有技术，并且引证反映该项技术的文件；

（四）发明或者实用新型的目的；

（五）清楚、完整地写明发明或者实用新型的内容，以所属技术领域的普通技术人员能够实现为准；

（六）发明或者实用新型与现有技术相比所具有的优点或者积极效果；

（七）如有附图，应当有图面说明；

（八）详细描述申请人认为实现发明或者实用新型的最好方式，有附图的应当对照附图。

发明或者实用新型说明书可以有化学式或者数学式，但不得有商业性宣传用语。

第十九条 发明或者实用新型的几幅附图可以绘在一张图纸上，每幅附图应当用阿拉伯数字编号，并且按照顺序排列。

附图的大小及清晰度，应当保证在该图缩小到三分之二时，仍能清楚地分辨出图中的各个细节。

同一申请中使用的附图标记应当前后一致。发明或者实用新型说明书未提及的标记不得在附图中出现。

附图中除必需的词语之外，不应当含有其他注释。

第二十条　权利要求书应当说明发明或者实用新型的技术特征，清楚和简要地表述请求保护的范围。

权利要求书有几项权利要求的，应当用阿拉伯数字顺序编号。

权利要求书中使用的科技术语应当与说明书中使用的一致，可以有化学式或者数学式，但不得有插图。除有绝对必要外，不得使用"如说明书……部分所述"或者"如图……所示"的用语。

第二十一条　权利要求书可以包括独立权利要求和从属权利要求。

独立权利要求应当从整体上反映发明或者实用新型的主要技术内容，记载构成发明或者实用新型必要的技术特征。

引用一项或者几项权利要求的从属权利要求，只能引用在前的权利要求。

第二十二条 除发明或者实用新型的性质需用其他方式表达的以外，独立权利要求应当按照下列规定撰写：

（一）前序部分：说明发明或者实用新型所属技术领域以及现有技术中与发明或者实用新型主题密切相关的技术特征；

（二）特征部分：使用"本发明（或者实用新型）的特征是……"或者类似的简明语言，说明发明或者实用新型的技术特征。这些特征，与前序部分说明的特征一起，构成要求保护的技术特征。

一项发明或者实用新型应当只有一个独立权利要求，并且写在同一发明或者实用新型的从属权利要求之前。

第二十三条 除发明或者实用新型的性质需要用其他方式表达的以外，从属权利要求应当按照下列规定撰写：

（一）引用部分：写明被引用的权利要求的编号，可能时把编号写在句首；

（二）特征部分：写明发明或者实用新型附加的技术特征，对引用部分的技术特征作进一步限定。

　　引用两项以上其他权利要求的从属权利要求，不得互相引用。

　　第二十四条　摘要应当写明发明或者实用新型所属的技术领域、需要解决的技术问题、主要技术特征和用途。摘要可以包含最能说明发明的化学式或者说明发明、实用新型的一幅附图。全文以不超过200个字为宜。

　　第二十五条　申请专利的发明是涉及新的微生物学方法或者其产品，而且使用的微生物是公众不能得到的，除申请应当符合专利法和本细则的有关规定外，申请人还应当办理下列手续：

　　（一）在申请日前，或者最迟在申请日，将该微生物菌种提交专利局指定的微生物菌种保藏单位保藏；

　　（二）在申请文件中，提供有关微生物特征的资料；

　　（三）在请求书中写明该微生物分类命名（注明拉丁文名称）和保藏该微生物菌种的单位名称、提交日期和保藏编号，并且附具该单位的证明。

　　第二十六条　有关微生物的发明专利申请公布后，任何单位或者个人需要将专利申请所涉及的微生物作为实验目的使用的，应当向专利局提出请求，写明下列事项：

（一）请求人的姓名或者名称和地址；

（二）请求人不向其他任何人提供菌种的保证；

（三）在授予专利权之前，只作为实验目的使用的保证。

第二十七条 依照专利法第二十七条规定提交的外观设计的图片或者照片，不得小于3厘米×8厘米，也不得大于19厘米×27厘米。

申请人可以就每件外观设计提交不同角度、不同侧面或者不同状态的图片或者照片，以清楚地显示请求保护的对象。每幅图片或者照片应当写明外观设计的角度、侧面和状态，并且在图片或者照片的背面左、右上方分别标上顺序编号和申请人的姓名或者名称。

第二十八条 请求保护色彩的外观设计专利申请，应当提交彩色和黑白的图片或者照片各一份，并且在黑白的图片或者照片上注明请求保护的色彩。

第二十九条 专利局认为必要时，可以要求外观设计专利申请人提交使用外观设计的产品样品或者模型。样品或者模型的体积不得超过30厘米×30厘米×30厘米，重量不得超过15公斤。易腐、易损或者危险品不得作为样品或者模型提交。

第三十条 专利法第二十四条第二项所称的学术会议或者技术会议是指国务院有关主管部门或者全国性学术团体组织召开的学术会议或者技术会议。

第三十一条 专利申请有专利法第二十四条第一项或者第二项规定情形的，申请人应当在提出专利申请时声明，并且自申请日起两个月内，提交有关国际展览会或者学术会议、技术会议的组织单位出具的有关发明创造已经展出或者发表，以及展出或者发表日期的证明文件。

专利申请有专利法第二十四条第三项规定情形的，专利局在必要时可以要求申请人提出证明文件。

第三十二条 发明专利的申请人要求优先权的，应当自其在外国第一次提出申请之日起十五个月内提交受理该项申请的国家给予的申请号。

第三十三条 申请人对一项专利申请要求两项以上优先权的，该申请的优先权期限从最早的优先权日起算。

第三十四条 在中国没有经常居所或者营业

所的外国人、外国企业或者外国其他组织申请专利的，专利局认为有疑义时可以要求其提供下列文件：

（一）国籍证明；

（二）外国企业或者外国其他组织总部所在地的证明文件；

（三）外国人、外国企业、外国其他组织的所属国，承认中国公民或者单位可以按照该国国民的同等条件，在该国享有专利权和其他与专利有关的权利的证明文件。

第三十五条 根据专利法第三十一条第一款的规定，发明或者实用新型专利申请的权利要求可以是下列各项之一：

（一）两项以上不能包括在一个权利要求以内的同类产品、方法的独立权利要求；

（二）产品和专用于制造该产品的方法的独立权利要求；

（三）产品和该产品的用途的独立权利要求；

（四）产品、专用于制造该产品的方法和该产品的用途的独立权利要求；

（五）产品、专用于制造该产品的方法和该方法的专用设备的独立权利要求；

（六）方法和为使用该方法而专门设计的专用设备的独立权利要求；

（七）方法和直接使用该方法制造的产品的独立权利要求。

第三十六条 依照专利法第三十一条第二款规定将两项以上外观设计作为一件申请提出的，应当将各件外观设计顺序编号，并且在请求书中写明使用每件外观设计的产品。外观设计的顺序编号应当标在每件使用外观设计产品的图片背面的左下方。

第三十七条 申请人撤回专利申请的，应当向专利局提出声明，写明发明创造的名称、申请号和申请日。

撤回专利申请的声明是在专利局作好公布专利申请文件的印刷准备工作之后提出的，申请文件仍予公布。

第三章 专利申请的审查和批准

第三十八条 对专利申请进行审查、复审的审查员或者专利复审委员会委员有下列情形之一的，应当自行回避，申请人或者其他利害关系人也可以要求其回避：

（一）是申请人或者专利代理人的近亲属

的;

　　（二）与专利申请有利害关系的;

　　（三）与申请人或者专利代理人有其他关系，可能影响对专利申请的公正审查的。

　　专利复审委员会委员曾参与原申请的审查的，适用前款的规定。

　　第三十九条　专利局收到发明或者实用新型专利申请的请求书、说明书（实用新型必须包括附图）和权利要求书，或者外观设计专利申请的请求书和外观设计的图片或者照片后，应当明确申请日，给予申请号，并且通知申请人。

　　第四十条　专利申请文件中缺少请求书、说明书或者权利要求书，或者不符合专利法第二十七条规定的，专利局不予受理，并且通知申请人。

　　第四十一条　在发明说明书中写有"对附图的说明"而无附图的，申请人应当在专利局指定的期限内补交附图或者声明取消"对附图的说明"。申请人补交附图的，以向专利局提交或者邮寄附图之日为申请日；取消"对附图的说明"的，保留原申请日。

　　第四十二条　一件专利申请包括两项以上发明、实用新型或者外观设计的，申请人可以在依照专利法第三十九条或者第四十条规定的公告前的任何时候，或者在公告后，专利局认为有提出分案申请的正当理由的时候，向专利局提出分案的请求，自行将其申请分为几个申请。

专利局认为专利申请不符合专利法第三十一条和本细则第三十五条规定的，应当通知申请人在指定的期限内将其专利申请分案；申请人无正当理由期满不答复的，该申请被视为撤回。

第四十三条 依照本细则第四十二条规定提出的分案申请，可以保留原申请日，但不得超出原说明书记载的范围。

第四十四条 经初步审查，专利局认为专利申请明显属于专利法第五条或者第二十五条规定，或者明显不符合专利法第十八条、第十九条或者本细则第二条规定的，应当通知申请人，要求其在指定期限内陈述意见；申请人无正当理由期满不答复的，其申请被视为撤回。

专利申请经申请人陈述意见后，专利局仍然认为明显不符合前款所列各条规定的，应当予以驳回。

第四十五条 专利申请有下列情形之一的，申请人应当在专利局指定的期限内补正：

（一）请求书未使用规定的格式或者填写不

符合要求的；

（二）发明或者实用新型说明书及其附图以及权利要求书不符合规定的；

（三）发明或者实用新型专利申请缺少摘要的；

（四）外观设计专利申请的图片或者照片不符合规定的；

（五）委托专利代理机构而未提交委托书的；

（六）其他应当予以补正的事项。

申请人无正当理由期满不补正的，其申请被视为撤回。专利申请经补正后，仍然不符合专利法或者本细则有关规定的，应当予以驳回。

第四十六条　申请人请求早日公布其发明专利申请的，应当向专利局声明。专利局对该申请进行初步审查之后，除予以驳回的以外，应当立即将申请予以公布。

第四十七条　申请人依照专利法第二十七条规定写明使用外观设计的产品及其所属类别时，应当使用专利局公布的外观设计产品分类表。未写明使用外观设计的产品所属类别或者所写的类别不确切的，专利局可以予以补充或者修改。

第四十八条　自发明专利申请公布之日起至

审定公告前，任何人均可以对不符合专利法规定的申请向专利局提出意见，并且说明理由。

第四十九条　发明专利申请人因有正当理由无法提交专利法第三十六条规定的检索资料或者审查结果资料的，应当向专利局声明，并且在得到该项资料后补交。

第五十条　专利局依照专利法第三十五条第二款规定对专利申请自行进行审查时，应当通知申请人。

第五十一条　发明专利申请人在自申请日起十五个月内，在提出实质审查请求或者在对异议提出答复时，可以对发明专利申请的说明书或者权利要求书主动提出修改。

发明或者实用新型专利申请的说明书或者权利要求书的修改部分，除个别文字修改或者增删外，应当按照规定格式提交替换页。

第五十二条　实用新型或者外观设计专利申请人自申请日起至申请公告前，或者在对异议提出答复时，可以对实用新型或者外观设计专利申请主动提出修改。对外观设计专利申请进行修改的，不得变更外观设计的基本组成部分。

第五十三条　依照专利法的规定，专利申请应当予以驳回的情形是指：

（一）申请不符合专利法第三条和本细则第二条规定的；

（二）申请属于专利法第五条、第二十五条规定或者不符合专利法第二十二条、第二十三条规定的；

（三）依照专利法第六条、第八条、第十八条规定申请人无权申请专利，或者依照专利法第九条规定不能取得专利权的；

（四）申请不符合专利法第二十六条第三款、第四款或者第三十一条规定的；

（五）申请的修改或者分案的申请超出原说明书记载范围的。

第五十四条 依照专利法第四十一条规定，对专利局公告的发明或者实用新型专利申请可以提出异议的情形是指：

（一）申请专利的发明不符合专利法第三条和本细则第二条第一款规定，申请专利的实用新型不符合专利法第三条和本细则第二条第二款规定的；

（二）申请人属于专利法第五条、第二十五条规定或者不符合专利法第二十二条规定的；

（三）申请人依照专利法第六条、第八条、第十八条规定无权申请专利，或者申请的主要内容是取自他人的说明书、附图、模型、设备等，或者取自他人使用的方法，而未经其同意的；

（四）申请不符合专利法第二十六条第三款或者第四款规定的；

（五）申请的修改或者分案的申请超出原说明书记载范围的。

第五十五条　依照专利法第四十一条规定，对专利局公告的外观设计专利申请可以提出异议的情形是指：

（一）申请专利的外观设计不符合专利法第三条和本细则第二条第三款规定的；

（二）申请专利的外观设计属于专利法第五条规定或者不符合第二十三条规定的；

（三）申请人依照专利法第六条、第八条、第十八条规定无权申请专利，或者依照专利法第九条规定不能取得专利权，或者申请专利的外观设计的基本组成部分是取自他人的设计、图片、照片、物品或者模型，而未经其同意的；

（四）对申请的修改，变更了外观设计的基本组成部分的。

第五十六条　任何人依照专利法第四十一条规定提出异议的，应当向专利局提交异议书一式两份，并且说明异议的理由。

第五十七条　专利局收到异议书后应当进行审查。对不符合规定的异议书，应当通知异议人在指定的期限内补正；未在指定的期限内补正的，被视为未提出异议。

异议书中未写明反对授予专利权的理由或者提出的理由不符合本细则第五十四条或者第五十五条规定的，不予受理。

第五十八条　专利复审委员会由专利局指定有经验的技术和法律专家组成，其主任委员由专利局局长兼任。

第五十九条　申请人依照专利法第四十三条第一款的规定向专利复审委员会请求复审的，应当提出复审请求书，说明理由并且附具有关的证明文件。请求书和证明文件应当一式两份。

申请人请求复审时，可以修改专利申请，但修改应当仅限于驳回申请的决定所涉及的部分。

第六十条　复审请求书不符合规定格式的，复审请求人应当在专利复审委员会指定的期限内补正；未在该期限内补正的，该复审请求被视为撤回。

第六十一条　专利复审委员会应当将受理的复审请求书转交原审查部门提出意见，由专利复审委员会作出决定，并且通知申请人。

第六十二条　专利复审委员会进行复审后，认为复审请求不符合专利法规定的，应当通知复审请求人，要求其在指定的期限内陈述意见；无正当理由期满不答复的，其复审请求被视为撤回。

第六十三条　复审请求人在专利复审委员会作出决定前，可以随时撤回其复审请求。

第六十四条　专利局作出授予专利权的决定后，应当通知申请人于两个月内缴纳专利证书费并且领取专利证书；申请人期满未缴纳专利证书费的，视为放弃取得专利权的权利。

第四章　专利权的无效宣告

第六十五条　依照专利法第四十八条规定，请求宣告专利权无效或者部分无效的，应当向专利复审委员会提出请求书，说明理由，必要时应当附具有关文件。无效宣告请求书和有关文件应当一式两份。

第六十六条　专利权无效宣告请求书不符合规定格式的，请求人应当在专利复审委员会指定的期限内补正；未在该期限内补正的，该无效宣告请求被视为撤回。

请求无效宣告的理由适用本细则第五十四

条、第五十五条的规定。

无效宣告请求书中未说明理由或者所提出的理由不符合本细则第五十四条、第五十五条规定的，不予受理。

第六十七条 专利复审委员会应当将专利权无效宣告请求书的副本和有关文件的副本送交专利权人，要求其在指定的期限内陈述意见；无正当理由期满不答复的，被视为无反对意见。

第五章 专利实施的强制许可

第六十八条 任何单位依照专利法第五十二条规定或者任何专利权人依照第五十三条规定，请求给予实施发明或者实用新型专利的强制许可的，该单位或者专利权人应当向专利局提交强制许可请求书，并且附具未能以合理条件与专利权人签订实施许可合同的证明文件，各一式两份。

任何单位依照专利法第五十二条规定请求给予实施发明或者实用新型专利的强制许可的，还应当提交该单位具备实施条件的说明文件一式两份。

专利局在受理强制许可请求书后，应当通知有关专利权人在指定期限内陈述意见；无正当理由期满不答复的，被视为无反对意见。

专利局在对强制许可请求书和有关专利权人的意见进行审查后，应当作出决定并且通知请求人和有关专利权人。

第六十九条 依照专利法第五十七条规定请求专利局裁决使用费数额的，当事人应当提出裁决请求书，并且附具双方不能达成协议的证明文件。专利局在收到请求书后应当在三个月内作出裁决，并且通知当事人。

第六章 对职务发明创造的发明人或者设计人的奖励

第七十条 专利法第十六条所称的奖励，包括发给发明人或者设计人的奖金和报酬。

第七十一条 专利权被授予后，专利权的持有单位应当对发现明人或者设计人发给奖金。一项发明专利的奖金最低不少于 200 元；一项实用新型专利或者外观设计专利的奖金最低不少于50元。

由于发明人或者设计人的建议被其所属单位采纳而完成的发明创造，专利权被授予后，专利权的持有单位应当从优发给奖金。

对上述奖金，企业单位可以计入成本，事业

单位可以从事业费中列支。

　　第七十二条　专利权的持有单位在专利权有效期限内，实施发明创造专利后，每年应当从实施发明或者实用新型所得利润纳税后提取0.5%～2%，或者从实施外观设计所得利润纳税后 提取0.05%～0.2%，作为报酬发给发明人或者 设计人；或者参照上述比例，发给发明人或者设计人一次性报酬。

　　第七十三条　发明创造专利权的持有单位许可其他单位或者个人实施其专利的，应当从收取的使用费中纳税后提取5%～10%作为报酬发给发明人或者设计人。

　　第七十四条　本细则规定的报酬，一律从制造专利产品、使用专利方法所获得的利润和收取的使用费中列支，不计入单位的奖金总额，不计征奖金税。但发明人或者设计人的个人所得，应当依法纳税。

　　第七十五条　本章关于奖金和报酬的规定，集体所有制单位和其他企业可以参照执行。

第七章　专利管理机关

　　第七十六条　专利法第六十条和本细则所称的专利管理机关是指国务院有关主管部门和各

省、自治区、直辖市、开放城市和经济特区人民政府设立的专利管理机关。

第七十七条　对于在发明专利申请公布后、专利权授予前使用发明而未支付适当费用的单位或者个人，在专利权授予后，专利权人可以请求专利管理机关进行调处，也可以直接向人民法院起诉。专利管理机关调处的时候，有权决定该单位或者个人在指定的期限内支付适当的费用。当事人对专利管理机关的决定不服的，可以向人民法院起诉。

前款规定准用于实用新型或者外观设计专利申请。

第七十八条　发明人或者设计人与其所属单位对其发明创造是否属于职务发明创造以及对职务发明创造是否提出专利申请有争议的，发明人或者设计人可以请求上级主管部门或者单位所在地区专利管理机关处理。

第七十九条　属于跨部门或者跨地区的侵权纠纷，当事人请求专利管理机关处理的，应当由发生侵权行为地区的专利管理机关或者侵权单位上级主管部门的专利管理机关处理。

第八章 专利登记和专利公报

第八十条 专利局设置专利登记簿，登记下列专利权有关事项：

（一）专利权的授予；

（二）专利权的转让；

（三）专利权期限的续展；

（四）专利权的终止和无效；

（五）专利实施的强制许可；

（六）专利权人的姓名或者名称、国籍和地址的变更。

第八十一条 专利局定期出版专利公报，公布或者公告下列内容：

（一）专利申请请求书中记载的著录事项；

（二）发明或者实用新型说明书的摘要；

（三）对发明专利申请的实质审查请求和专利局对该项申请自行进行实质审查的决定；

（四）发明专利申请的审定和实用新型、外观设计专利申请的公告；

（五）专利申请的驳回；

（六）异议的审查决定和对专利申请的修改；

（七）专利权的授予；

（八）专利权的终止；

（九）专利权的无效宣告；

（十）专利权的转让；

（十一）专利实施的强制许可的给予；

（十二）专利权期限的续展；

（十三）专利申请的撤回、视为撤回和放弃；

（十四）专利权人的姓名或者名称、地址的变更；

（十五）对地址不明的申请人的通知；

（十六）其他有关事项。

发明或者实用新型说明书及其附图、权利要求书和外观设计专利申请的图片或者照片，另行全文出版。

第九章　费　　用

第八十二条　向专利局申请专利和办理其他手续时，应当按照情况缴纳下列费用：

（一）申请费和申请维持费；

（二）审查费、复审费和异议费；

（三）年费；

（四）办理其他专利事务手续费：专利权期限续展费、著录事项变更费、专利证书费、优先权证明费、无效宣告请求费、强制许可请求费和强制许可使用费的裁决请求费。

上述各种费用数额，由专利局另行规定。

第八十三条 专利法和本细则规定的各种费用，可以通过邮局或者银行汇付，也可以直接向专利局缴纳。

通过邮局或者银行汇付的，应当在汇单上写明费用名称、发明创造的名称、申请号或者专利号。没有申请号或者专利号的，应当注明提出申请的日期。

通过邮局或者银行汇付费用的，以费用汇出日为缴款日。

第八十四条 申请专利未按时缴纳或者未缴足申请费的，申请人可以自提交申请之日起一个月内缴纳或者缴足；期满未缴纳或者未缴足的，其申请被视为撤回。

第八十五条 申请人请求实质审查或者请求复审，任何人提出异议或者请求宣告专利权无效，未按规定缴纳费用的可以在自提出请求或者异议之日起十五天内缴纳，但缴费日不得超过专利法规定请求实质审查、复审或者提出异议的期限；期满未缴纳的被视为未提出请求或者异议。

第八十六条 发明专利申请人自申请日起满

二年尚未被授予专利权的，自第三年度起每年缴纳申请维持费。第一次申请维持费应当在第三年度的第一个月内缴纳，以后的申请维持费应当在前一年度期满前一个月内预缴。

第八十七条　第一次年费应当于领取专利证书时缴纳。在授予专利权时已经缴纳当年申请维持费的，专利权人应当按照当年年费数额补缴差额。以后的年费应当在前一年度期满前一个月内预缴。

第八十八条　申请人或者专利权人未按时缴纳申请维持费或者年费，以及缴纳的申请维持费或者年费数额不足的，专利局应当通知申请人在应当缴纳申请维持费或者年费期满之日起六个月内补缴，同时缴纳金额为申请维持费或者年费的25％的滞纳金；期满未缴纳的，自应当缴纳申请维持费或者年费期满日起，其申请被视为撤回或者专利权终止。

第八十九条　依照专利法第四十五条第二款规定，申请续展实用新型或者外观设计专利权期限的，应当在专利权期满前六个月内提出请求，并且缴纳续展费；期满未缴纳续展费的，被视为未提出请求。

第九十条　个人申请专利和办理其他手续，

缴纳本细则第八十二条规定的各种费用有困难的，可以按规定向专利局提出减缴或者缓缴的请求。

减缴或者缓缴的办法由专利局另行规定。

第十章　附　　则

第九十一条　任何人经专利局同意后，可以查阅或者复制已经公布或者公告的专利申请案卷、专利登记簿和有关证明文件。

第九十二条　申请人向专利局提交的文件应当使用专利局制定的统一格式，由申请人或者其专利代理人签字或者盖章。

第九十三条　向专利局提交有关申请或者专利权的文件或者物品时，应当标明申请号或者专利号和发明创造的名称。邮寄文件或者物品必须挂号。

第九十四条　各类申请文件应当打字或者印刷，字迹应当整齐清晰，不得涂改。纸张只限使用正面。

附图应当用制图工具和黑色墨水绘制，线条应当均匀清晰。

第九十五条　本细则由专利局负责解释。

第九十六条　本细则自1985年4月1日起施

行。

专利收费标准

（单位：人民币元）

（一）申请费
    （1）发明专利申请费：150
    （2）实用新型专利申请费：100
    （3）外观设计专利申请费：80

（二）发明专利申请维持费每年：100

（三）发明专利申请审查费：400

（四）复审费
    （1）发明专利申请复审费：200
    （2）实用新型专利申请复审费：100
    （3）外观设计专利申请复审费：80

（五）异议费
    （1）发明专利申请异议费：30
    （2）实用新型专利申请异议费：20
    （3）外观设计专利申请异议费：20

（六）实用新型或者外观设计专利权有效期续展费：100

（七）著录事项变更手续费：10

（八）专利证书费

　　（1）发明专利证书费：100

　　（2）实用新型专利证书费：50

　　（3）外观设计专利证书费：50

（九）优先权证明费：20

（十）无效宣告请求费

　　（1）发明专利权无效宣告请求费：300

　　（2）实用新型专利权无效宣告请求费：200

　　（3）外观设计专利权无效宣告请求费：150

（十一）强制许可请求费

　　（1）发明专利实施的强制许可请求费：300

　　（2）实用新型专利实施的强制许可请求费：200

（十二）强制许可的专利使用费裁决请求费：100

（十三）年费

　　（1）发明专利年费：

　　　　第一年至第三年每年200

　　　　第四年至第六年每年300

　　　　第七年至第九年每年600

　　　　第十年至第十二年每年1200

　　　　第十三年至第十五年每年2400

　　（2）实用新型专利年费：

第一年至第三年每年100

第四年第五年每年200

第六年第八年300

（3）外观设计专利年费：

第一年至第三年每年50

第四年至第五年每年100

第六年至第八年每年200

注：（1）外国申请人和专利权人缴纳上述各项费用，按缴
纳时的汇率折合后，以外币支付。

（2）第十三项所列的年度，自申请日起算。年费从授
予专利权的当年开始按该年的标准缴纳。

INTERIM PROVISIONS OF PATENT AGENCIES

*(Approved by the State Council on September 4, 1985
and promulgated by the Patent Office of China
on September 12, 1985)*

Article 1 These Provisions are formulated specifically for the purpose of implementing the provisions of patent agencies stated in the Patent Law of the People's Republic of China.

Article 2 Patent agencies shall accept the entrustment of applicants for patent rights and other persons concerned to handle patent applications and other patent matters in accordance with Articles 19 and 20 of the Patent Law of the People's Republic of China.

Article 3 The patent agencies mentioned in these Provisions refer to

(1) Patent agencies designated by the State Council;

(2) Patent agencies established with the approval of the competent authorities under the State Council and patent administration offices under the governments of provinces, autonomous regions, municipalities directly under the Central Government, cities open to the outside and the special economic zones;

(3) Attorney's offices that deal with patent-agency business with the approval of patent administration offices under the governments of provinces, autonomous regions, municipalities directly under the Central Govern-

ment, open cities and special economic zones.

The patent agencies mentioned in Articles 2 and 3 shall register with the Patent Office of China through patent administration offices.

Article 4 A patent agency that undertakes patent entrusted to it must have a power of attorney from the client explicitly prescribing the scope of power entrusted and bearing the seal or signature of the clients.

Patent agencies shall charge fees for the work entrusted to them according to the Provisions.

Article 5 A patent agency shall have patent agents to handle matters:

(1) Advice on patent matters;

(2) Writing applications for patent rights;

(3) Requesting examinations as to substance and re-examinations;

(4) Filing objections to and requesting an invalidation of a patent right;

(5) Undertaking matters concerning the transfer and approval of patent rights;

(6) Related patent matters.

A patent agent can accept engagement to serve as a patent adviser.

Article 6 Citizens of the People's Republic of China who have the right to vote and to stand for election in accordance with the law can apply to and register themselves with the Patent Office of China as patent agents if they meet the following requirements:

(1) College graduates (or persons having the equivalent academic level) in science and engineering who have mastered one foreign language and done scientific and technological work for three years or work related to

science and technology for five years;

(2) People trained in patent law and the patent business and, therefore, knowledgeable as to the basic patent laws relating to patent agencies.

Patent agents engaged in work concerned with foreign countries or foreign nationals must, in addition to the requirements mentioned above, be well versed in national and international laws and treaties on the protection of industrial property rights and must be proficient in one foreign language.

Article 7 The Assessment Committee of Patent Agents formed by the Patent Office of China, the Ministry of Justice, the China Council for the Promotion of International Trade, and other departments and organizations concerned is responsible for the following tasks;

(1) Examining applicants for work as patent agents;

(2) Supervising and instructing the work of patent agents.

Article 8 After the Assessment Committee's examination, applicants for work as patent agents are registered in the Patent Office of China and issued certificates of qualification as patent agents.

Article 9 Patent agents shall work at patent agencies, perform tasks assigned to them by the patent agencies, and must not themselves accept entrustment.

Article 10 Patent agents performing tasks according to the law are protected by national law, and no units or individuals shall interfere with them.

Article 11 The conduct of patent agents and of clients with regard to entrustment has equal legal effect within the limits of authority.

Article 12 It is the duty of the patent agents to

observe the secrecy of the inventions and creations that have come to their knowledge in the course of their work, except those that have already been announced or published.

Article 13   The Assessment Committee of Patent Agents has the right to annul the status of a patent agent if any of the following circumstances apply to him:

(1) He has plagiarized the invention or creation of a client, intentionally revealed the nature of an invention or creation, or performed other acts seriously detrimental to the interests of the clients;

(2) He is quite unqualified.

The Assessment Committee of Patent Agents shall inform the Patent Office of China of any decision annulling the status of a patent agent, whereby the Patent Office of China shall cancel the patent agent's registration and retrieve his certificate.

Article 14   If a patent agent has committed the first act in the first item of the previous article, he shall be disciplined by his unit; if the circumstances are serious, the criminal liability of the patent agent shall be investigated according to the law.

Article 15   These Provisions shall be interpreted by the Patent Office of China.

Article 16   These Provisions shall go into effect on the day they are promulgated.

专利代理暂行规定

（一九八五年九月四日国务院批准；
一九八五年九月十二日中国专利局发布）

第一条　为实施《中华人民共和国专利法》有关专利代理的规定，特制定本规定。

第二条　专利代理机构依照《中华人民共和国专利法》第十九条和第二十条的规定，接受专利申请人或者其他当事人的委托，办理申请专利和其他专利事务。

第三条　本规定所称的专利代理机构是指：

（一）　国务院指定的专利代理机构；

（二）国务院有关主管部门和省、自治区、直辖市、开放城市、经济特区人民政府专利管理机关批准成立的专利代理机构；

（三）经省、自治区、直辖市、开放城市和经济特区人民政府专利管理机关同意可以办理专利代理事务的律师事务所。

前款第二项和第三项的专利代理机构，应当由专利管理机关向中国专利局备案。

第四条　专利代理机构接受委托，承办业务，应当有委托人提交的委托书，写明委托权限，并由委托人盖章或者签字。

专利代理机构接受委托，承办业务，按照规定收取费用。

第五条　专利代理机构设专利代理人，承办下列事务：

（一）为专利事务提供咨询；

（二）撰写专利申请文件、申请专利的有关事务；

（三）请求实质审查、请求复审的有关事务；

（四）提出异议、请求宣告专利权无效的有关事务；

（五）专利权转让、专利许可的有关事务；

（六）其他有关专利事务。

专利代理人可以接受聘请，担任专利顾问。

第六条　依法有选举权和被选举权的中华人民共和国公民具备下列条件的，可以向中国专利局申请登记为专利代理人：

（一）高等院校理工科专业毕业（或者具有同等学力），掌握一门外语，做过三年以上科技工作或者做过五年以上与科技有关的其他工作；

（二）受过专利法以及有关专利业务训练，掌握与专利代理工作有关的法律基本知识。

从事涉外专利代理工作的，除具备前款所列条件外，还应当熟悉有关国家和国际间保护工业产权的法律和条约，并且熟练掌握一门外语。

第七条　中国专利局与司法部、中国国际贸易促进委员会等有关部门和团体组成专利代理人考核委员会，负责下列工作：

（一）对申请登记为专利代理人的人员进行考核；

（二）在业务上监督和指导专利代理工作。

第八条　申请登记为专利代理人的人员经专利代理人考核委员会考核合格，由中国专利局登记为专利代理人，并且发给专利代理人证书，即取得专利代理人资格。

第九条　专利代理人必须在专利代理机构执行职务，由专利代理机构委派工作，不得自行接受委托。

第十条　专利代理人依法执行职务，受国家法律保护，任何单位和个人不得干涉。

第十一条　专利代理人在委托权限内的行为与委托人的行为有同等法律效力。

第十二条　专利代理人对在业务活动中所了

解的发明创造，除专利申请已经公布或者公告的以外，有保守秘密的责任。

第十三条 专利代理人有下列情形之一的，专利代理人考核委员会有权取消其专利代理人资格：

（一）剽窃委托人的发明创造，故意泄露委托人的发明创造内容，或者有其他严重损害委托人利益行为的；

（二）严重不称职的。

专利代理人考核委员会应当将取消专利代理人资格的决定通知中国专利局，由中国专利局注销专利代理人登记，并缴销专利代理人证书。

第十四条 专利代理人有前条第一款第一项行为的，由所在单位给予行政处分；情节严重的，依法追究法律责任。

第十五条 本规定由中国专利局负责解释。

第十六条 本规定自发布之日起施行。

TARIFF RAGULATIONS ON IMPORTS AND EXPORTS OF THE PEOPLE'S REPUBLIC OF CHINA

(Promulgated by the State Council on March 7, 1985)
(Revised and Promulgated by the State Council on September 12, 1987)

CHAPTER I GENERAL RULES

Article 1 These regulations are formulated in accordance with the Customs Law of the People's Republic of China to implement the policy of opening to the outside world and to promote foreign trade and national economic development.

Article 2 All imported and exported goods permitted by the People's Republic of China will have duties imposed on them, according to the Regulations on Customs Duties for Imports and Exports of the People's Republic of China, hereinafter referrd to as Regulations on Customs Duties for Imports and Exports, unless otherwise specified by the state.

The Regulations on Customs Duties on Imports and Exports are a component part of these Regulations.

Article 3 The State Council has established a Tariff Regulations Commission, responsible for proposing the guide-lines, policies and principles formulating and revising the Tariff Regulations on Imports and Exports and Regulations on Customs Duties on Imports and Ex·

ports, studying drafts for revision of customs regulations, fixing temporary tariff rates and examining and approving partial adjustment in tariff rates.

The composition of the Tariff Regulations Commission is decided by the State Council.

Article 4 The shippers and consignees of imported or exported cargoes shall pay the import or export duties. The agents appointed to go through the relevant formalities shall abide by the various provisions concerning their clients in these Regulations.

Article 5 Regulations on import duties on incoming passenger's belongings and personal postal matter will be specified by the Tariff Regulations Commission.

CHAPTER II   THE APPLICATION OF TARIFF RATES

Article 6 Duties on imports are divided into general tariff rates and minimum tariff rates. General tariff rates are applicable on imports from countries that do not have a mutually favourable clause in their trade agreements or treaties with the People's Republic of China. Minimum duties are applicable on imports from countries that have such a clause.

Article 7 Items without tariff rates being listed in the Regulations on Customs Duties for Imports and Exports shall not be charged customs duties.

Article 8 Imports and exports shall be charged customs duty according to the tariff rates on the day when the consignees, shippers or their agents file a declaration for importation or exportation.

For those declaring in advance, as permitted by Customs, duties will be imposed according to the tariff rates on the day the cargo carrier files its declaration.

CHAPTER III   DETERMINATION OF DUTIABLE VALUE

Article 9 The dutiable value of imported goods shall be the C.I.F. based on regular transaction prices, as appraised by Customs. The C.I.F. includes the cost and expenses for packaging, shipping, insurance and other service charges incurred before unloading at the importing port in the People's Republic of China.

Article 10 If the transaction prices of imported goods cannot be estimated by Customs, their dutiable value shall be determined by basing the C.I.F. on transaction prices of the same or similar goods imported from the same country or region.

If the dutiable value cannot be determined in the ways mentioned, the wholesale prices of the same or similar imported goods on the domestic market with import duties, and other taxes incurred in the course of importing, regular expenses for transportation, storage, sales and profit subtracted, shall be taken as the dutiable value.

Under special circumstances the dutiable value shall be reasonably estimated by Customs.

Article 11 Machinery and instruments, transportation vehicles or other cargoes shipped out of China for repair, declared to Customs upon exportation and reimported within the time limit set by Customs, shall have regular reparation costs and costs of parts and materials appraised by Customs as the dutiable value.

Article 12 The dutiable value of goods to be processed abroad, declared to Customs upon exportation and reimported within the time limit set by Customs, shall be the difference between the C.I.F. of the processed goods upon importation and the C.I.F. of the unprocessed goods or the same or similar goods upon importation.

Article 13   The dutiable value of leased or rented imports shall be the regular rental fee of the imports as appraised by Customs.

Article 14   The dutiable value of exported goods shall be the F.O.B. of the goods sold overseas, as appraised by Customs, with export duties subtracted.

Article 15   The consigners and consignees or their agents, upon handing in Customs import or export declarations, should deliver invoices listing the goods' true prices and shipping, insurance and other costs (including the manufacturer's invoice if any), a detailed account of packaging and any other pertinent certificates.

All certificates must bear the signatures or seals of the consigners, consignees or their agents to prove their authenticity.

Article 16   Shippers, consignees or their agents shall present invoices and other certificates to Customs when it examines the dutiable value of the goods. Customs can inspect contracts, account books, vouchers and other documents pertaining to the transaction or implement other types of investigation. It can also inspect the relevant documents of goods that have already had customs duties levied and been allowed to pass.

Article 17   If upon delivering the import or export declaration, the shippers, consignees or their agents do not present the certificates required in Article 15, they shall pay duties according to the dutiable value appraised by Customs. When the certificates are handed in later, the duty amounts shall not be changed.

Article 18   The C.I.F. or F.O.B. of imports and exports, rental, or cost of reparation, parts and materials calculated in a foreign currency shall be converted into RMB according to the middle rate between the buying and selling rates listed in the Chart of Exchange Rates Between RMB and Foreign Currencies announced by the State Foreign Exchange Administration on the day the note for payment of the customs duties is issued by Customs. If the foreign currency is not listed, the exchange rate for conversion into RMB shall be decided by the State Foreign Exchange Administration.

CHAPTER IV   THE PAYMENT AND REFUNDING OF CUSTOMS DUTIES

Article 19   The shippers, consignees or their agents shall pay duties at an appointed bank within seven days (excluding Sundays and holidays) from the day when the note for payment of customs duties is issued by Customs. In case of failure to pay on time, a daily surcharge of 0.1 percent of the total sum of duties for delayed payment shall be imposed by Customs from the day the duties are due to the day the payment is made in full.

Article 20   Customs shall collect duties and surcharges for delayed payment in RMB, unless otherwise specified.

Article 21   Upon collection of duties and surcharges, Customs shall issue receipts, the forms of which are to be decided by the General Administration of Customs.

Article 22   Within one year from the day of payment of duties, import or export consigners, consignees or their agents can present a written statement, with receipts for payment of duties, to Customs for refunds in any of the following circumstances, but a request later than a year shall not be considered:

(1) More duties were paid than should have been, owing to mistakes by Customs.

(2) Imports exempt from customs examination, as approved by Customs, for which full duties have been paid, are found to have been imcompletely unloaded, a fact checked and approved by Customs.

(3) Goods whose export duties have been paid fail for some reason to be exported, a fact checked and approved by Customs.

Article 23 If the duties imposed are found to be insufficient, Customs can demand that the shippers, consignees or their agents pay the difference within one year from the day duties are paid for imported or exported goods. If the difference has been caused by violation of regulations on the part the shippers, consignees or their agents, the demand can be made within three years.

CHAPTER V EXEMPTION FROM AND REDUCTION OF CUSTOMS DUTIES AND PROCEDURES FOR THEIR EXAMINATION AND APPROVAL

Article 24 The following items are duty-free if Customs agrees that no mistake has been made:

(1) Goods with duties of less than 10 yuan RMB;

(2) Advertisements and samples of no commercial value;

(3) Goods presented gratis by international organizations and foreign governments;

(4) Fuel, materials, food and beverages needed on the way by transporting vehicles crossing borders.

Exported domestic products that are returned for some reason may be exempt from duties if the original shippers or their agents, in declaring them as imports, present the original export certificates, examined and approved by Customs. However, the original export duties shall not be refunded.

Article 25   The following imports will have their duties reduced by Customs:

(1) Those that suffer damage or loss during shipping or unloading;

(2) Those that suffer damage or loss owing to force majeure after being unloaded and before passing Customs;

(3) Those found to be broken, damaged or rotten upon inspection by Customs, with the damage proved not to have been caused by insufficient caution.

Article 26   Duties shall be reduced or exempted on goods as stipulated in international treaties of which the People's Republic of China is a signatory or a contracting party.

Article 27   Import or export duties will not be imposed on product samples, exhibition items, construction machinery, engineering vehicles, equipment and tools for installation, television and movie filming equipment, cargo containers, and costumes and stage properties of performing troupes if they are examined and approved by Customs for temporary importation or exportation and are guaranteed to be exported or imported within six months, provided shippers or consignees pay a cash deposit equal to the duties or provide a guarantee for the imported or exported goods.

The six-month limit can be extended by Customs according to actual conditions.

Article 28 Raw materials, auxiliary materials, parts, assemblies, components, and packaging materials imported to be processed or assembled for foreign businesses, or to be manufactured for export, shall be exempted from import duties according to the actual quantity processed and exported.

Article 29 Imposition and exemption of customs duties for imports and exports on an item-for-item basis will be specified by the General Administration of Customs.

Article 30 Duties shall be reduced or exempted on imports, exports and other items that by law enjoy a reduction or exemption of customs duties for special economic zones and other special areas, Chinese-foreign joint ventures, Chinese-foreign cooperative enterprises, foreign-owned enterprises and other special enterprises.

Article 31 If the consigners, consignees or their agents wish temporary reduction or exemption of customs duties on their imports and exports, they shall apply to Customs with a written statement stating the reason, and other necessary documents and certificates before the importation or exportation of the goods. After verification by Customs, the application will be sent to the General Administration of Customs for examination and approval, or for examination and approval jointly by the General Administration of Customs and the Ministry of Finance, according to the regulations of the State Council.

CHAPTER VI   APPEAL PROCEDURE

Article 32 When a payer of import and export duties disagrees with the classification and dutiable value of his cargoes determined by Customs in accordance with the Regulations on Customs Duties, he is to pay customs duties, as decided by Customs, first before appealing to Customs in written form within thirty days from the day note for payment of customs duties is issued. Appeals after the expiration date will not be considered by Customs.

Article 33 Customs shall consider the case and make a new decision within fifteen days from the day it receives the appeal. If the payer of the import or export duties still disagrees with the decision, he should re-appeal to the General Adminstration of Customs within fifteen days from the day he receives the new decision.

Article 34 Upon receiving the re-appeal of the payer of the import or export duties, the General Administration of Customs should consider the case again and make another decision within thirty days and request Customs to pass the written verdict on to the appealing party or announce it if undeliverable.

If the payer still disagrees with the decision, he may sue in a people's court within fifteen days from the day he receives the written decision.

CHAPTER VII   PENALTY CODE

Article 35 Smuggling and other activities in violation of these Regulations or other acts violating the supervisory regulations of Customs shall be dealt with according to the Customs Law of the People's Republic of China, Rules for the Implementation of the Customs Law of the People's Republic of China Concerning Disciplinary Penalties, and other related regulations.

CHAPTER VIII   APPENDIX

Article 36   Any individual or unit exposing or helping in the seizure of persons evading customs duties in violation of the Regulations hereof shall be rewarded and his or its identity kept secret by Customs.

Article 37   These Regulations are to be interpreted by the General Administration of Customs of the People's Republic of China.

Article 38   These Regulations take effect as of October 15,1987.

中华人民共和国进出口关税条例

（一九八五年三月七日国务院发布，
一九八七年九月十二日国务院修订发布）

第一章 总 则

第一条 为了贯彻对外开放政策，促进对外经济贸易和国民经济的发展，根据《中华人民共和国海关法》的有关规定，制定本条例。

第二条 中华人民共和国准许进出口的货物，除国家另有规定的以外，应当由海关按照《中华人民共和国海关进出口税则》（以下简称《海关进出口税则》）征收进口税或者出口税。

《海关进出口税则》是本条例的组成部分。

第三条 国务院成立关税税则委员会，其职责是提出制订或者修订《进出口关税条例》、《海关进出口税则》的方针、政策、原则，审议税则修订草案，制订暂定税率，审定局部调整税率。

国务院关税税则委员会的组成由国务院规定。

第四条 进口货物的收货人、出口货物的发货人，是关税的纳税义务人。

接受委托办理有关手续的代理人，应当遵守本条例对其委托人的各项规定。

第五条　进境的旅客行李物品和个人邮递物品征税办法，由国务院关税税则委员会另行制订。

第二章　税率的运用

第六条　进口税设普通税率和最低税率。对产自与中华人民共和国未订有关税互惠条款的贸易条约或者协定的国家的进口货物，按照普通税率征税；对产自与中华人民共和国订有关税互惠条款的贸易条约或者协定的国家的进口货物，按照最低税率征税。

第七条　《海关进出口税则》中未订有出口税率的货物，不征出口税。

第八条　进出口货物，应当按照收发货人或者他们的代理人申报进口或者出口之日实施的税率征税。

进口货物到达前，经海关核准先行申报的，应当按照装载此项货物的运输工具申报进境之日实施的税率征税。

第三章 完税价格的审定

第九条 进口货物以海关审定的正常成交价格为基础的到岸价格作为完税价格。到岸价格包括货价，加上货物运抵中华人民共和国关境内输入地点起卸前的包装费、运费、保险费和其他劳务费等费用。

第十条 进口货物的成交价格经海关审查未能确定的，应当以从该货物的同一出口国或者地区购进的相同或者类似货物的成交价格为基础的到岸价格作为完税价格。

按照前款规定，完税价格仍未能确定的，应当以相同或者类似进口货物在国内市场的批发价格，减去进口关税、进口环节其它税收以及进口后的正常运输、储存、营业费用及利润作为完税价格。

如有特殊情形，货物的完税价格可由海关按照合理的方法估定。

第十一条 运往境外修理的机械器具、运输工具或者其他货物，出境时已向海关报明并在海关规定期限内复运进境的，应当以海关审定的正常修理费和料件费作为完税价格。

第十二条 运往境外加工的货物，出境时已向海关报明并在海关规定期限内复运进境的，应当以加工后的货物进境时的到岸价格与原出境货物或者相同、类似的货物在进境时的到岸价格之间的差额，作为完税价格。

第十三条　租赁（包括租借）方式进口的货物，应当以海关审定的货物的正常租金，作为完税价格。

第十四条　出口货物应当以海关审定的货物售与境外的离岸价格，扣除出口税后，作为完税价格。

第十五条　进出口货物的收发货人或者他们的代理人，在向海关递交进出口货物报关单时，应当交验载明货物的真实价格、运费、保险费和其他费用的发票（如有厂家发票应附在内）、包装清单和其他有关单证。

前款各项单证应当由货物的收发货人或者他们的代理人签印证明无讹。

第十六条　海关审核进出口货物完税价格时，收发货人或者他们的代理人应当交验发票等单证；必要时海关可以检查买卖双方的有关合同、帐册、单据和文件等，或者作其他调查。对于已经海关完税放行的货物，海关仍可检查货物的上述有关资料。

第十七条 进出口货物的收发货人或者他们代理人，在递交进出口货物报关单时未交验第十五条规定的各项单证的，应当按照海关估定的完税价格完税；事后补交单证的，税款不予调整。

第十八条 进出口货物的到岸价格、离岸价格或者租金、修理费、料件费等以外币计价的，应当由海关按照填发税款缴纳证之日国家外汇管理部门公布的《人民币外汇牌价表》的买卖中间价，折合人民币。《人民币外汇牌价表》未列入的外币，按照国家外汇管理部门确定的汇率折合人民币。

第四章 税款的缴纳、退补

第十九条 进出口货物的收发货人或者他们的代理人，应当在海关填发税款缴纳证次日起七日内（星期日和节假日除外），向指定银行缴纳税款。逾期不缴的，除依法追缴外，由海关自到期之日起至缴清税款之日止，按日征收欠缴税款额1‰的滞纳金。

第二十条 海关征收关税、滞纳金等，除另有规定的以外，应当按人民币计征。

第二十一条 海关征收关税、滞纳金等，应当制发收据。收据格式由海关总署规定。

第二十二条 有下列情形之一的，进出口货物的收发货人或者他们的代理人，可以自缴纳税款之日起一年内，书面声明理由，连同纳税收据向海关申请退税，逾期不予受理：

（一）因海关误征，多纳税款的；

（二）海关核准免验进口的货物，在完纳关税后，发现有短卸情事，经海关审查认可的；

（三）已征出口税的货物，因故未装运出口申报退关，经海关查验属实的。

第二十三条 进出口货物完税后，如发现少征或者漏征税款，海关应当自缴纳税款或者货物放行之日起一年内，向收发货人或者他们的代理人补征。因收发货人或者他们的代理人违反规定而造成的少征或者漏征，海关在三年内可以追征。

第五章 关税的减免及审批程序

第二十四条 下列货物，经海关审查无讹，可以免税：

（一）一票货物的关税税额在人民币十元以下的；

（二）无商业价值的广告品及货样；

（三）国际组织、外国政府无偿赠送的物

资；

（四）进出境运输工具装载的途中必需的燃料、物料和饮食用品。

因故退还的我国出口货物，由原发货人或者他们的代理人申报进境，并提供原出口单证，经海关审查核实，可以免征进口税。但是，已征收的出口税，不予退还。

第二十五条 有下列情形之一的进口货物，海关可以酌情减免税：

（一）在境外运输途中或者在起卸时，遭受损坏或者损失的；

（二）起卸后海关放行前，因不可抗力遭受损坏或者损失的；

（三）海关查验时已经破漏、损坏或者腐烂，经证明不是保管不慎造成的。

第二十六条 中华人民共和国缔结或者参加的国际条约规定减征、免征关税的货物、物品，海关应当按照规定予以减免关税。

第二十七条 经海关核准暂时进境或者暂时出境并在六个月内复运出境或者复运进境的货样、展览品、施工机械、工程车辆、供安装用的仪器和工具、电视或者电影摄制器械、盛装货物的容器以及剧团服装道具，在货物收发货人向海关缴纳相当于税款的保证金或者提供担保后，准予暂时免纳关税。

前款规定的六个月期限，海关可以根据情况酌予延长。

第二十八条 为境外厂商加工、装配成品和为制造外销产品而进口的原材料、辅料、零件、部件、配套件和包装物料，海关按照实际加工出口的数量免征进口税。

第二十九条 无代价抵偿的进出口货物的关税征免办法，由海关总署另行规定。

第三十条 经济特区等特定地区进出口的货物，中外合资经营企业、中外合作经营企业、外资企业等特定企业进出口的货物以及其他依法给予关税减免优惠的进出口货物，按照有关规定减税或者免税。

第三十一条 收发货人或者他们的代理人，要求对其进出口货物临时减征或者免征进出口关税的，应当在货物进出口前书面写明理由，随附必要的证明和资料向海关申请。海关审查属实后，转报海关总署，由海关总署或者海关总署会同财政部按照国务院的规定审查批准。

第六章   申诉程序

第三十二条 纳税义务人对货物在《海关进出口税则》上的归类和完税价格的审定有异议时，应当先按海关核定的税额缴纳税款，然后自海关填发税款缴纳证之日起三十日内，向海关书面申请复议。逾期申诉的，海关可以不受理。

第三十三条 海关应当自收到复议申请之日起十五日内作出复议决定。

纳税义务人对复议决定不服的，可以自接到复议决定书之日起十五日内向海关总署申请复议。

第三十四条 海关总署接到纳税义务人的复议申请后，应当在三十日内作出复议决定，并制成决定书交海关送达申诉人。无法送达的，应当予以公告。

纳税义务人对海关总署的复议决定仍然不服的，可以自收到复议决定书之日起十五日内，向人民法院起诉。

第七章   罚   则

第三十五条 违反本条例的规定构成走私或者违反海关监管规定的行为的，由海关按照《中

华人民共和国海关法》、《中华人民共和国海关法
行政处罚实施细则》和其他有关规定处理。

第八章　附　　则

　　第三十六条　海关对检举或者协助查获违反
本条例的偷税漏税行为的单位和个人，应当按照
规定给予奖励，并负责保密。

　　第三十七条　本条例由中华人民共和国海关
总署负责解释。

　　第三十八条　本条例自一九八七年十月十五
日起施行。

LAW OF THE PEOPLE'S REPUBLIC OF CHINA ON ECONOMIC CONTRACTS INVOLVING FOREIGN INTERESTS

(Adopted at the Tenth Session of the Standing Committee of the Sixth National People's Congress and Promulgated on March 21, 1985)

CHAPTER I GENERAL PROVISIONS

Article 1 This Law is formulated with a view to protecting the lawful rights and interests of the parties to Chinese-foreign economic contracts and to promoting the development of China's foreign economic relations.

Article 2 This Law shall apply to economic contracts concluded between enterprises or other economic organizations of the People's Republic of China and foreign enterprises, other economic organizations or individuals (hereinafter referred to as "contracts"). However, these provisions shall not apply to international transport contracts.

Article 3 Contracts shall be concluded according to the principle of equality and mutual benefit and the principle of achieving agreement through consultation.

Article 4 In concluding a contract, the parties must abide by the law of the People's Republic of China and shall not harm the public interest of the People's Republic of China.

Article 5 The parties to a contract may choose the proper law applicable to the settlement of contract dis-

putes. In the absence of such a choice by the parties, the
law of the country that has the closest connection with
the contract shall apply.

The law of the People's Republic of China shall apply
to contracts that are to be performed within the territory
of the People's Republic of China, namely contracts for
Chinese-foreign joint ventures, Chinese-foreign cooperative enterprises and Chinese-foreign cooperative exploration and development of natural resources.

Matters not covered by the law of the People's Republic of China shall be dealt with through international
practice.

Article 6   Where an international treaty, of which
the People's Republic of China is a contracting party or a
signatory, differs from the law of the People's Republic
of China in matters relating to a contract, the provisions
of the international treaty shall prevail, with the exception
of clauses about which the People's Republic of China has
declared reservation.

CHAPTER II   CONCLUSION OF CONTRACTS

Article 7   A contract shall take form as soon as the
parties to it have reached agreement in writing on the
terms and attached their signatures. If agreement is reached by means of letters, telegrams or telex and one party
requests a signed letter of confirmation, the contract shall
take form only after the letter of confirmation is signed.

Contracts subject to approval by the state, as provided for by the laws or administrative regulations of the
People's Republic of China, shall take form only after
such approval is granted.

Article 8   The annexes to contracts are component

parts of these contracts.

Article 9   Contracts that violate the law or the public interest of the People's Republic of China shall be void.

If any terms in a contract violate the law or the public interest of the People's Republic of China, the validity of the contract shall not be affected if such terms are cancelled or modified by the parties through consultation.

Article 10   Contracts concluded by means of fraud or duress shall be void.

Article 11   A party responsible for the invalidity of a contract shall be liable for losses suffered by the other party as a result of the contract's invalidity.

Article 12   A contract shall, in general, contain the following terms:

(1) The corporate or personal names of the contracting parties, their nationalities and their principal places of business or domicile;

(2) The date and place of the signing of the contract;

(3) The type of contract and the nature and scope of its objective;

(4) The technical conditions, quality, standards, specifications and quantity pertaining to the contract's objective;

(5) The time limit, place and method of performance;

(6) The price, amount and method of payment, and various incidental charges;

(7) If the contract is assignable, the conditions for its assignment;

(8) Liability to pay compensation and other liabilities for breach of contract;

(9) Methods for settling contract disputes;

(10) The language(s) in which the contract is to be written and its validity.

Article 13   So far as may be required, a contract shall provide for the limits of the risks to be borne by the parties in performing the objective; if necessary, it shall provide for insurance coverage.

Article 14   Where a contract needs to be in effect over a long period, the parties shall set a limit of validity for the contract and may also stipulate conditions for its extension or termination before its expiry.

Article 15   In the contract the parties may agree to provide a guaranty. The guarantor shall be held liable within the agreed scope of guaranty.

CHAPTER III   PERFORMANCE OF CONTRACTS AND LIABILITY FOR BREACH OF CONTRACT

Article 16   A contract shall be legally binding as soon as it is formulated in accordance with the law. The parties shall perform the obligations stipulated in the contract. No party shall unilaterally modify or rescind the contract.

Article 17   A party may temporarily suspend its performance of the contract if it has conclusive evidence that the other party is unable to perform its part. However, it shall immediately inform the other party of such suspension and resume performance if and when the other party provides a sure guarantee of performance. If a party suspends performance of a contract without conclusive evidence of the other party's inability to perform, it shall be liable for breach of contract.

Article 18   If a party fails to perform the contract

or its performance of the contractual obligations does not conform to the agreed terms, constituting a breach of contract, the other party is entitled to claim damages or demand other reasonable remedial measures. If the losses suffered by the other party cannot be completely made up after adoption of such remedial measures, the other party shall still have the right to claim damages.

Article 19 The liability of a party to pay compensation for breach of contract shall be equal to the loss suffered by the other party as a consequence of the breach. However, such compensation may not exceed the loss that the party responsible for the breach ought to have foreseen at the time of the conclusion of the contract as a possible consequence of a breach of contract.

Article 20 The parties may agree in a contract that if one party breaches the contract, it shall pay a certain amount of damages to the other party; they may also agree upon a method for calculating the damages resulting from such a breach.

The damages stipulated in the contract shall be regarded as compensation for losses resulting from breach of contract. However, if the contractually agreed breach of contract damages are far more or far less than is necessary to compensate for losses resulting from the breach, the party concerned may request an arbitration body or a court to reduce or increase them appropriately.

Article 21 If both parties breach the contract, each shall be commensurately liable for the breach of contract that is its responsibility.

Article 22 A party suffering losses resulting from a breach of contract by the other party shall promptly take appropriate measures to prevent the losses from increasing.

If the losses are aggravated as a result of its failure to adopt appropriate measures, it shall not be entitled to claim compensation for the aggravated part of the losses.

Article 23 If a party fails to pay on time any amount stipulated as payable in the contract or any other payable amount related to the contract, the other party is entitled to interest on the amount in arrears. The method for calculating the interest may be specified in the contract.

Article 24 If a party is prevented from performing all or part of its obligations owing to force majeure, it shall be relieved of all or part of its obligations.

If a party cannot perform its obligations within the contractually agreed time limit owing to force majeure, it shall be relieved of the liability for delayed performance during the aftereffect of the event.

Force majeure means an event that the parties could not have foreseen at the time of conclusion of the contract, both parties being unable to either avoid or overcome its occurrence and consequences.

The scope of force majeure may be specified in the contract.

Article 25 The party that fails to perform wholly or in part its contractual obligations owing to force majeure shall promptly inform the other party so as to mitigate possible losses inflicted on the other party and shall also provide a certificate issued by the relevant agency within a reasonable period of time.

CHAPTER IV THE ASSIGNMENT OF CONTRACTS

Article 26 When a party assigns, wholly or in part, its contractual rights and obligations to a third party, it must obtain the consent of the other party.

Article 27   In the case of a contract that, according to the laws or administrative regulations of the People's Republic of China, is to be approved by the state, the assignment of conractual rights and obligations shall be subject to approval by the authority that approved the contract, unless otherwise stipulated in the approved contract.

CHAPTER V   MODIFICATION, RESCISSION AND TERMINATION OF CONTRACTS

Article 28   A contract may be modified if both parties agree after consultation.

Article 29   A party shall have the right to notify the other party that a contract is rescinded in any of the following situations:

(1) If the other party has breached the contract, thus adversely affecting the economic benefits to be expected from the conclusion of the contract;

(2) If the other party fails to perform the contract within the time limit agreed upon in the contract or fails to perform it within a reasonable period of time allowed for delayed performance;

(3) If all the obligations under the contract cannot be performed owing to force majeure;

(4) If the contractually agreed conditions for rescission of the contract are present.

Article 30   For a contract consisting of several independent parts, some may be rescinded according to the provisions of the preceding article while the other parts remain valid.

Article 31   A contract shall be terminated in any one of the following situations:

(1) If the contract has already been performed in accordance with the agreed terms;

(2) If an arbitration body or a court has decided that the contract shall be terminated;

(3) If the parties agree through consultation to terminate the contract.

Article 32   Notices or agreements on the modification or rescission of contracts shall be made in writing.

Article 33   In the case of a contract that, according to the laws or administrative regulations of the People's Republic of China, is to be established with the approval of the state, any significant modification of the contract shall be subject to approval by the authority that approved the contract, and rescission of the contract shall be filed with the same authority for the record.

Article 34   The modification, rescission or termination of a contract shall not affect the rights of the parties to claim damages.

Article 35   The contractually agreed terms for the settlement of disputes shall not become invalid because of the rescission or termination of a contract.

Article 36   The contractually agreed terms for the settlement of accounts and liquidations of a contract shall not become invalid because of the rescission or termination of the contract.

CHAPTER VI   SETTLEMENT OF DISPUTES

Article 37   If disputes over a contract develop, the parties shall, as far as possible, settle them through consultation or through mediation by a third party.

If the parties are unwilling to settle their dispute through consultation or mediation, or if consultation or mediation proves unsuccessful, they may, in accordance with the arbitration clause provided in the contract or a written arbitration agreement reached by the parties afterwards, submit the dispute to a Chinese arbitration body or any other arbitration body for arbitration.

Article 38 If no arbitration clause is provided in the contract and a written arbitration agreement is not reached afterwards, the parties may bring suit in a people's court.

CHAPTER VII SUPPLEMENTARY PROVISIONS

Article 39 The time limit for filing suit or applying for arbitration in a dispute over a contract for the purchase and sale of goods shall be four years, counting from the day when the party was aware or ought to have been aware of its rights' being infringed upon. The time limit for filing suit or applying for arbitration in a dispute over any other contract shall be stipulated separately by law.

Article 40 If new legal provisions are formulated while contracts for Chinese-foreign joint ventures, Chinese-foreign cooperative enterprises, or Chinese-foreign cooperative exploration and development of natural resources, which have been concluded with the approval of the state, are being performed within the territory of the People's Republic of China, the performance may still be based on the terms of the contracts.

Article 41 This Law may apply to contracts concluded before it goes into effect if this is agreed to by the parties through consultation.

Article 42 The State Council shall, in accordance with this Law, formulate rules for its implementation.

Article 43 This law shall go into effect on July 1, 1985.

中华人民共和国涉外经济合同法

（一九八五年三月二十一日第六届全国人民代表大会常务委员会第十次会议通过并公布）

第一章 总 则

第一条 为了保障涉外经济合同当事人的合法权益，促进我国对外经济关系的发展，特制定本法。

第二条 本法的适用范围是中华人民共和国的企业或者其他经济组织同外国的企业和其他经济组织或者个人之间订立的经济合同（以下简称合同）。但是，国际运输合同除外。

第三条 订立合同，应当依据平等互利、协商一致的原则。

第四条 订立合同，必须遵守中华人民共和国法律，并不得损害中华人民共和国的社会公共利益。

第五条 合同当事人可以选择处理合同争议所适用的法律。当事人没有选择的，适用与合同有最密切联系的国家的法律。

在中华人民共和国境内履行的中外合资经营企业合同、中外合作经营企业合同、中外合作勘探开发自然资源合同，适用中华人民共和国法律。

中华人民共和国法律未作规定的，可以适用国际惯例。

第六条　中华人民共和国缔结或者参加的与合同有关的国际条约同中华人民共和国法律有不同规定的，适用该国际条约的规定。但是，中华人民共和国声明保留的条款除外。

第二章　合同的订立

第七条　当事人就合同条款以书面形式达成协议并签字，即为合同成立。通过信件、电报、电传达成协议，一方当事人要求签订确认书的，签订确认书时，方为合同成立。

中华人民共和国法律、行政法规规定应当由国家批准的合同，获得批准时，方为合同成立。

第八条　合同订明的附件是合同的组成部分。

第九条　违反中华人民共和国法律或者社会公共利益的合同无效。

合同中的条款违反中华人民共和国法律或者

社会公共利益的，经当事人协商同意予以取消或者改正后，不影响合同的效力。

第十条　采取欺诈或者胁迫手段订立的合同无效。

第十一条　当事人一方对合同无效负有责任的，应当对另一方因合同无效而遭受的损失负赔偿责任。

第十二条　合同一般应当具备以下条款：

一、合同当事人的名称或者姓名、国籍、主营业所或者住所；

二、合同签订的日期、地点；

三、合同的类型和合同标的的种类、范围；

四、合同标的的技术条件、质量、标准、规格、数量；

五、履行的期限、地点和方式；

六、价格条件、支付金额、支付方式和各种附带的费用；

七、合同能否转让或者合同转让的条件；

八、违反合同的赔偿和其他责任；

九、合同发生争议时的解决方法；

十、合同使用的文字及其效力。

第十三条　合同应当视需要约定当事人对履行标的承担风险的界限；必要时应当约定对标的

的保险范围。

第十四条 对于需要较长期间连续履行的合同，当事人应当约定合同的有效期限，并可以约定延长合同期限和提前终止合同的条件。

第十五条 当事人可以在合同中约定担保。担保人在约定的担保范围内承担责任。

第三章 合同的履行和违反合同的责任

第十六条 合同依法成立，即具有法律约束力。当事人应当履行合同约定的义务，任何一方不得擅自变更或者解除合同。

第十七条 当事人一方有另一方不能履行合同的确切证据时，可以暂时中止履行合同，但是应当立即通知另一方；当另一方对履行合同提供了充分的保证时，应当履行合同。当事人一方没有另一方不能履行合同的确切证据，中止履行合同的，应当负违反合同的责任。

第十八条 当事人一方不履行合同或者履行合同义务不符合约定条件，即违反合同的，另一方有权要求赔偿损失或者采取其他合理的补救措施。采取其他补救措施后，尚不能完全弥补另一方受到的损失的，另一方仍然有权要求赔偿损失。

第十九条 当事人一方违反合同的赔偿责任，应当相当于另一方因此所受到的损失，但是不得超过违反合同一方订立合同时应当预见到的因违反合同可能造成的损失。

第二十条 当事人可以在合同中约定，一方违反合同时，向另一方支付一定数额的违约金；也可以约定对于违反合同而产生的损失赔偿额的计算方法。

合同中约定的违约金，视为违反合同的损失赔偿。但是，约定的违约金过分高于或者低于违反合同所造成的损失的，当事人可以请求仲裁机构或者法院予以适当减少或者增加。

第二十一条 当事人双方都违反合同的，应当各自承担相应的责任。

第二十二条 当事人一方因另一方违反合同而受到损失的，应当及时采取适当措施防止损失的扩大；没有及时采取适当措施致使损失扩大的，无权就扩大的损失要求赔偿。

第二十三条 当事人一方未按期支付合同规定的应付金额或者与合同有关的其他应付金额的，另一方有权收取迟延支付金额的利息。计算利息的方法，可以在合同中约定。

第二十四条 当事人因不可抗力事件不能履

行合同的全部或者部分义务的，免除其全部或者部分责任。

当事人一方因不可抗力事件不能按合同约定的期限履行的，在事件的后果影响持续的期间内，免除其迟延履行的责任。

不可抗力事件是指当事人在订立合同时不能预见、对其发生和后果不能避免并不能克服的事件。

不可抗力事件的范围，可以在合同中约定。

第二十五条　当事人一方因不可抗力事件不能履行合同的全部或者部分义务的，应当及时通知另一方，以减轻可能给另一方造成的损失，并应在合理期间内提供有关机构出具的证明。

第四章　合同的转让

第二十六条　当事人一方将合同权利和义务的全部或者部分转让给第三者的，应当取得另一方的同意。

第二十七条　中华人民共和国法律、行政法规规定应当由国家批准成立的合同，其权利和义务的转让，应当经原批准机关批准。但是，已批准的合同中另有约定的除外。

第五章　合同的变更、解除和终止

第二十八条　经当事人协商同意后，合同可以变更。

第二十九条　有下列情形之一的，当事人一方有权通知另一方解除合同：

一、另一方违反合同，以致严重影响订立合同所期望的经济利益；

二、另一方在合同约定的期限内没有履行合同，在被允许推迟履行的合理期限内仍未履行；

三、发生不可抗力事件，致使合同的全部义务不能履行；

四、合同约定的解除合同的条件已经出现。

第三十条　对于包含几个相互独立部分的合同，可以依据前条的规定，解除其中的一部分而保留其余部分的效力。

第三十一条　有下列情形之一的，合同即告终止：

一、合同已按约定条件得到履行；

二、仲裁机构裁决或者法院判决终止合同；

三、双方协商同意终止合同。

第三十二条　变更或者解除合同的通知或者协议，应当采用书面形式。

第三十三条 中华人民共和国法律、行政法规规定应当由国家批准成立的合同，其重大变更应当经原批准机关批准，其解除应当报原批准机关备案。

第三十四条 合同的变更、解除或者终止，不影响当事人要求赔偿损失的权利。

第三十五条 合同约定的解决争议的条款，不因合同的解除或者终止而失去效力。

第三十六条 合同约定的结算和清理条款，不因合同的解除或者终止而失去效力。

第六章 争议的解决

第三十七条 发生合同争议时，当事人应当尽可能通过协商或者通过第三者调解解决。

当事人不愿协商、调解的，或者协商、调解不成的，可以依据合同中的仲裁条款或者事后达成的书面仲裁协议，提交中国仲裁机构或者其他仲裁机构仲裁。

第三十八条 当事人没有在合同中订立仲裁条款，事后又没有达成书面仲裁协议的，可以向人民法院起诉。

第七章　附　　则

第三十九条　货物买卖合同争议提起诉讼或者仲裁的期限为四年，自当事人知道或者应当知道其权利受到侵犯之日起计算，其他合同争议提起诉讼或者仲裁的期限由法律另行规定。

第四十条　在中华人民共和国境内履行经国家批准成立的中外合资经营企业合同、中外合作经营企业合同、中外合作勘探开发自然资源合同，在法律有新的规定时，可以仍然按照合同的规定执行。

第四十一条　本法施行之日前成立的合同，经当事人协商同意，可以适用本法。

第四十二条　国务院依据本法制定实施细则。

条四十三条　本法自1985年7月1日起施行。

PENALTIES FOR VIOLATIONS OF FOREIGN EXCHANGE REGULATIONS

(Approved by the State Council on March 25, 1985 and promulgated by the State Foreign Exchange Administration on April 5, 1985)

Article 1 The following detailed regulations have been made to ensure implementation of Articles 31 and 33 of the Interim Regulations on Foreign Exchange Control of the People's Republic of China.

Article 2 The following activities shall be considered illegal procurement of foreign exchange:

(1) Imports and other items that should be paid for with foreign exchange but are paid for in RMB, unless approved by the State Foreign Exchange Administration and its sub-administrations (hereinafter referred to as SFEA) or specified by the State;

(2) Institutions in China that pay in RMB for expenses in China of Chinese missions abroad, foreign missions in China, enterprises with overseas Chinese investments, enterprises with foreign investments, Chinese-foreign joint ventures, or private persons of temporary entry and are repaid with foreign exchange that is not sold to the State;

(3) Chinese missions abroad that use RMB in China to pay expenses for others and are repaid with foreign exchange;

(4) Foreign missions in China, enterprises with overseas Chinese investments, enterprises with foreign investments, and Chinese-foreign joint ventures and their staff members that pay expenses for others in RMB and are repaid with foreign exchange or similar means;

(5) Delegations, work groups, and their members sent to foreign countries or the regions of Hong Kong and Macao who use business funds or revenue from business activities to purchase commodities or use them in other ways without permission from SFEA;

(6) Institutions in China that use foreign exchange revenue from exports or other sources to pay for imports or other expenses.

Article 3   The following penalties will be imposed on parties for illegal procurement of foreign exchange:

(1) If the party has not yet used the foreign exchange, it will be ordered to exchange it for RMB. If it has used the foreign exchange, it will be ordered to deliver foreign exchange of an equal amount for exchange into RMB or will suffer corresponding reductions in its foreign exchange quotas. If the foreign exchange has been spent and cannot be made up, the difference between purchase prices at home and abroad must be paid for the commodities purchased with foreign exchange. A fine of 10 to 30 percent of the amount of foreign exchange illegally procured can be imposed in addition to the punishments above.

(2) The illegal supplier of foreign exchange will be fined 10 to 30 percent of the amount of the foreign exchange provided.

Article 4   The following activities will be considered evasions of foreign exchange control:

(1) Institutions in China retain, use or deposit their foreign exchange earnings abroad without permission from SFEA.

(2) Institutions in China, overseas-Chinese-invested enterprises, foreign enterprises, and Chinese-foreign joint ventures retain or deposit without authorization funds resulting from understatement of foreign exchange earnings in understating export prices or commission fees or from overstatement of foreign exchange expenditure in overstating import prices, costs and commission fees.

(3) Chinese missions abroad and the Chinese side of Chinese-foreign joint ventures overseas use profits from their businesses that should be transferred back to China, as required by State regulations.

(4) Delegations, work groups and their personnel sent abroad do not use the foreign exchange in accordance with their specific plans, deposit abroad their overseas-mission budgets or the profits made from their businesses, or use the funds in other ways.

Article 5 Penalties will be imposed on evaders of foreign exchange control according to specific cases:

(1) If the foreign exchange has not been used, the evaders or their superior departments will be ordered to exchange it into RMB within a set time limit, or all or part of their foreign exchange will be confiscated. A fine of 10 to 50 percent of the amount of the foreign exchange may also be imposed.

(2) If the foreign exchange has been used, the evaders will be ordered to turn in foreign exchange of equivalent value for exchange into RMB or confiscation. An additional fine of 10 to 50 percent of the amount can be imposed.

(3) If the foreign exchange has been used and cannot be made up, the evaders will be fined more than 30 percent up to 100 percent of the amount of the foreign exchange, or their illegal income will be confiscated, or a fine and confiscation will both be imposed.

Article 6 The following activities are considered disruptions of the money market:

(1) Foreign exchange businesses are run without being authorized by the State Foreign Exchange Administration or go beyond their authorized extent.

(2) Institutions in China, without approval from the State Council or its authorized institutions, issue negotiable securities of foreign exchange values in China or abroad or accept loans from banks or enterprises in foreign countries or the regions of Hong Kong and Macao.

(3) Institutions in China make settlements, loans, transfers or pledges in foreign currencies, or circulate or use foreign exchange, without permission from SFEA.

(4) Foreign exchange is bought and sold without authorization or in covert ways. It is bought and sold at higher exchange rates than those fixed by the State Foreign Exchange Administration. Speculation in foreign exchange is engaged in.

Article 7 Penalties imposed on the violations defined in the above article follow:

(1) Offenders defined in item 1 will be ordered to cease their foreign exchange businesses or to stop running the businesses beyond their authorized extent, their illegal income will be confiscated, or a fine of no more than their total illegal sales will be imposed, or a fine and confiscation will be imposed at the same time.

(2) Offenders defined in item 2 will be prohibited

from issuing new negotiable securities or accepting new loans and may be fined no more than 20 percent of the amount of the securities or the loans.

(3) Offenders defined in items 3 and 4 will be forced to exchange their illegal foreign exchange into RMB and their illegal income will be confiscated, or they will be fined no more than the equivalent of the foreign exchange, or a fine and confiscation will be imposed at the same time.

Article 8   Other violations of foreign exchange control, as defined in Articles 2, 4, and 6, should be handled in accordance with the regulations most applicable to specific cases.

Article 9   Light offenders of the foreign exchange regulations can be punished leniently or exempted from punishment if they admit frankly to their offences to SFEA, show sincere regret for their misdeeds, or inform as to offences by others as a way to contribute to exposure of wrongdoing.   They will be heavily penalized according to Articles 3, 5, and 7 if they refuse to confess, try to cover up their violations, or commit offences repeatedly regardless of penalties.

Article 10   Consequent cases of illegal procurement of foreign exchange, evasion of foreign exchange control, and disruption of the money market will be passed on to judicial authorities for punishment by law.

Article 11   In penalizing offenders of foreign exchange control and to avoid transfer of funds by work units liable for punishment, SFEA may notify the bank to put a freeze on the concerned funds but the freeze cannot be for more than two months and cessation is automatic when the time is up.   In special cases where the freeze has to be retained, SFEA must renew procedures of notification. Money that the offending work units refuse to pay will be deducted from their bank accounts by SFEA.

Article 12 In handling violations of foreign exchange control SFEA should issue letters of penalty to the liable work units or individuals. If the liable parties plead not guilty, they can apply for reconsideration to SFEA at a higher level within 15 days from the day they receive the letters of penalty. They can appeal to a local people's court if they do not accept the decision after reconsideration.

Article 13 Violations of foreign exchange regulations will be handled by SFEA. Illegal procurement of foreign exchange and evasion of foreign exchange control that represent smuggling because of involvement with entry into or exit from China of commodities, luggage, personal belongings, mail and transportation vehicles should be handled by Customs. Speculation involving foreign exchange or foreign exchange certificates should be handled by industrial and commercial administrative institutions.

Article 14 Penalties for violations of foreign exchange regulations in the special economic zones will be imposed by the people's governments of the provinces of Guangdong and Fujian in accordance with the regulations announced herein.

Article 15 The State Foreign Exchange Administration is responsible for interpreting the regulations announced herein.

Article 16 These regulations take effect the day of their promulgation.

违反外汇管理处罚施行细则

（一九八五年三月二十五日国务院批准，
一九八五年四月五日国家外汇管理局公布）

第一条 为贯彻执行《中华人民共和国外汇管理暂行条例》第三十一条、第三十三条的规定，特制定本细则。

第二条 下列行为，都属于套汇：

一、除经国家外汇管理局及其分局（以下简称管汇机关）批准或者国家另有规定者外，以人民币偿付应当以外汇支付的进口货款或者其他款项的；

二、境内机构以人民币为驻外机构、外国驻华机构、侨资企业、外资企业、中外合资经营企业、短期入境个人支付其在国内的各种费用，由对方付给外汇，没有卖给国家的；

三、驻外机构使用其在中国境内的人民币为他人支付各种费用，由对方付给外汇的；

四、外国驻华机构、侨资企业、外资企业、中外合资经营企业及其人员，以人民币为他人支付各种费用，而由他人以外汇或者其他相类似的形式偿还的；

　　五、未经管汇机关批准，派往外国或者港澳等地区的代表团、工作组及其人员，将出国经费或者从事各项业务活动所得购买物品或者移作他用，以人民币偿还的；

　　六、境内机构以出口收入或者其他收入的外汇抵偿进口物品费用或其他支出的。

　　第三条　对套汇者区别情况作如下处罚：

　　一、套入方所得外汇尚未使用的，责令其限期调回，强制收兑；套入方所得外汇已被使用，责令其补交等值的外汇，强制收兑，或者扣减相应的外汇额度；套入方所得外汇已被使用而无外汇归还的，补交所购物品的国内外差价；以上并可另按套汇金额处以10％至30％的罚款。

　　二、对套出外汇方，根据情节轻重，按套汇金额处以10％至30％的罚款。

　　第四条　下列行为，都属于逃汇：

　　一、未经管汇机关批准，境内机构将收入的外汇私自保存、使用、存放境外的；

　　违反《对侨资企业、外资企业、中外合资企业外汇管理施行细则》的规定，将收入的外汇存放境外的；

二、境内机构、侨资企业、外资企业、中外合资经营企业以低报出口货价、佣金等手段少报外汇收入，或者以高报进口货价、费用、佣金等手段多报外汇支出，将隐匿的外汇私自保存或者存放境外的；

三、驻外机构以及在境外设立的中外合资经营企业的中方投资者，不按国家规定将应当调回的利润留在当地营运或者移作他用的；

四、除经管汇机关批准，派往外国或者港澳等地区的代表团、工作组及其人员不按各该专项计划使用外汇，将出国经费或者从事各项业务活动所得外汇存放境外或者移作他用的。

第五条 对逃汇者区别情况作如下处罚：

一、逃汇所得外汇尚未使用的，责令违法者或者其主管部门限期调回，强制收兑，或者没收全部或者部分外汇，并可另按逃汇金额处以10%至50%的罚款；

二、逃汇所得外汇已被使用的，责令其补交等值的外汇，强制收兑或者予以没收，并可另按逃汇金额处以10%至50%的罚款；

三、逃汇所得外汇已被使用而无外汇归还的，按逃汇金额处以30%以上、等值以下的罚款，或者没收非法所得，或者罚、没并处。

第六条　下列行为，都属于扰乱金融：

一、未经国家外汇管理局批准经营外汇业务，或者超越批准经营范围扩大外汇业务的；

二、未经国务院或者国务院授权机关批准，境内机构在国内外发行具有外汇价值的有价证券，按受外国或者港澳等地区的银行、企业贷款的；

三、除经管汇机关批准，境内机构以外汇计价结算、借贷、转让、质押，或者以外币流通、使用的；

四、私自买卖外汇、变相买卖外汇，或者超过国家外汇管理局规定价格买卖外汇，以及倒买倒卖外汇的。

第七条　对犯有前条违法行为者区别情况作如下处罚：

一、对犯有第一项违法行为者，分别责令其停止经营外汇业务、停止超越批准经营范围的外汇业务，或者没收非法所得，或者处以非法经营额等值以下的罚款，或者罚、没并处；

二、对犯有第二项违法行为者，不准其发行新的债券或者接受新的贷款，并可按其债券或者贷款金额处以20％以下的罚款；

三、对犯有第三、四项违法行为者，强制收

兑违法外汇，没收非法所得，或者处以违法外汇等值以下的罚款，或者罚、没并处。

第八条 对第二、四、六条未作具体规定的其他违反外汇管理的违法行为，可以区别情况，参照本细则最相类似的条款处理。

第九条 违反外汇管理，情节轻微，或者主动向管汇机关坦白交待违法事实、真诚悔改、检举立功的，可以从宽处理直至免予处罚；抗拒检查、掩盖违法事实、屡教不改的，按照本细则第三、五、七条的规定从重处罚。

第十条 套汇、逃汇、扰乱金融，情节严重的案件，应当移送司法机关依法处理。

第十一条 管汇机关查处违反外汇管理案件，为了防止违法单位转移资金，可以通知银行冻结其违法款项，冻结时间不超过两个月，届期自动解冻。遇有特殊情况需要适当延长冻结时间的，管汇机关应当重新办理通知手续。对于拒不缴付罚没款项的违法单位，管汇机关可以从其开户银行帐户中强制扣款。

第十二条 管汇机关处理违反外汇管理案件，应当制发处罚决定书，通知被查处的单位或者个人，当事人对管汇机关的处罚决定不服，可以在接到处罚决定书之日起的十五日内，向上一级管汇机关申请复议；当事人不服复议决定的，可以向当地人民法院起诉。

第十三条　违反外汇管理的案件，由管汇机关处理；通过货物、行李物品、邮递物品、运输工具进出国境，从而具有走私性质的套汇、逃汇案件，由海关处理；利用外汇、外币票证进行投机倒把的案件，由工商行政管理机关处理。

第十四条　经济特区违反外汇管理处罚办法，由广东省、福建省人民政府参照本细则另行制定。

第十五条　本细则由国家外汇管理局负责解释。

第十六条　本细则自公布之日起施行。

ADMINISTRATIVE REGULATIONS OF THE PEOPLE'S REPUBLIC OF CHINA ON FOREIGN BANKS AND CHINESE-FOREIGN JOINT BANKS IN SPECIAL ECONOMIC ZONES

(Promulgated by the State Council on April 2, 1985)

Article 1 These Regulations are formulated for the purpose of expanding international economic and financial cooperation, facilitating the importation of foreign capital and technology, and benefiting the development of the Special Economic Zones.

Article 2 As used in these Regulations, "foreign banks" refers to branches established in the Special Economic Zones by banks with foreign capital headquartered in a foreign country or in Hong Kong or Macao and registered in accordance with local law and to banks with foreign capital headquartered in the Special Economic Zones and registered in accordance with the law of the People's Republic of China.

"Chinese-foreign joint banks" refers to the banks jointly operated in the Special Economic Zones by banks or financial agencies with foreign capital and banks or financial agencies with Chinese capital.

Article 3 Foreign banks and Chinese-foreign joint banks must abide by the laws and regulations of the People's Republic of China and their justifiable business activities and legitimate rights and interests are entitled to the protection of the law of the People's Republic of China.

Article 4 A written application for the establishment of a foreign bank or a Chinese-foreign joint bank in the Special Economic Zones must be submitted to the People's Bank of China; the People's Bank of China will then proceed with examination and approval based on the needs of the Special Economic Zones in their development and on the principle of equality and mutual benefit.

The Special Economic Zone branches of the People's Bank of China administer and supervise foreign banks and Chinese-foreign joint banks.

The State Foreign Exchange Administration issues the licence to conduct foreign exchange business to foreign banks and Chinese-foreign joint banks.

Article 5 An application for establishment of a foreign bank or a Chinese-foreign joint bank is subject to the following regulations:

1. If a foreign bank wishes to establish a branch in a Special Economic Zone, the bank's headquarters should submit an application, including the following credentials and data:

(1) An application form signed by the chairman of the board of directors or the general manager, authorized by the board of directors, and certified by a notary public, including the following items: the name of the branch, the total funds allocated by the head bank, the résumé and written authorizations of the chief responsible persons, the types of business the branch proposes to conduct, and any other pertinent matters;

(2) The head bank's articles of association, list of directors record of assets and liabilities, statement of profit and loss, and report of business activity for the three

years prior to the application;

(3) A business permit (copy), approved and issued by the competent authorities of the country or area in which the foreign bank is located;

(4) A written liability guaranty from the head bank for tax and debt.

2. If a foreign bank wishes to be headquartered in a Special Economic Zone, the foreign investor should submit an application, including the following credentials and data:

(1) An application for establishment of a foreign bank, including the following items: the bank's name, its registered capital and called-up capital, a list of chief responsible personnel and the types of business the bank proposes to conduct;

(2) Articles of association;

(3) List of candidates for chairman and vice-chairman and other directors of the board of directors of the proposed bank nominated by the investor;

(4) The investor's assets and liabilities and attached documents, certified by a notary public.

3. If a Chinese-foreign joint bank wants to be established in a Special Economic Zone, the parties to the joint bank should jointly submit an application, including the following credentials and data:

(1) An application for establishment of a joint bank, including the following items: the joint bank's name, names of the parties to the joint bank, the registered capital and called-up capital, the ratio of investment contributed by each of the parties, list of candidates for the chief responsible personnel, the types of business the joint bank proposes to conduct;

(2)   A feasibility-study report jointly prepared by the parties to the joint bank;

(3)   The joint bank's agreement, contract and articles of association, initialled by authorized representatives of each of the parties to the joint bank;

(4)   List of candidates for chairman and vice-chairman and other directors of the board of directors of the joint bank, nominated by the parties to the joint bank.

4.   If a foreign bank or a Chinese-foreign joint bank established in a Special Economic Zone, wants to open a branch in the Special Economic Zone, the bank must submit an application to be approved by the Special Economic Zone's branch of the People's Bank of China.

If any of the credentials and data referred to in Article 5.1 are written in a foreign language, a Chinese version must be attached.

Article 6   The People's Bank of China shall approve the conduct of part or all of the following business by a foreign bank or a Chinese-foreign joint bank in accordance with its application:

1.   Lending of national currency and foreign currency and discounting of bills;

2.   Collection of remittance and foreign exchange from foreign countries and the Hong Kong and Macao areas;

3.   Export trade balances and documentary bills;

4.   Exchange of foreign currency and bills;

5.   National and foreign currency investments;

6.   National and foreign currency guarantees:

7.   Buying and selling of shares and securities;

8.   Trust and safe-deposit business and credit information and consultation service;

9.   Outward remittances and import trade balances and documentary bills relating to overseas Chinese enterprises, foreign enterprises, Chinese-foreign joint ventures and Chinese-foreign cooperative enterprises;

10.   National and foreign currency deposits and overdrafts relating to overseas Chinese enterprises, foreign enterprises, Chinese-foreign joint ventures and Chinese-foreign cooperative enterprises and national and foreign currency deposits and overdrafts relating to foreigners, overseas Chinese and compatriots from Hong Kong and Macao;

11.   Foreign exchange deposits and loans of foreign countries, Hong Kong and Macao;

12.   Other business.

Article 7   The registered capital of a foreign bank's head office or a Chinese-foreign joint bank established in a Special Economic Zone must amount to no less than the foreign exchange equivalent of 80 million RMB and its called-up capital must be no lower than 50 percent of the registered capital. A branch of a foreign bank established in a Special Economic Zone must possess operating capital of no less than the foreign exchange equivalent of 40 million RMB, allocated by the head office.

Within thirty days of the date of approval of its establishment, the foreign bank or Chinese-foreign joint bank must raise the called-up capital or operating capital in full, and such capital must be verified by an accountant registered in the People's Republic of China.

Article 8   Within thirty days of the date of approval of establishment a foreign bank or Chinese-foreign joint bank must register with the Administrative Bureau for Industry and Commerce and obtain a business licence, and within thirty days of the date of beginning operations, such banks must register with the local tax authorities.

If a foreign bank or Chinese-foreign joint bank does not begin operations within twelve months of the date of its notification of approval, the original certificate of approval automatically loses effect.

Article 9   The head office of a foreign bank or a Chinese-foreign joint bank establishel in a Special Economic Zone must not loan more than 30 percent of its total called-up capital plus reserve funds to an enterprise in the Special Economic Zone, and its total investment in the Special Economic Zone must not exceed 30 percent of its total called-up capital plus reserve funds.

Article 10   The foreign bank or Chinese-foreign joint bank, in the exchange and balance of national and foreign currency, should abide by the exchange rate and relevant regulations promulgated by the State Foreign Exchange Administration.

The foreign bank and Chinese-foreign joint bank, in deciding the interest rate for varieties of national and foreign currency deposits, loans, overdrafts, and discounting of bills in the Special Economic Zone, may refer to the interest rate established by the Special Economic Zone's branch of the People's Bank of China.

Article 11   A foreign bank or Chinese-foreign joint bank that wants to handle deposits of any national or foreign currency in the Special Economic Zones should deposit reserve funds in the Special Economic Zone's branch of the People's Bank of China.

Article 12   Foreign banks or Chinese-foreign joint banks should transmit the following business reports to the Special Economic Zone's branch of the People's Bank of China.

1.   Before the tenth day of the month the previous month's assets and liabilities;

2.   Before the fifteenth day of the first month in a quarter the previous quarter's deposit and loan analysis table, outward and inward remittance amounts, import and export balance analysis table, and investment analysis table;

3.   Before the end of th third month in a year the previous year's assets and liabilities list, profit and loss statement and balance table, attached to the inspection report written by an accountant registered in the People's Republic of China.

Article 13   The Special Economic Zone's branch of the People's Bank of China has the power to inspect the foreign bank's or Chinese-foreign joint bank's business and financial condition to order the bank to provide relevant materials, and to appoint personnel to examine the bank's account books and file.

Article 14   After paying tax according to the law, the branch office of a foreign bank can remit its profit out of China.

After payment of tax, the head office of a foreign bank or a Chinese-foreign joint bank established in a Special Economic Zone should, according to regulations, withdraw from their profit reserve funds, staff and workers' monetary awards, welfare funds, and business development fund; the bank's foreign investors can remit out of China that part of the profit that is their gains.

Workers and staff of foreign banks or Chinese-foreign joint banks from foreign countries, Hong Kong and Macao, can remit their wages and salaries and other legitimate income out of China after paying tax according to the law.

Article 15 Within thirty days of terminating business operations a foreign or a Chinese-foreign joint bank must submit a written report to the People's Bank of China for approval.

The foreign bank or Chinese-foreign joint bank terminating business operations should carry out liquidation in accordance with the regulations of the People's Republic of China on the breakup and settlement of foreign enterprises and Chinese-foreign joint ventures and under the supervision of the Special Economic Zone's branch of the People's Bank of China and relevant departments. After payment of tax and debt the capital of the foreign banks or the capital owned by or apportioned to foreign investors of the Chinese-foreign joint banks can be remitted out of China.

After completing liquidation, foreign banks or Chinese-foreign joint banks should file for cancellation with the agency that issued the original certificate of approval.

Article 16 If a foreign bank or Chinese-foreign joint bank violates these Regulations or any other financial laws and regulations, the Special Economic Zone's branch of the People's Bank of China has the right to give the banks a warning or impose a fine, based on the seriousness of the case. If the bank objects, it may petition the People's Bank of China, and the People's Bank of China will decide as to the objection's validity.

If a foreign bank or Chinese-foreign joint bank commits an especially grave violation of the law, the People's Bank of China can order it to stop business operations and even close its office.

Article 17 These Regulations are applicable accordingly to banks and financial agencies with overseas Chinese capital or with capital from Hong Kong and Macao established in the Special Economic Zones.

Article 18 These Regulations shall be interpreted by the People's Bank of China.

Article 19 These Regulations shall go into effect on the day they are promulgated.

中华人民共和国经济特区
外资银行、中外合资银行管理条例

（一九八五年四月二日国务院发布）

第一条 为了扩大国际经济、金融合作，有助于引进外资、引进技术，有益于经济特区的发展，特制定本条例。

第二条 本条例所称外资银行是指总行设在外国或香港、澳门地区，依照当地法律注册的外国资本的银行在经济特区设立的分行，以及总行设在经济特区，依照中华人民共和国法律注册的外国资本的银行。

本条例所称中外合资银行是指外国资本的银行、金融机构同中国资本的银行、金融机构在经济特区合资经营的银行。

第三条 外资银行、中外合资银行必须遵守中华人民共和国的法律、法规，其正当业务活动和合法权益受中华人民共和国法律保护。

第四条 在经济特区设立外资银行、中外合资银行，必须向中国人民银行提出申请；中国人民银行根据经济特区发展的需要和平等互利的原则进行审批。

中国人民银行经济特区分行对外资银行、中外合资银行进行管理和监督。

国家外汇管理局对外资银行、中外合资银行颁发经营外汇业务许可证。

第五条　申请设立外资银行、中外合资银行，分别按照以下规定办理：

（一）外国资本的银行在经济特区设立分行，应当由其总行提出申请并提交下列证件、资料：

1.由董事会授权董事长或总经理签署、并经公证机构证明的申请书，其内容包括：分行名称、总行拨给的营运资金数额、主要负责人员的简历和授权书、申请经营业务种类等；

2.总行组织章程，董事会董事名单，申请设行前三年的资产负债表、损益计算书、业务状况报告；

3.所在国或地区的有关主管当局核发的营业执照（副本）；

4.总行承担税务、债务的责任担保书。

（二）在经济特区设立外资银行总行，应当由外国投资者提出申请，并提交下列证件、资料：

1.设立外资银行的申请书，其内容包括：总行名称、注册资本和实收资本、主要负责人员名单、申请经营业务种类等；

2.组织章程；

3.投资者提出的董事长、副董事长、董事人选名单；

4.投资者的资产、负债状况，并附经公证机构证明的文件。

（三）在经济特区设立中外合资银行，应当由合资各方共同提出申请，并提交下列证件、资料：

1.设立合资银行的申请书，其内容包括：合资银行名称、合资各方名称、注册资本和实收资本、各方出资比例、主要负责人员人选名单、申请经营业务种类等；

2.合资各方共同编制的可行性研究报告；

3.由合资各方授权代表草签的合资银行协议、合同和章程的草案；

4.由合资各方提出的合资银行董事长、副董事长、董事人选名单。

（四）设在经济特区的外资银行、中外合资银行在特区另设分支机构，应当提出申请并由中国人民银行经济特区分行批准。

本条第一款各项所指的证件、资料，凡用外文书写的，都应附具中文译本。

第六条　中国人民银行根据外资银行、中外合资银行的申请，批准其经营下列业务项目的部分或全部：

（一）本、外币放款和票据贴现；

（二）国外和香港、澳门地区汇入汇款和外汇托收；

（三）出口贸易结算和押汇；

（四）外币和外币票据兑换；

（五）本、外币投资业务；

（六）本、外币担保业务；

（七）股票、证券买卖；

（八）信托，保管箱业务，资信调查和咨询服务；

（九）侨资企业、外资企业、中外合资经营企业和中外合作经营企业的汇出汇款、进口贸易结算和押汇；

（十）侨资企业、外资企业、中外合资经营企业和中外合作经营企业的本、外币存款及透支，外国人、华侨和港澳同胞的本、外币存款及透支；

（十一）办理国外或香港、澳门地区的外汇存款和外汇放款；

（十二）其他业务。

第七条　设在经济特区的外资银行总行、中外合资银行，其注册资本不得少于八千万元人民币的等值外汇，实收资本不得低于注册资本的50%；在经济特区设立的外资银行分行必须持有其总行拨给的不少于四千万元人民币等值外汇的营运资金。

外资银行、中外合资银行的实收资本或营运资金应当自批准设立之日起三十天内筹足，并由在中华人民共和国注册的会计师验证。

第八条　外资银行、中外合资银行自批准之日起三十天内，应当向工商行政管理局办理登记手续，领取营业执照，并应自开业之日起三十天内向当地税务机关办理税务登记。

外资银行、中外合资银行自批准之日起十二个月内未开业者，原批准证件自动失效。

第九条　设在经济特区的外资银行总行、中外合资银行对经济特区一个企业的放款不得多于该行实收资本加储备基金总数的30%；对经济特区的投资总额不得多于该行实收资本加储备基金总数的30%。

第十条　外资银行、中外合资银行经营本币对外币的兑换和结算，应当按照国家外汇管理局公布的汇价和有关规定办理。

外资银行、中外合资银行办理特区内各种本、外币存款、放款、透支、票据贴现的利率，可以参照中国人民银行经济特区分行规定的利率制定。

第十一条　外资银行、中外合资银行办理特区内各种本、外币存款，应当向中国人民银行经济特区分行缴存存款准备金。

第十二条　外资银行、中外合资银行应当向中国人民银行经济特区分行报送下列业务报表：

（一）每月10日前报送上月末资产负债表；

（二）每季首月15日前报送上季度的存款放款分析表，汇出汇入款项、进出口结算分析表和投资项目分析表；

（三）每年3月底前，报送上年度资产负债表、损益计算书和科目余额表，随附在中华人民共和国登记注册会计师的审查报告。

第十三条　中国人民银行经济特区分行有权检查外资银行、中外合资银行的业务和财务状况，令其报送或提供有关情况和资料，并派出人员对其帐册、案卷等进行检查。

第十四条　外资银行分行依法纳税后的利润可以汇出。

设在经济特区的外资银行总行、中外合资银行纳税后的利润，应当按照规定提取储备基金、职工奖励金和福利基金、企业发展基金，国外投资者所得部分可以汇出。

外资银行、中外合资银行的外籍职工和港澳职工依法纳税后的工资和其他正当收益，可以汇出。

第十五条　外资银行、中外合资银行终止业务活动，必须在终止前三十天，以书面形式向中国人民银行提出报告，由中国人民银行批准。

依法停业的外资银行、中外合资银行，应当按照中华人民共和国关于外资企业、中外合资经营企业解散和清算的规定，在中国人民行银经济特区分行和有关部门的监督下，进行清理。在交清税款、偿还债务后，外资银行的资金或中外合资银行的国外投资者所有的或分得的资金，都可以汇出。

前款外资银行、中外合资银行清理完毕，应当向原发证机关办理注销登记手续。

第十六条　外资银行、中外合资银行违反本条例或其他金融法规，中国人民银行经济特区分行有权视其情节给予警告或者处以罚款。如有异议，可以向中国人民银行申诉，由中国人民银行作出裁定。

对违法情节特别严重的外资银行、中外合资银行，中国人民银行可以令其停业直至撤消机构。

第十七条　本条例对华侨资本和香港、澳门地区资本的银行、金融机构，比照适用。

第十八条　本条例由中国人民银行负责解释。

第十九条　本条例自公布之日起施行。

PROVISIONAL REGULATIONS OF THE MINISTRY OF FINANCE ON THE IMPOSITION OF CONSOLIDATED INDUSTRIAL AND COMMERCIAL TAX AND ENTERPRISE INCOME TAX ON RESIDENT REPRESENTATIVE AGENCIES OF FOREIGN ENTERPRISES

(Approved by the State Council, April 11, 1985 and promulgated by the Ministry of Finance, May 14, 1985)

In accordance with Article 2 and Article 8 of the Regulations on Consolidated Industrial and Commercial Tax of the People's Republic of China, Article 1 of the Income Tax Law of the People's Republic of China Concerning Foreign Enterprises and Article 2 and Article 4 of its Rules for Implementation, Article 9 of the Interim Provisions of the State Council of the People's Republic of China for Administration of Resident Representative Agencies of Foreign Enterprises in the People's Republic of China, and relevent provisions of the tax agreements between the Chinese government and foreign governments, the following regulations are hereby formulated for the taxation on resident representative agencies of foreign enterprises:

1. Consolidated industrial and commercial tax and enterprise income tax shall not be imposed on resident representative agencies for marketing surveying, pro-

viding market information and other business, liaison, consultations and services to their head offices without charge.

Taxes shall not be imposed on income of resident representative agencies from offshore agent activities, entrusted by enterprises in China, which are performed mainly outside China.

2. Taxes shall be levied on the following incomes of resident representative agencies:

(1) Brokerage fees, commissions, rebates and service charges for liaison work in business negotiations and transactions in China, on behalf of the head office, entrusted by other enterprises.

(2) Payments at fixed rates periodically or on a service-item basis for providing marketing surveying, business liaison service, collecting business information and consultation, performed in China, for the clients of the resident representative agencies (including the clients of their head offices).

(3) Brokerage fees, commissions, service charges of resident representative agencies for agent services in China for another enterprise, or as liaison or intermediate between other enterprises for business negotiation and transaction.

3. Taxes levied on commissions of liaison service, negotiation or intermediation received by resident representative agencies shall be based on the amount as specified in the contracts. Taxes shall be imposed by the tax authority according to the amount of transaction with reference to the regular brokerage rates. If not specified, and no sufficient support documents for accurate amount of commission can be provided. In case of the condition

as mentioned in 2(1), if hte work of an assignment is partly performed by the head office outside China, relative documentation should be delivered to the tax authority by the resident representative agency for assessing the tax amount to be paid in China.

4. Tax on brokerage fees, commissions and service charges earned by resident representative agencies for agent services and intermediation, which is a taxable item listed in the Rates of Consolidated Industrial and Commercial Tax, may be levied at a reduction rates of 5 percent. Unless sufficient supporting documentation can be provided for cost and expenses to assess taxable income, income tax should be imposed on the basis of a deemed profit rate, which is provisionally calculated at 15 percent of the business revenue, according to the provisions of Article 24, of the Rules for the Implementation of the Income Tax Law of the People's Republic of China covering foreign enterprises.*

5. The term "enterprise" as used in these Regulations applies also to "companies" and "economic organizations."

6. The right to interpret these Regulations resides

---

* A notice was issued by the Ministry of Finance on October 6, 1986 to the effect that in order to encourage the resident representative agencies to develop their business and considering the uneven profit rates among the agencies, it was decided and approved by the State Council that, beginning from October 1, 1986, the deemed profit rate of the resident representative agencies was reduced from 15 percent to 10 percent of their business revenue.

in the Ministry of Finance of the People's Republic of China.

7.   These Regulations shall go into effect as from 1985.

中华人民共和国财政部
对外国企业常驻代表机构征收工商
统一税、企业所得税的暂行规定

（一九八五年四月十一日国务院批准，
一九八五年五月十四日财政部公布）

根据《中华人民共和国工商统一税条例》第二条、第八条，《中华人民共和国外国企业所得税法》第一条及其《施行细则》，第二条、第四条，《中华人民共和国国务院关于管理外国企业常驻代表机构的暂行规定》第九条，以及中国政府同外国政府缔结的税收协定的有关规定，现对外国企业常驻代表机构的征税问题，作如下规定：

一、常驻代表机构为其总机构进行了解市场情况、提供商情资料以及其他业务联络、咨询、服务活动，凡没有营业收入、服务收入的，不征收工商统一税、企业所得税。

常驻代表机构接受中国境内企业的委托，在中国境外从事代理业务，其活动主要是在中国境外进行的，所取得的收入不征税。

二、常驻代表机构有下列收入的，应当征税：

（一）常驻代表机构为其总机构在中国境外接受其他企业委托的代理业务，在中国境内从事联络洽谈、介绍成交，所收取的佣金、回扣、手续费；

（二）常驻代表机构为其客户（包括其总机构客户）在中国境内负责了解市场情况、联络事务、收集商情资料、提供咨询服务，由客户按期定额付给的报酬或者按代办事项业务量付给的报酬；

（三）常驻代表机构在中国境内为其他企业从事代理业务，为其他企业之间的经济贸易交往从事联络洽谈、居间介绍，所收取的佣金、回扣、手续费。

三、常驻代表机构从事联络洽谈、居间介绍所收取的佣金，在合同中载明佣金金额的，按合同规定的金额计算征税；在合同中没有载明佣金金额，不能提供准确的证明文件和正确申报佣金收入额的，可以由当地税务机关参照一般佣金水平，按介绍成交额核定相应的金额计算征税。其中属于本规定第二条第一项所列情况，在一项代理业务中，有一部分工作是由其总机构在中国境外进行的，应由常驻代表机构申报并提出有关凭证资料，报送当地税务机关核定其应在中国申报纳税的金额。

　　四、常驻代表机构从事代理业务或居间介绍所收取的佣金、回扣、手续费，属于《工商统一税税目税率表》列举征税项目的，可以减按5%的税率征税。应征收的企业所得税，除了能够提供准确的成本、费用凭证，正确计算应纳税所得额的以外，应按照《中华人民共和国外国企业所得税法施行细则》第二十四条规定，核定利润率，暂以业务收入额的15%为应纳税的所得额，计算征收所得税*。

　　五、本规定所称"企业"，包括"公司"，"经济组织"。

　　六、本规定由财政部负责解释。

　　七、本规定自1985年度起施行。

------

　　*据财政部1986年10月6日通知：为了进一步鼓励代机构开展业务，照顾到代表机构之间利润率水平高低不一的实际情况，经报国务院批准，决定自1986年10月1日起，对常驻代表机构的核定利润率由15%减按10%执行。

ADMINISTRATIVE REGULATIONS OF THE PEOPLE'S REPUBLIC OF CHINA ON CONTRACTS INVOLVING THE IMPORT OF TECHNOLOGY

(Promulgated by the State Council on May 24, 1985)

Article 1 These Regulations are formulated to expand foreign economic and technological cooperation, improve China's scientific and technological level and promote the development of the national economy.

Article 2 As used in these Regulations, "the import of technoloy" refers to the acquisition of technology by companies, enterprises, organizations or individuals within the territory of the People's Republic of China (hereinafter referred to as the "recipient"), through trade or economic and technological cooperation, from companies, enterprises, organizations or individuals outside the territory of the People's Republic of China (hereinafter referred to as the "supplier"). This applies to the following items:

(1) Transfer or permit of patent right or other industrial property rights;

(2) Patented technoloy on technological process, formulas, design of products, quality control and management provided in the form of drawings, technological data and technological norms;

(3) Technological service.

Article 3 The imported technology must be appropriate and advanced and should meet at least one of the following requirements:

(1) Capable of developing and producing new products;

(2) Capable of improving the quality and function of products and reducing the cost of production and the use of energy and materials;

(3) Conducive to full use of domestic resources;

(4) Capable of expanding product exports and increasing foreign exchange income;

(5) Conducive to environmental protection;

(6) Contributing to safety in production;

(7) Contributing to improvement in management and administration;

(8) Contributing to raising scientific and technological levels.

Article 4 The recipient and the supplier must sign a written contract for the import of technology (hereinafter referred to as the "contract"), and within thirty days after the date of signing, the recipient shall submit a written application to the Ministry of Foreign Economic Relations and Trade of the People's Republic of China or to other agencies authorized by the Ministry to undertake examination and approval (hereinafter referred to as the "examining and approving agency"). Within sixty days after the date of receipt of application the examining and approving agency shall decide whether or not to approve it. The approved contract takes effect on the date of approval. If the examining and approving agency does not come to a decision within the designated period, the contract is considered approved and automatically comes into effect.

Article 5   Contracts involving the import of technology must abide by the Law of the People's Republic of China on Economic Contracts Involving Foreign Interests and by relevant provisions in other laws.

The parties must make the following points clear in the contract:

(1)   Contents, scope and essential explanation of the technology to be imported and a detailed list of technologies involving patent rights and trademarks;

(2)   The proposed technological objectives and the time limits and measures for reaching such objectives;

(3)   Payment, make-up and means of payment.

Article 6   The supplier must guarantee that he is the legitimate owner of the technology to be supplied and guarantee the integrity, correctness and effectiveness of the technology and its ability to achieve the objectives of the contract.

Article 7   With regard to any part of the technology that is still secret, the recipient shall keep it confidential within the scope and time limit negotiated by both parties.

Article 8   The time limit of the contract must suit the length of time the recipient needs to master the technology, but it must not exceed ten years without special approval by the examining and approving agency.

Article 9   The supplier must not force the recipient to accept unreasonable restrictive requirement.   Without special approval of the examining and approving agency the contract must not include the following restrictive items:

(1)   A demand that the recipient accept items that have nothing to do with the technology to be imported, such as unnecessary technology, technological service, raw

materials, equipment or products;

(2) Restrictions on the recipient's buying freely from different sources raw materials, spare and component parts or equipment;

(3) Restrictions on the recipient's developing and improving the imported technology;

(4) Refusal to allow the recipient to obtain from other sources similar technology or competitive technology of the same type;

(5) Unequal bases for the parties' exchange of improved technology;

(6) A limit on the number, assortment or selling price of the products the recipient will produce with the technology to be imported;

(7) Unreasonable restrictions on the recipient's sales channels or export market;

(8) Refusal to allow the recipient to continue using the imported technology after expiration of the contract period;

(9) A demand that the recipient pay for or bear responsibility for an unemployed or invalid patent.

Article 10 When the contract is submitted for approval, the following documents must be attached:

(1) Application for submission and approval;

(2) A copy and a translation of the contract;

(3) Documents that identify the legal status of the parties signing the contract.

Article 11 Revision or extension of the contract must be handled in accordance with Article 4 and Article 10 of these Regulations.

Article 12 Interpretation of these Regulations and the formulation of rules for their implementation are the responsibility of the Ministry of Foreign Economic Relations and Trade.

Article 13   These Regulations shall take effect the day of promulgation.

中华人民共和国技术引进
合同管理条例

（一九八五年五月二十四日国务院发布）

第一条 为了进一步扩大对外经济技术合作，提高我国科学技术水平，促进国民经济发展，特制定本条例。

第二条 本条例规定的技术引进是指中华人民共和国境内的公司、企业、团体或个人（以下简称受方），通过贸易或经济技术合作的途径，从中华人民共和国境外的公司、企业、团体或个人（以下简称供方）获得技术，其中包括：

（一）专利权或其他工业产权的转让或许可；

（二）以图纸、技术资料、技术规范等形式提供的工艺流程、配方、产品设计、质量控制以及管理等方面的专有技术；

（三）技术服务。

第三条 引进的技术必须先进适用，并且应当符合下列一项以上的要求：

（一）能发展和生产新产品；

（二）能提高产品质量和性能，降低生产成本，节约能源或材料；

（三）有利于充分利用本国的资源；

（四）能扩大产品出口，增加外汇收入；

（五）有利于环境保护；

（六）有利于生产安全；

（七）有利于改善经营管理；

（八）有利于提高科学技术水平。

第四条　受方和供方必须签订书面的技术引进合同（以下简称合同），并由受方在签字之日起三十天内提出申请书，报中华人民共和国对外经济贸易部或对外经济贸易部授权的其他机关（以下简称审批机关）审批；审批机关应当在收到申请书之日起的六十天内决定批准或不批准；经批准的合同自批准之日起生效。在规定的审批期限内，如果审批机关没有作出决定，即视同获得批准，合同自动生效。

第五条　技术引进合同的签订，应当遵守《中华人民共和国涉外经济合同法》和其他法律的有关规定。

下列事项，双方应当在合同中加以明确：

（一）引进的技术的内容、范围和必要的说

明，其中涉及专利和商标的应当附具清单；

（二）预计达到的技术目标以及实现各该目标的期限和措施；

（三）报酬、报酬的构成和支付方式。

第六条　供方应当保证自己是所提供的技术的合法拥有者，并且保证所提供的技术完整、无误、有效，能够达到合同规定的目标。

第七条　受方应当按照双方商定的范围和期限，对供方提供的技术中尚未公开的秘密部分，承担保密义务。

第八条　合同的期限应当同受方掌握引进技术的时间相适应，未经审批机关特殊批准不得超过十年。

第九条　供方不得强使受方接受不合理的限制性要求；未经审批机关特殊批准，合同不得含有下列限制性条款：

（一）要求受方接受同技术引进无关的附带条件，包括购买不需要的技术、技术服务、原材料、设备或产品；

（二）限制受方自由选择从不同来源购买原材料、零部件或设备；

（三）限制受方发展和改进所引进的技术；

（四）限制受方从其他来源获得类似技术或

与之竞争的同类技术；

（五）双方交换改进技术的条件不对等；

（六）限制受方利用引进的技术生产产品的数量、品种或销售价格；

（七）不合理地限制受方的销售渠道或出口市场；

（八）禁止受方在合同期满后，继续使用引进的技术；

（九）要求受方为不使用的或失效的专利支付报酬或承担义务。

第十条　合同报批必须提交下列文件：

（一）报批申请书；

（二）合同副本和合同译文文本；

（三）签约双方法律地位的证明文件。

第十一条　修订合同或延长合同期限，都应当比照本条例第四条、第十条的规定办理。

第十二条　本条例由对外经济贸易部负责解释；施行细则由对外经济贸易部制定。

第十三条　本条例自发布之日起施行。

INTERIM PROVISIONS OF THE STATE COUNCIL FOR PREFERENTIAL TREATMENT IN CHINESE-FOREIGN COOPERATIVE CONSTRUCTION OF PORTS AND DOCKS

(Promulgated by the State Council on September 30, 1985)

Article 1 These Interim Provisions are formulated to expand foreign economic cooperation and exchange of technology and to speed up the construction of ports and docks to keep up with the development of China's socialist modernization.

Article 2 For joint ventures by foreign companies, enterprises or individuals (hereinafter referred to as the "foreign joint venturers") and Chinese companies and enterprises, (hereinafter referred to as "joint ventures") established within the territory of the People's Republic of China engaging in the construction of ports and docks, besides subject to the relevant laws, regulations and rules on joint ventures, will be given preferential treatment in line with these Interim Provisions, provided the actual situation calls for a larger investment and a prolonged construction cycle and the venture manifests a low rate of profit.

Article 3 The joint ventures are permitted a longer joint operation period, exceeding thirty years; the specific time limit shall be negotiated by the parties to the joint

160

venture. The time limit can be extended upon expiration of the joint operation period if the parties to the joint venture agree and apply to the Ministry of Foreign Economic Relations and Trade of the People's Republic of China or to the agencies entrusted by the Ministry for approval.

Article 4 The joint venture, upon application, examination by local tax authorities and approval by the Ministry of Finance, can use accelerated depreciation of fixed assets as a way for return of investment.

Article 5 Raw materials, loading and unloading equipment, means of transport, and other facilities indispensable to the construction of docks imported by the joint venture with capital within the total investment shall be free of customs duties and consolidated industrial and commercial tax.

Article 6 The income tax of joint ventures shall be paid at a reduced rate of 15 percent. Joint ventures newly established with an operation period exceeding fifteen years, after approved by the tax authority of provinces, autonomous regions or municipalities directly under the central government where the joint venture is located, shall enjoy five years' tax holiday since the first profitable year, and 50 percent tax reduction from the sixth year to the tenth year.

If a joint venture, after expiration of the tax-exempt period and tax reduction period, still has difficulty in paying tax, after approved by the Ministry of Finance of the People's Republic of China, the tax exemption or reduction period can be extended for an appropriate period.

The exemption or reduction of local sur-tax shall be decided by the people's government of the province, autonomous region or municipality directly under the central government where the joint venture is located.

Article 7   Foreign joint venturers' share of joint-venture profits to be remitted out of China shall be exempt from income tax.

Article 8   Rates for cargo handling fees and other fees at docks built by joint ventures shall be decided by the joint ventures themselves and reported to the competent authority of the joint ventures and the competent local department of price administration for the record.

Article 9   If the foreign joint venturer reinvests the profit alloted to him by the joint venture in cooperative construction of a new berth or dock and the time limit is not less than five years, upon application to and the approval of the tax authorities, 40 percent of the income tax on the reinvested profit shall be refunded.

Article 10   The joint venture is permitted simultaneous operation of projects demanding a smaller investment and shorter construction cycle and obtaining a higher rate of profit; matters concerned shall be handled in accordance with current regulations.

Article 11   Establishment of joint ventures engaging in the construction of ports and docks by companies, enterprises or individuals with joint venturers from Hong Kong and Macao shall be handled in accordance with these Interim Provisions.

Article 12   These Interim Provisions shall take effect the day of their promulgation.

中华人民共和国国务院关于
中外合资建设港口码头优
惠待遇的暂行规定

（一九八五年九月三十日国务院发布）

第一条 为了扩大对外经济合作和技术交流，加速港口码头的建设，以适应我国社会主义现代化建设事业的发展，特制定本规定。

第二条 外国公司、企业或个人（以下简称外国合营者），在中华人民共和国境内，同中国的公司、企业共同投资兴办合营企业（以下简称合营企业）建设港口码头，除适用有关合营企业的法律、法规、规章外，根据其投资大、建设周期长和资金利润率低的实际情况，按照本规定给予优惠待遇。

第三条 允许合营企业有较长的合营期，可以超过三十年，具体合营期限由合营各方协商确定。合营期满后，如合营各方同意并报中华人民共和国对外经济贸易部或其委托机构批准，还可以延长合营期限。

第四条　经合营企业申请，当地税务机关审核并报中华人民共和国财政部批准，企业可以采取固定资产加速折旧的办法回收投资。

第五条　合营企业以投资总额内的资金进口建设码头必需的原材料、装卸设备、运输工具和其他生产设施，免征关税和工商统一税。

第六条　合营企业按百分之十五的税率缴纳所得税。对新办的合营企业，合营期在十五年以上的，经企业申请，所在地的省、自治区、直辖市税务机关批准，从开始获利的年度起，第一年至第五年免征所得税，第六年至第十年减半征收所得税。

合营企业按照前款规定免税、减税期满后，纳税仍有困难的，经中华人民共和国财政部批准，还可以适当延长免税、减税的年限。

对合营企业征收的地方所得税，需要减征或免征的，由合营企业所在地的省、自治区、直辖市人民政府决定。

第七条　合营企业的外国合营者将从企业分得的利润汇出境外，免征所得税。

第八条　合营企业所建码头的装卸费等费率标准，由企业自定，报企业主管部门和当地物价主管部门备案。

第九条　合营企业的外国合营者，将从企业分得的利润，再投资合营建设新的泊位或码头，期限不少于五年的，经外国合营者申请，税务机关批准，退还再投资部分已纳所得税税款的百分之四十。

第十条　允许合营企业兼营投资较少、建设周期较短、资金利润率较高的项目，其有关事宜按照现行规定办理。

第十一条　香港、澳门地区的公司、企业或个人投资兴办合营企业建设港口码头的，比照本规定办理。

第十二条　本规定自发布之日起施行。

LAW OF THE PEOPLE'S REPUBLIC OF CHINA ON ENTRY AND EXIT OF ALIENS

(Adopted by the Standing Committee of the Sixth National People's Congress at Its Thirteenth Session on November 22, 1985)

CHAPTER I GENERAL PROVISIONS

Article 1 The present Law is enacted for the purpose of safeguarding the sovereignty and maintaining the security and public order of the People's Republic of China and facilitating international exchanges.

The present Law shall apply to aliens entering, leaving or passing through the territory of the People's Republic of China and to aliens residing or travelling in China.

Article 2 Aliens must obtain permission from the competent authorities of the Chinese Government for their entry, transit and residence in China.

Article 3 For entry, exit and transit, aliens shall pass through the ports open to aliens or other designated ports and shall be subject to inspection at border checkposts.

For entry, exit and transit, foreign-owned means of transport shall pass through the ports open to aliens or other designated ports and shall be subject to inspection and supervision at border checkposts.

Article 4 The Chinese Government protects the legitimate rights and interests of aliens within Chinese territory.

The personal freedom of aliens shall be inviolable. Aliens shall not be liable to arrest unless a warrant or decision is made by a people's procuratorate or a decision is made by a people's court and such a warrant or decision is executed by a public security organ or state security organ.

Article 5 Aliens in China shall abide by Chinese law and shall not endanger the national security of China, harm its public interests or disturb its public order.

CHAPTER II ENTRY

Article 6 For entry into China, aliens shall apply for visas to the Chinese diplomatic missions or consular posts or other agencies abroad authorized by the Ministry of Foreign Affairs of the People's Republic of China. In specific situations and in compliance with the stipulations of the State Council, aliens may also apply for visas to visa offices at the ports designated by the competent authorities of the Chinese Government.

The entry of nationals of a country having a visa agreement with the Chinese Government shall be dealt with in accordance with the said agreement.

In cases where a country has special regulations regarding the entry and transit of Chinese citizens, the competent authorities of the Chinese Government may take corresponding measures, contingent on the circumstances.

Visas are not required for aliens who hold tickets for continuing international flights and who are in immediate transit and stay no longer than twenty-four hours at an airport in China. Aliens wishing to leave the airport temporarily may obtain permission from the border checkposts.

Article 7 In applying for visas, aliens shall present valid passports and, if necessary, provide pertinent certificates.

Article 8 Aliens invited or employed to work in China shall, in applying for visas, produce letters of invitation or employment.

Article 9 Aliens wishing to reside in China permanently shall, in applying for visas, present residence confirmation forms, which may be obtained upon application from the public security organs at the intended places of residence.

Article 10 The competent authorities of the Chinese Government shall issue appropriate visas to aliens according to the purposes stated in their entry applications.

Article 11 When an airborne vehicle or a vessel in international operation arrives at a Chinese port, the captain or his agent must submit a passenger list to the border checkpost; in the case of a foreign aircraft or vessel, a list of crew members must be provided as well.

Article 12 An alien considered a potential threat to China's national security and public order shall not be permitted to enter China.

CHAPTER III RESIDENCE

Article 13 Aliens residing in China shall possess identity cards or residence certificates issued by the competent authorities or the Chinese Government.

The term of validity of an identity card or residence certificate shall be decided according to the purposes of entry.

Aliens residing in China shall submit certificates for examination to the local public security organs within the prescribed period of time.

Article 14   Aliens who, in compliance with Chinese law, wish to have long-term residence in China for the purpose of investing in China or engaging in cooperative projects with Chinese enterprises or institutions in the economic, scientific-technological and cultural fields or for other purposes may be granted the status of long-term or permanent residence upon approval by the competent authorities of the Chinese Government.

Article 15   An alien who seeks asylum for political reasons shall be permitted to reside in China upon approval by the competent authorities of the Chinese Government.

Article 16   An alien who fails to abide by Chinese law may have his stay in China shortened or his status of residence in China annulled by the competent authorities of the Chinese Government.

Article 17   Aliens wishing to make temporary overnight stays in China shall complete registration procedures pursuant to the relevant stipulations.

Article 18   Aliens holding residence certificates who wish to change places of residence in China shall complete removal formalities pursuant to the relevant stipulations.

Article 19   Aliens who have no residence certificates or are on a study programme in China shall not be employed in China without permission of the competent authorities of the Chinese Government.

CHAPTER IV   TRAVEL

Article 20   Aliens who hold valid visas or residence certificates may travel to places declared open to aliens by the Chinese Government.

Article 21   Aliens wishing to travel to places not open to aliens shall apply to the local public security organs for travel permits.

CHAPTER V   EXIT

Article 22   For exit from China, aliens shall present their valid passports or any other valid certificates.

Article 23   Aliens shall not be allowed to leave China if they come under any of the following categories:

(1)   A defendant in a criminal procedure or a criminal suspect listed by a public security organ or people's procuratorate or people's court;

(2)   A person under notice by a people's court to be denied exit for an unsettled civil procedure;

(3)   A person awaiting decision for any other violation of Chinese law whose case, in the opinion of the competent authorities, calls for investigation.

Article 24   Border checkposts have the power to withhold exit of aliens in any of the following categories and to subject them to rules of the law:

(1)   A holder of an invalid exit certificate;

(2)   A holder of an exit certificate other than his own;

(3)   A holder of a forged or altered exit certificate.

CHAPTER VI   ADMINISTRATIVE ORGANS

Article 25   China's diplomatic missions and consular posts and other agencies abroad authorized by the Ministry of Foreign Affairs are the agencies of the Chinese Government abroad to handle aliens' applications for entry and transit.

The Ministry of Public Security, its authorized local public security organs, the Ministry of Foreign Affairs and its authorized local foreign affairs offices are the agencies of the Chinese Government at home to handle aliens' application for entry, transit, residence and travel.

Article 26 The authorities handling aliens' applications for entry, transit, residence and travel have the power to decline issuing visas and certificates or to cancel or annul visas and certificates already issued.

The Ministry of Public Security and the Ministry of Foreign Affairs may, if necessary, alter decisions made by their respectively authorized organs.

Article 27 An alien illegally entering or residing in China may be detained for investigation or placed under residential surveillance or deportation by public security organs at and above county level.

Article 28 Police in charge of aliens' affairs in the public security organs at and above county level have, in performing their duties, the power to examine aliens' passports and other certificates. When conducting such examinations, the said police shall produce their own service cards, and the organizations or individuals concerned are obliged to cooperate.

CHAPTER VII   PENALTIES

Article 29 Whoever illegally enters, leaves, resides or stops over in China, travels to places not open to aliens without a valid travel permit, or forges, alters, misuses or negotiates an entry or exit certificate in contravention of the provisions of the present law may be subjected to such penalties as warning, fine or detention for not more than ten days by public security organs at and above county level. Offenders whose violations are serious enough to constitute crimes shall be prosecuted in accordance with the law.

If an alien being fined or detained by a public security organ refuses to accept the penalty, he may, within fifteen days of receiving notification, appeal to the next higher public security organ, which shall make final judgement, and/or file suit directly in a local people's court.

Article 30 The Ministry of Public Security may order serious offenders, as listed in Article 29 of the present Law, to leave the country within a limited time or may expel them.

CHAPTER VIII   ANCILLARY PROVISIONS

Article 31 The term "alien" used in this Law refers to any person not having Chinese nationality under the Nationality Law of the People's Republic of China.

Article 32 Transitory entry into and exit from China by aliens who are nationals of countries adjacent to China and reside in contiguous areas between the two countries shall be handled pursuant to agreements between the two countries; in absence of such agreement, transitory entry and exit shall be handled in accordance with the relevant stipulations of the Chinese Government.

Article 33 Rules for implementation of the present Law shall be formulated according to the law by the Ministry of Public Security and the Ministry of Foreign Affairs and shall come into force upon approval by the State Council.

Article 34 Matters concerning the members of foreign diplomatic missions and consular posts in the People's Republic of China and other aliens who enjoy privileges and immunities, after their entry into China, shall be dealt with in accordance with the relevant stipulations of the State Council and its competent authorities.

Article 35 This Law shall come into force as of February 1, 1986.

中华人民共和国外国人
入境出境管理法

（一九八五年十一月二十二日）第六届全国人民代表大
会常务委员会第十三次会议通过）

第一章　总　　则

第一条　为维护中华人民共和国的主权、安
全和社会秩序，有利于发展国际交往，特制定本
法。

外国人入、出、通过中华人民共和国国境和
在中国居留、旅行，适用本法。

第二条　外国人入境、过境和在中国境内居
留，必须经中国政府主管机关许可。

第三条　外国人入境、出境、过境，必须从
对外国人开放的或者指定的口岸通行，接受边防
检查机关的检查。

外国的交通工具入境、出境、过境，必须从
对外国人开放的或者指定的口岸通行，接受边防
检查机关的检查和监护。

第四条　中国政府保护在中国境内的外国人

的合法权利和利益。

外国人的人身自由不受侵犯，非经人民检察院批准或者决定或者人民法院决定，并由公安机关或者国家安全机关执行，不受逮捕。

第五条 外国人在中国境内，必须遵守中国法律，不得危害中国国家安全、损害社会公共利益、破坏社会公共秩序。

第二章　入　　境

第六条 外国人入境，应当向中国的外交代表机关、领事机关或者外交部授权的其他驻外机关申请办理签证。在特定情况下，依照国务院规定，外国人也可以向中国政府主管机关指定口岸的签证机关申请办理签证。

同中国政府订有签证协议的国家的人员入境，按照协议执行。

外国对中国公民入境、过境有专门规定的，中国政府主管机关可以根据情况采取相应措施。

持联程客票搭乘国际航班直接过境，在中国停留不超过二十四小时不出机场的外国人，免办签证。要求临时离开机场的，需经边防检查机关批准。

第七条 外国人申请各项签证，应当提供有效护照，必要时提供有关证明。

第八条　应聘或者受雇来中国工作的外国人，申请签证时，应当持有应聘或者受雇证明。

第九条　来中国定居的外国人，申请签证时，应当持有定居身份确认表。定居身份确认表，由申请人向申请定居地的公安机关申请领取。

第十条　中国政府主管机关根据外国人申请入境的事由，发给相应的签证。

第十一条　从事国际航行的航空器或者船舶抵达中国口岸时，机长、船长或者代理人必须向边防检查机关提交旅客名单；外国的飞机、船舶还必须提供机组、船员名单。

第十二条　被认为入境后可能危害中国的国家安全、社会秩序的外国人，不准入境。

第三章　居　　留

第十三条　外国人在中国居留，必须持有中国政府主管机关签发的身份证件或者居留证件。

身份证件或者居留证件的有效期限，根据入境的事由确定。

在中国居留的外国人，应当在规定的时间内到当地公安机关缴验证件。

第十四条　依照中国法律在中国投资或者同中国的企业、事业单位进行经济、科学技术、文化合作以及其他需要在中国长期居留的外国人，经中国政府主管机关批准，可以获得长期居留或者永久居留资格。

第十五条　对因为政治原因要求避难的外国人，经中国政府主管机关批准，准许在中国居留。

第十六条　对不遵守中国法律的外国人，中国政府主管机关可以缩短其在中国停留的期限或者取消其在中国居留的资格。

第十七条　外国人在中国境内临时住宿，应当依照规定，办理住宿登记。

第十八条　持居留证件的外国人在中国变更居留地点，必须依照规定办理迁移手续。

第十九条　未取得居留证件的外国人和来中国留学的外国人，未经中国政府主管机关允许，不得在中国就业。

第四章　旅　　行

第二十条　外国人持有效的签证或者居留证件，可以前往中国政府规定的对外国人开放的地区旅行。

第二十一条　外国人前往不对外国人开放的地区旅行，必须向当地公安机关申请旅行证件。

第五章　出　　境

第二十二条　外国人出境，凭本人有效护照或者其他有效证件。

第二十三条　有下列情形之一的外国人，不准出境：

（一）刑事案件的被告人和公安机关或者人民检察院或者人民法院认定的犯罪嫌疑人；

（二）人民法院通知有未了结民事案件不能离境的；

（三）有其他违反中国法律的行为尚未处理，经有关主管机关认定需要追究的。

第二十四条　有下列情形之一的外国人，边防检查机关有权阻止出境，并依法处理：

（一）持用无效出境证件的；

（二）持用他人出境证件的；

（三）持用伪造或者涂改的出境证件的。

第六章　管理机关

第二十五条　中国政府在国外受理外国人入境、过境申请的机关，是中国的外交代表机关、领事机关和外交部授权的其他驻外机关。

中国政府在国内受理外国人入境、过境、居留、旅行申请的机关，是公安部、公安部授权的地方公安机关和外交部、外交部授权的地方外事部门。

第二十六条　受理外国人入境、过境、居留、旅行申请的机关有权拒发签证、证件；对已经发出的签证、证件，有权吊销或者宣布作废。

公安部和外交部在必要时，可以改变各自授权的机关所作出的决定。

第二十七条　对非法入境、非法居留的外国人，县级以上公安机关可以拘留审查、监视居住或者遣送出境。

第二十八条　县级以上公安机关外事民警在执行任务时，有权检验外国人的护照和其他证件。外事民警查验时，应当出示自己的工作证件，有关组织或者个人有协助的责任。

第七章　处　　罚

第二十九条　对违反本法规定，非法入境、出境的，在中国境内非法居留或者停留的，未持有效旅行证件前往不对外国人开放的地区旅行的，伪造、涂改、冒用、转让入境、出境证件的，县级以上公安机关可以处以警告、罚款或者十日以下的拘留处罚；情节严重，构成犯罪的，依法追究刑事责任。

受公安机关罚款或者拘留处罚的外国人，对处罚不服的，在接到通知之日起十五日内，可以向上一级公安机关提出申诉，由上一级公安机关作出最后的裁决，也可以直接向当地人民法院提起诉讼。

第三十条　有本法第二十九条所列行为情节严重的，公安部可以处以限期出境或者驱逐出境处罚。

第八章　附　　则

第三十一条　本法所称的外国人是指依照《中华人民共和国国籍法》不具有中国国籍的人。

第三十二条　同中国毗邻国家的外国人，居住在两国边境接壤地区的，临时入中国国境、出中国国境，有两国之间协议的按照协议执行，没有协议的按照中国政府的规定执行。

第三十三条　公安部和外交部根据本法制定实施细则，报国务院批准施行。

第三十四条　外国驻中华人民共和国外交代表机关、领事机关成员以及享有特权和豁免的其他外国人入境后的管理，按国务院及其主管机关的有关规定办理。

第三十五条　本法自一九八六年二月一日起施行。

RULES FOR IMPLEMENTATION OF THE LAW OF THE PEOPLE'S REPUBLIC OF CHINA ON ENTRY AND EXIT OF ALIENS

(Approved by the State Council on December 3, 1986, and promulgated by the Ministry of Public Security and the Ministry of Foreign Affairs on December 27, 1986)

The present Rules are formulated in accordance with the provisions of Article 33 of the Law of the People's Republic of China on Entry and Exit of Aliens (hereinafter referred to as the Law on Entry and Exit of Aliens)

CHAPTER I ENTRY

Article 1 For entry into China, aliens shall apply for visas to Chinese diplomatic missions, consular posts or other foreign-based agencies authorized by the Ministry of Foreign Affairs of the People's Republic of China.

In case of an urgent need to travel to China and a lack of time to apply for visas to the above mentioned Chinese agencies abroad, aliens holding letters or telegrams from authorized organizations in China and ordinary passports issued by countries that have diplomatic relations or official trade contacts with China may apply for visas at port visa agencies authorized by the Ministry of Public Security for any of the following reasons:

(1) Invited at short notice by the Chinese side to attend a trade fair in China;

(2) Invited to China to enter a bid or to formally sign an economic or trade contract;

(3) Under contract to supervise an export shipment, inspect an import commodity or check on the completion of a contract;

(4) Invited to instal equipment or make rush repairs;

(5) Requested by the Chinese side to settle claims;

(6) Invited to China for scientific or technological consulting services;

(7) Last-minute replacement or addition, approved by the Chinese side, to an invited delegation or group that has already obtained visas for travelling to China;

(8) To visit a patient in critical condition or make funeral arrangements;

(9) Persons in immediate transit who, because of force majeure, are unable to leave China by the original aircraft within twenty-four hours or have to leave China by other means of transport;

(10) Other invitees who do not have enough time to apply for visas to the above-mentioned Chinese agencies abroad but hold letters or telegrams from designated competent authorities approving the application for visas at port visa agencies.

Port visa agencies shall not handle visa applications of aliens who do not come under the categories listed above.

Article 2 Port visa agencies authorized by the Ministry of Public Security are set up at the following ports:

Beijing, Shanghai, Tianjin, Dalian, Fuzhou, Xiamen, Xi'an, Guilin, Hangzhou, Kunming, Guangzhou (Baiyun Airport), Shenzhen (Luohu, Shekou) and Zhuhai (Gongbei).

Article 3 In accordance with their status and the type of passport they hold, aliens coming to China shall be issued a diplomatic, courtesy, service or ordinary visa.

Article 4 Ordinary visas shall be marked with Chinese phonetic letters and issued to aliens according to the stated purpose of their visit to China.

(1) Visa D to aliens who are to reside permanently in China;

(2) Visa Z to aliens and their accompanying family members who come to China to take up posts or employment;

(3) Visa X to aliens who come to China for study, advanced studies or job training for a period of six months or more;

(4) Visa F to aliens who are invited to China for a visit or a study, lecture or business tour, for scientific and technological or cultural exchanges, for short-term refresher courses or for job training for a period of not more than six months;

(5) Visa L to aliens who come to China for sightseeing, visiting relatives or other private purposes (group visa may be issued to a group of nine or more aliens on a sightseeing trip to China);

(6) Visa G to aliens passing through China;

(7) Visa C to train attendants, airline crews and seamen and their accompanying family members in international operations.

Article 5 In applying for visas, aliens shall provide such pertinent information as requested and complete the following procedures;

(1)   Present valid passports or replacement certificates;

(2)   Fill in visa application forms and submit recent two-inch, half-length, bareheaded, full-face photos;

(3)   Submit for examination papers supporting the application for entry into or transit through China.

Article 6   The supporting papers mentioned in Article 5 (3) of these Rules refer to the following:

(1)   In applying for Visa D, a permanent residence confirmation form, which may be obtained by the alien or his/her designated relatives in China by applying to the exit-and-entry department of the municipal or county public security bureau at the place of the applicant's intended residence;

(2)   In applying for Visa Z, a letter of appointment or employment from the sponsor or employer organization in China or a letter or telegram from an authorized organization;

(3)   In applying for Visa X, a certificate from the receiving organization or the competent department;

(4)   In applying for Visa F, a letter or telegram from the authorized organization;

(5)   In applying for Visa L for a tourist trip in China, a certificate of reception from a Chinese travel service;

(6)   In applying for Visa G, a valid visa for entering the country (region) of destination or connecting tickets in case such a visa is exempt;

(7)   In applying for Visa C, relevant certificates in accordance with the agreements concerned.

Aliens who come to China for permanent residence or for residence of one year and up shall, in applying for entry visas, submit for examination a health certificate issued by a health or medical institution designated by the government of the country of their current residence or one issued by a health or medical institution and certified by a notary public. Health certificates are valid for six months from the date of issue.

Article 7 Aliens coming under the following categories shall not be allowed to enter China:

(1) An alien expelled by the Chinese Government whose period of prohibited re-entry has not yet expired.

(2) An alien considered likely to engage in terrorism, violence or subversion in China;

(3) An alien considered likely to engage in smuggling, drug trafficking or prostitution in China;

(4) An alien suffering from mental disorder, leprosy, AIDS, venereal diseases, contagious tuberculosis or other infectious diseases;

(5) An alien who cannot guarantee to cover his/her own expenses during his/her stay in China;

(6) An alien considered likely to engage in other activities prejudicial to China's national security and interests.

Article 8 Transit visas are not required for aliens who are in immediate transit through China on continuing international flights, hold connecting flight tickets and booked seats, and stay for no more than twenty-four hours at the airport of the in-transit city. Aliens wishing to leave the airport shall apply to the border checkposts for stopover permits.

Article 9 When vessels in international service

anchor at Chinese ports, foreign crew members and their accompanying family members wishing to disembark shall apply to border checkposts for disembarkation permits, or lodging permits if they desire to stay overnight on land. Those who, for proper reasons, need to travel to areas beyond the port city or cannot leave China on the original vessel shall apply to the local public security bureau for appropriate visas.

CHAPTER II INSPECTION OF ENTRY AND EXIT CERTIFICATES

Article 10 Upon arrival at Chinese port aliens shall submit their valid passport, Chinese visas and certificates to border checkposts for examination and shall fill in entry and exit forms. They may enter China after the border checkposts complete inspection and affix inspection seals.

Article 11 When a foreign airborne vehicle or vessel arrives at a Chinese port, the person in charge shall fulfil the following obligations:

(1) The captain or his/her agent must submit lists of the crew members and passengers to the border checkpost;

(2) Report, immediately upon discovery, cases of persons aboard attempting to illegally cross China's borders to the border checkpost for action;

(3) See that persons not permitted to enter China leave on the original means of transport and that the expenses during the stay in China of persons who cannot promptly leave the country through force majeure are covered along with their travel expenses for departure.

Article 12 Border checkposts have the right to prevent the entry or exit of aliens coming under the following categories:

(1) Those who do not hold valid passports, certificates or visas;

(2) Those who hold forged, altered or other than their own passports or certificates;

(3) Those who refuse to have their certificates examined;

(4) Those who are under notice by the Ministry of Public Security or the Ministry of State Security forbidding their entry or exit.

Article 13 For exit, aliens shall submit for examination their valid passports or other valid certificates as well as visas or residence certificates permitting their stay in China.

Article 14 Aliens and their means of transport, required by visa agencies to pass through designated ports, shall enter or depart only through said ports.

Article 15 Aliens denied entry under Article 12 of the present Rules who cannot promptly leave on the original means of transport may have the area of their activities limited and be ordered to leave China on the next available means of transport by the border checkpost.

CHAPTER III RESIDENCE

Article 16 Aliens holding visas D, Z or X shall, within ten days of entry into China, obtain aliens' residence cards or aliens' temporary residence cards from the city or county public security bureau at the place of their residence. The period of validity of the aforementioned certificates is the duration of the holders' permitted stay in China.

Aliens' residence cards are issued to those who stay in China for one year or more.

Aliens' temporary residence cards are issued to those who stay less than one year in China.

Aliens holding visas F, L, G or C may stay in China for the period prescribed in their visas without obtaining residence certificates.

Article 17 In applying for residence certificates, aliens shall provide such information as requested and complete the following procedures:

(1) Submit for examination their passports, visas and papers supporting their purposes of residence;

(2) Fill in residence application forms;

(3) In applying for aliens' residence cards submit for examination health certificates and recent two-inch, half-length, bareheaded, full-face photos.

Article 18 An alien's residence card's period of validity, from one to five years, shall be decided by the city or county public security bureau according to the alien's purpose of residence.

Public security organs may issue residence certificates valid for one to five years to aliens who come under the provisions of Article 14 of the Law on Entry and Exit of Aliens and may issue certificates of permanent residence to those with meritorious performance.

Article 19 Aliens exempt from visas under agreements signed between the Chinese and foreign governments shall, in case they wish to stay in China thirty days or longer, apply upon entry into China for residence certificates in accordance with Articles 16 and 17 of the present Rules. This does not apply, however, to aliens referred to in Article 34 of the Law on Entry and Exit of Aliens.

Article 20 Aliens who need to prolong their stay or residence in China beyond the expiration of their visas or residence certificates shall apply for an extension before the expiration of their visas or certificates.

Chinese authorities in charge of public health discovering aliens, during their stay in China, afflicted with diseases specified in Article 7 (4) of the present Rules may request the public security organs concerned to order them to advance their date of exit from China.

Article 21 In case of any changes in the information written in an alien's residence card (such as name, nationality, occupation, status, place of work, address, passport number and accompanying children), the holder of the card shall, within ten days, register such changes with the public security bureau at the place of his/her residence.

Article 22 The holder of an alien's residence card who wishes to move out of the city or county of residence shall, before moving, register the move with the public security bureau at the original place of residence and, within ten days of arrival at the new place of residence, register with the public security bureau at the new place of residence.

An alien residing permanently in China who wishes to apply for a change of residence shall apply in advance to the public security bureau at the new place of residence for a certificate permitting the move and register the move on the strength of the certificate in accordance with the provisions of the previous paragraph.

Article 23   For the sake of national security, public order or other public interests, a city or county public security bureau may declare certain areas out of bounds for the establishment of residences or offices by aliens or foreign institutions.   Residences and offices already established in these restricted areas shall be moved to nonrestricted areas within the time limit prescribed in the removal notice issued by the city or county public security bureau.

Article 24   Aliens residing permanently in China shall, once every year and at a prescribed time, submit their residence cards for examination to the public security bureau at their place of residence.

The public security bureau may, when necessary, ask an alien to submit his/her residence card to the exit-and-entry department for examination, and the alien shall do so at the time prescribed in the notice.

Article 25   Aliens sixteen and up who reside or stay in China shall carry with them their residence certificates or passports for possible examination by police in charge of foreign affairs.

Article 26   The parents of an alien infant born in China or their agent shall, within one month after its birth, report to the local public security bureau with the birth certificate and complete registration procedures.

Article 27   When an alien dies in China, his/her family members, guardian or agent shall, within three days, report to the local public security bureau with the death certificate and hand in the deceased's residence certificate or visa for cancellation.

In case of the unnatural death of an alien, the per-

sons concerned or the discoverer shall promptly report
to the public security organ.

Article 28 The competent authorities of the
Chinese Government referred to in Article 19 of the Law
on Entry and Exit of Aliens are the Ministry of Labour
and Personnel of the People's Republic of China.

CHAPTER IV   ACCOMMODATION REGISTRATION

Article 29   For lodging at a guesthouse, hotel, inn,
hostel, school or other enterprise or institution or at a
government or other Chinese organization, aliens shall
present valid passports or residence certificates and fill
in registration forms of temporary accommodation. They
shall present travel permits when seeking accommodation
in areas closed to aliens.

Article 30   When an alien wishes to lodge at the
home of a Chinese resident in urban areas, the host or
the lodger shall, within twenty-four hours of the lodger's
arrival, report to the local public security organ with the
lodger's passport and certificate as well as the host's residence booklet and fill in registration forms of temporary
accommodation.   In rural areas, the host or lodger shall
report to the local police station or residence registration
office within seventy-two hours of the lodger's arrival.

Article 31   When an alien lodges at a foreign institution in China or at the home of an alien in China,
the institution in question, the host or the lodger shall,
within twenty-four hours of the lodger's arrival, report
to the local public security organ with the lodger's passport or residence certificate and fill in registration forms
of temporary accommodation.

Article 32 Aliens having long-term residence in China who wish to lodge temporarily in a place other than their own residence shall report and register accommodation in accordance with the provisions of Articles 29, 30 and 31 of the present Rules.

Article 33 Aliens who lodge temporarily in movable living facilities shall, within twenty-four hours of arrival, report to the local public security organ. The institutions or individuals furnishing sites for the aliens' movable living facilities shall report to the local public security organ twenty-four hours ahead of time.

CHAPTER V TRAVEL

Article 34 An alien wishing to travel to cities or counties closed to aliens shall apply in advance for a travel permit to the public security bureau of the city or county where he/she stays and may travel only with permission. To apply for a travel permit, the following procedures must be completed:

(1) Submit passport or residence certificate for examination;

(2) Provide papers supporting the purpose of travel;

(3) Fill in a travel application form.

Article 35 An alien's travel permit shall be valid for one year at the most and may not exceed the period of validity of his/her visa or residence certificate.

Article 36 An alien who wishes to extend the validity of travel permit, tour more places closed to aliens or increase the number of accompanying persons shall apply to the public security bureau for extension or alteration of the permit.

Article 37   Aliens shall not enter places closed to aliens without permission.

CHAPTER VI   EXIT

Article 38   Aliens shall leave China within the time limit prescribed in visas or within the period of validity of their residence certificates.

Article 39   The holder of an alien's residence certificate who wishes to leave and then re-enter China within the period of validity of the said certificate shall, before leaving China, apply to the local public security organ for a re-entry visa in accordance with the relevant provisions of Articles 5 and 6 of the present Rules.

An alien holding a residence certificate who does not wish to return to China after exit shall hand in his/ her residence certificate for cancellation to the border checkpost upon exit.

CHAPTER VII   PENALTIES

Article 40   Aliens who enter China illegally may be fined 500 to 2000 yuan (RMB) or be detained three to ten days and may simultaneously be ordered to leave the country within a specified time or be expelled from the country.   Those whose offences are serious enough to constitute a crime shall be prosecuted for criminal responsibility according to law.

Article 41   A person in charge of a means of transport or his/her agent who refuses to bear responsibility in contravention of the provisions of Article 11 of the present Rules may be fined 500 to 2000 yuan or be detained three to ten days.

Article 42 Aliens who illegally stay in China in contravention of the provisions of Articles 16, 19, 20, 21, 22, and 23 of the present Rules or violate the regulations on residence control may be served a warning, be fined 100 to 500 yuan, or be detained one to three days. Those whose offences are serious may also be ordered to leave the country within a specified time.

Article 43 Aliens who, in contravention of the provisions of Articles 24 and 25 of the present Rules, fail to submit their residence certificates for examination as required or to carry their passports or residence certificates with them or refuse to produce their certificates to police for examination may be served a warning or be fined 20 to 50 yuan, and those whose offences are serious may also be ordered to leave the country within a specified time.

Article 44 Aliens who have been employed without permission from the Ministry of Labour and Personnel of the People's Republic of China shall have their posts or employment terminated and may also be fined 200 to 1000 yuan; those whose offences are serious may also be ordered to leave the country within a specified time.

Article 45 Whoever is held responsible for failing to register accommodation or report such registration to the public security organ or for accommodating aliens without valid certificates in contravention of the provisions of Chapter IV of the present Rules may be served a warning or be fined 10 to 50 yuan.

Article 46 Aliens who travel to areas closed to

aliens without prior permission in contravention of the
provisions of Articles 34, 36, and 37 of the present Rules
may be served a warning or be fined 30 to 100 yuan;
those whose offences are serious may also be ordered to
leave the country within a specified time.

Article 47 Aliens who forge, alter, misuse or
transfer visas or certificates shall have the said visas or
certificates revoked or confiscated and may be fined 500
to 2000 yuan or be detained three to ten days and may
also be ordered to leave the country within a specified
time; those whose offences are serious enough to constitute a crime shall be prosecuted for their criminal responsibility according to law.

Article 48 Whoever out of force majeure acts in
contravention of the Law on Entry and Exit of Aliens
and the present Rules may be exempted from penalties.

Aliens who are unable to pay a fine may be subjected to detention instead.

Article 49 Penalties such as fines and detention
provided for in this Chapter shall also apply to persons
held responsible for assisting aliens to enter or leave
China illegally, causing aliens to reside or stay illegally
in China, employing aliens who seek jobs without permission, or providing facilities for aliens to travel without
valid travel permits to areas closed to aliens.

Article 50 If an alien being fined or detained by
a public security organ refuses to accept such penalty,
he/she may, within fifteen days of receiving notification,
appeal to the original adjudication organ or directly to
the next higher public security organ, which shall make
the final judgement within three days of receiving the
appeal. The person being penalized may also file suit

directly on a local people's court.

Article 51 The penalties provided for in this Chapter shall be executed by public security organs.

CHAPTER VIII   OTHER PROVISIONS

Article 52 Aliens who wish to apply for extension or alteration of visas or certificates shall complete the following procedures:

(1) Submit their passports, visas and certificates for examination;

(2) Fill in application forms for extension or alteration;

(3) Provide papers supporting reasons for extension or alteration.

Article 53 Aliens applying for visas and certificates or for their extension or alteration shall pay visa and certificate fees according to the prescribed rates.

The rates of visa and certificate fees shall be prescribed by the Ministry of Public Security and the Ministry of Foreign Affairs.

Persons from countries that have agreements on visa fees with the Chinese Government shall act in accordance with the pertinent agreements.

Article 54 An alien child under the age of sixteen who travels on the same passport as his/her parent or guardian, need not, while visiting China with his/her parent or guardian, go through entry, transit, residence or travel procedures separately.

Article 55 An alien whose Chinese visa or certificate is lost or damaged shall promptly report to the exit-and-entry department of the local public security bureau and apply for a replacement. An alien who has lost his/her residence card shall declare the lost card invalid in an official local newspaper.

Article 56 The format of the various visas, certificates and application forms referred to in the present Rules shall be decided upon by the Ministry of Public Security and the Ministry of Foreign Affairs.

Article 57 The present Rules shall be implemented from the date of their promulgation.

中华人民共和国外国人入境出境管理法实施细则

（一九八六年十二月三日国务院批准，
一九八六年十二月二十七日公安部、外交部公布）

根据《中华人民共和国外国人入境出境管理法》（以下简称《外国人入境出境管理法》）第三十三条的规定，制定本实施细则。

第一章　入　　境

第一条　外国人入境，应当向中国的外交代表机关、领事机关或者外交部授权的其他驻外机关申请办理签证。

外国人持有中国国内被授权单位的函电，并持有与中国有外交关系或官方贸易往来国家的普通护照，因下列事由确需紧急来华而来不及在上述中国驻外机关申办签证的，也可以向公安部授权的口岸签证机关申请办理签证：

（一）中方临时决定邀请来华参加交易会的；

（二）应邀来华参加投标或正式签订经贸合同的；

（三）按约来华监装出口、进口商检或参加合同验收的；

（四）应邀参加设备安装或工程抢修的；

（五）应中方要求来华解决索赔问题的；

（六）应邀来华提供科技咨询的；

（七）应邀来华团组办妥签证后，经中方同意临时增换的；

（八）看望危急病人或处理丧事的；

（九）直接过境人员由于不可抗拒的原因不能在二十四小时内乘原机离境或需改乘其他交通工具离境的；

（十）其他被邀请确实来不及在上述中国驻外机关申请签证，并持有指定的主管部门同意在口岸申办签证的函电的。

不属上述情况者，口岸签证机关不得受理其签证申请。

第二条 公安部授权的口岸签证机关设立在下列口岸：北京、上海、天津、大连、福州、厦门、西安、桂林、杭州、昆明、广州（白云机场）、深圳（罗湖、蛇口）、珠海（拱北）。

第三条 根据外国人来中国的身份和所持护

照的种类，分别发给外交签证、礼遇签证、公务签证、普通签证。

第四条 签发普通签证时，根据外国人申请来中国的事由，在签证上标明相应的汉语拼音字母：

（一）D字签证发给来中国定居的人员；

（二）Z字签证发给来中国任职或就业的人员及其随行家属；

（三）X字签证发给来中国留学、进修、实习六个月以上的人员；

（四）F字签证发给应邀来中国访问、考察、讲学、经商、进行科技文化交流及短期进修、实习等活动不超过六个月的人员；

（五）L字签证发给来中国旅游、探亲或因其他私人事务入境的人员，其中九人以上组团来中国旅游的，可以发给团体签证；

（六）G字签证发给经中国过境的人员；

（七）C字签证发给执行乘务、航空、航运任务的国际列车乘务员、国际航空机机组人员及国际航行船舶的海员及其随行家属。

第五条 外国人申请签证须回答被询问的有关情况并履行下列手续：

（一）提供有效护照或者能够代替护照的证

件；

（二）填写签证申请表，交近期二寸半身正面免冠照片；

（三）交验与申请入境、过境事由有关的证明。

第六条　本实施细则第五条（三）项所说的有关证明是指：

（一）申请D字签证，须持有定居身份确认表。定居身份确认表由申请人或委托其在中国的亲属向申请定居地的市、县公安局出入境管理部门申请领取；

（二）申请Z字签证，须有中国聘雇单位的聘请或雇用证明，或被授权单位的函电；

（三）申请X字签证，须有接受单位或主管部门的证明；

（四）申请F字签证，须有被授权单位的函电；

（五）申请L字签证，来华旅游的，须有中国旅游部门的接待证明；

（六）申请G字签证，须持有前往国家（地区）的有效签证。如果申请人免办前往国家（地区）的签证，须持有联程客票；

（七）申请C字签证，按协议提供有关的证

明。

外国人来中国定居或者居留一年以上的，在申请入境签证时，还须交验所在国政府指定的卫生医疗部门签发的，或者卫生医疗部门签发的并经过公证机关公证的健康证明书。健康证明书自签发之日起六个月有效。

第七条 下列外国人不准入境：

（一）被中国政府驱逐出境，未满不准入境年限的；

（二）被认为入境后可能进行恐怖、暴力、颠覆活动的；

（三）被认为入境后可能进行走私、贩毒、卖淫活动的；

（四）患有精神病和麻疯病、艾滋病、性病、开放性肺结核病等传染病的；

（五）不能保障其在中国期间所需费用的；

（六）被认为入境后可能进行危害我国国家安全和利益的其他活动的。

第八条 外国人持有联程客票并已定妥联程座位搭乘国际航班从中国直接过境，在过境城市停留不超过二十四小时，不出机场的，免办过境签证；要求离开机场的，须向边防检查站申请办理停留许可手续。

第九条　国际航行船舶在中国港口停泊期间，外国船员及其随行家属要求登陆，不出港口城市的，向边防检查站申请登陆证，要求在陆地住宿的，申请住宿证。有正当理由需要前往港口城市以外的地区，或不能随原船出境的，须向当地公安局申请办理相应的签证。

第二章　入出境证件检查

第十条　外国人抵达口岸，必须向边防检查站缴验有效护照和中国的签证、证件，填写入出境卡，经边防检查站查验核准加盖验讫章后入境。

第十一条　外国航空器或者船舶抵达中国口岸时，其负责人负有下列责任：

（一）机长、船长或代理人必须向边防检查站提交机组人员、船员名单和旅客名单；

（二）如果载有企图偷越国境的人员，发现后应立即向边防检查站报告，听候处理；

（三）对于不准入境的人员，必须负责用原交通工具带走，对由于不可抗拒的原因不能立即离境的人，必须负责其在中国停留期间的费用和离开时的旅费。

第十二条　对下列外国人，边防检查站有权

阻止入境或出境：

（一）未持有效护照、证件或签证的；

（二）持伪造、涂改或他人护照、证件的；

（三）拒绝接受查验证件的；

（四）公安部或者国家安全部通知不准入境、出境的。

第十三条　外国人出境，须缴验有效护照或者其他有效证件，以及准予在中国停留的签证或者居留证件。

第十四条　被签证机关指定通行口岸的外国人和外国人的交通工具，必须从指定的口岸入、出境。

第十五条　对于本实施细则第十二条所列被阻止入境的外国人，如不能立即随原交通工具返回，边防检查站可以采取必要的措施限制其活动范围，并令其乘最近一班交通工具离境。

第三章　居　　留

第十六条　持标有 D、Z、X 字签证的外国人，必须自入境之日起十日内到居住地市、县公安局办理外国人居留证或外国人临时居留证。上述居留证件的有效期即为准许持证人在中国居留的期限。

外国人居留证，发给在中国居留一年以上的人员。

外国人临时居留证，发给在中国居留不满一年的人员。

持标有F、L、G、C字签证的外国人，可以在签证注明的期限内在中国停留，不需办理居留证件。

第十七条　外国人申请居留证件须回答被询问的有关情况并履行下列手续：

（一）交验护照、签证和与居留事由有关的证明；

（二）填写居留申请表；

（三）申请外国人居留证的，还要交验健康证明书，交近期二寸半身正面免冠照片。

第十八条　外国人居留证有效期可签发一年至五年，由市、县公安局根据外国人居留的事由确定。

对符合《外国人入境出境管理法》第十四条规定的外国人，公安机关可以发给一年至五年长期居留资格的证件；有显著成效的可以发给永久居留资格的证件。

第十九条　根据中国政府同外国政府签定的协议免办签证的外国人，需在中国停留三十日以上的，应于入境后按本实施细则第十六、十七条申请居留证件。

但是，《外国人入境出境管理法》第三十四条规定的外国人，不适用前款的规定。

第二十条 外国人在签证或居留证件有效期满后需继续在中国停留或居留，须于期满前申请延期。

外国人在中国居留期间，如果发现患有本实施细则第七条第四项规定的疾病，中国卫生主管机关可以提请公安机关令其提前出境。

第二十一条 在外国人居留证上填写的项目内容（姓名、国籍、职业或身份、工作单位、住址、护照号码、偕行儿童等）如有变更，持证人须于十日内到居住地公安局办理变更登记。

第二十二条 持外国人居留证的人迁出所在市、县，须于迁移前向原居住地的公安局办理迁移登记，到达迁入地后，须于十日内向迁入地公安局办理迁入登记。

定居的外国人申请迁移，须事先向迁入地公安局申请准予迁入的证明，凭该证明按前款规定办理迁移登记。

第二十三条 出于维护国家安全、社会秩序或其他公共利益的原因，市、县公安局可以限制外国人或外国机构在某些地区设立住所或办公处所；已在上述限制地区设立住所或办公处所，必须在市、县公安局迁移通知书指定的期限内迁至许可的地区。

第二十四条　在中国定居的外国人必须每年一次在指定的时间到居住地的公安局缴验外国人居留证。

公安局认为必要时，可通知外国人到出入境管理部门缴验外国人居留证，外国人应按通知指定的时间前往缴验。

第二十五条　在中国居留或停留的年满十六周岁以上的外国人必须随身携带居留证件或者护照，以备外事民警查验。

第二十六条　在中国出生的外国婴儿，须于出生后一个月内，由其父母或代理人持出生证明向当地公安局申报，办理登记手续。

第二十七条　外国人在中国死亡，其家属或监护人或代理人须于三日内持死亡证明向当地公安局申报并缴销死者的居留证件或签证。

外国人非正常死亡，有关人员或发现者应当立即向公安机关报告。

第二十八条　《外国人入境出境管理法》第十九条所称的中国政府主管机关是指中华人民共和

国劳动人事部。

第四章　住宿登记

第二十九条　外国人在宾馆、饭店、旅店、招待所、学校等企业、事业单位或者机关、团体及其他中国机构内住宿，应当出示有效护照或者居留证件，并填写临时住宿登记表。在非开放地区住宿还要出示旅行证。

第三十条　外国人在中国居民家中住宿，在城镇的，须于抵达后二十四小时内，由留宿人或本人持住宿人的护照、证件和留宿人的户口簿到当地公安机关申报，填写临时住宿登记表；在农村的，须于七十二小时内向当地派出所或者户籍办公室申报。

第三十一条　外国人在中国的外国机构内或在中国的外国人家中住宿，须于住宿人抵达后二十四小时内，由留宿机构、留宿人或者本人持住宿人的护照或居留证件，向当地公安机关申报，并填写临时住宿登记表。

第三十二条　长期在中国居留的外国人离开自己的住所临时在其他地方住宿，应当按本实施细则第二十九、三十、三十一条规定申报住宿登记。

第三十三条　外国人在移动性住宿工具内临时住宿,须于二十四小时内向当地公安机关申报。为外国人的移动性住宿工具提供场地的机构或个人,应于二十四小时前向当地公安机关申报。

第五章　旅　行

第三十四条　外国人前往不对外国人开放的市、县旅行,须事先向所在市、县公安局申请旅行证,获准后方可前往。申请旅行证须履行下列手续:

（一）交验护照或居留证件;

（二）提供与旅行事由有关的证明;

（三）填写旅行申请表。

第三十五条　外国人旅行证的有效期最长为一年,但不得超过外国人所持签证或居留证件的有效期限。

第三十六条　外国人领取旅行证后,如要求延长旅行证有效期、增加不对外国人开放的旅行地点、增加偕行人数,必须向公安局申请延期或者变更。

第三十七条　外国人未经允许,不得进入不对外开放的场所。

第六章 出 境

第三十八条 外国人应当在签证准予停留的期限内或者居留证件的有效期内出境。

第三十九条 持有外国人居留证件的人，在其居留证件有效期内出境并需返回中国的，应当在出境前按本实施细则第五、六条有关规定向当地公安机关申请办理返回中国的签证。

持有居留证件的外国人出境后不再返回中国的，出境时应向边防检查站缴销居留证件。

第七章 处 罚

第四十条 对非法进入中国境内的外国人，可以处五百元以上、二千元以下的罚款，或处三日以上、十日以下的拘留，也可以并处限期出境或驱逐出境；情节严重，构成犯罪的，依法追究刑事责任。

第四十一条 对违反本实施细则第十一条规定，拒绝承担责任的交通工具负责人或其代理人，可以处五百元以上、二千元以下的罚款，或处三日以上、十日以下的拘留。

第四十二条 对违反本实施细则第十六、十九、二十、二十一、二十二、二十三条规定，非法居留或者违反居留管理规定的外国人，可以处警告或一百元以上、五百元以下的罚款，或处一日以上、三日以下的拘留；情节严重的，并处限期出境。

第四十三条 对违反本实施细则第二十四、二十五条规定，不按要求缴验居留证，不随身携带护照或者居留证件，或者拒绝民警查验证件的外国人，可以处警告，或处二十元以上、五十元以下的罚款；情节严重的，并处限期出境。

第四十四条 对未经中华人民共和国劳动人事部批准私自谋职的外国人，在终止其任职或就业的同时，可以处二百元以上、一千元以下的罚款；情节严重的，并处限期出境。

第四十五条 对违反本实施细则第四章规定，不办理住宿登记或者不向公安机关申报住宿登记或者留宿未持有效证件外国人的责任者，可以处警告，或处十元以上、五十元以下的罚款。

第四十六条 对违反本实施细则第三十四、三十六、三十七条规定，未经批准前往不对外国人开放地区旅行的外国人，可以处警告，或处三十元以上、一百元以下的罚款；情节严重的，并处限期出境。

第四十七条 对伪造、涂改、冒用、转让签证、证件的外国人，在吊销或没收原签证、证件的同时，可以处五百元以上、二千元以下的罚款，或处三日以上、十日以下的拘留，也可以并处限期出境；情节严重，构成犯罪的，依法追究刑事责任。

第四十八条 由于不可抗拒的原因而违反《外国人入境出境管理法》及本实施细则的，可免予处罚。

外国人无力缴纳罚款的，可以改处拘留。

第四十九条 本章规定的各项罚款、拘留处罚，也适用于协助外国人非法入境或出境、造成外国人非法居留或停留、聘雇私自谋职的外国人、为未持有效旅行证件的外国人前往不对外国人开放的地区旅行提供方便的有关责任者。

第五十条 被处罚人对公安机关的罚款、拘留处罚不服的，在接到通知之日起十五日内，可以通过原裁决机关或者直接向上一级公安机关申诉，上一级公安机关自接到申诉之日起三日内作出最后裁决。被处罚人也可以直接向当地人民法院提起诉讼。

第五十一条 本章规定的处罚，由公安机关执行。

第八章　其他规定

第五十二条　外国人申请各项签证、证件的延期或者变更，须履行下列手续：

（一）交验护照和签证、证件；

（二）填写延期申请表或者变更申请表；

（三）提供与延期或者变更事由有关的证明。

第五十三条　外国人申请各项签证、证件或者申请签证、证件延期、变更，必须按规定缴纳签证、证件费。

各项签证、证件的收费标准，由公安部和外交部另行制定。

同中国政府订有签证费协议国家的人员，按有关协议执行。

第五十四条　不满十六周岁的外国少年儿童，与其父母或监护人使用同一护照的，随其父母或监护人来中国时，可以不单独办理入境、过境、居留、旅行手续。

第五十五条　外国人所持中国的签证、证件如有遗失或损坏，应当立即向当地公安局出入境管理部门报告，申请补领或换发。遗失外国人居留证的，须在当地政府报纸上声明作废。

第五十六条 本实施细则涉及的各种签证、证件和申请表的式样，由公安部和外交部另行制定。

第五十七条 本实施细则自公布之日起施行。

PROVISIONS OF THE STATE COUNCIL ON BALANCE OF PAYMENT OF FOREIGN EXCHANGE IN CHINESE-FOREIGN JOINT VENTURES

(Promulgated by the State Council on January 15, 1986)

Article 1 These Provisions are formulated to encourage foreign partners to initiate Chinese-foreign joint ventures in China, achieve balance of payment of foreign currencies in the joint ventures and facilitate production operations and the remittance by foreign partners of their lawful profits out of China.

Article 2 Chinese-foreign joint ventures should increase the export of their products in order to earn more foreign exchange and achieve balance of payment of foreign exchange.

Article 3 When adjustments are needed for balance of payment of foreign exchange in Chinese-foreign joint ventures established according to law, they will be handled by administrations at different levels within their authority for examination and approval.

Balances of payment of foreign exchange for Chinese-foreign joint ventures established with the approval of the competent departments of the State will be adjusted by these departments with foreign currency revenues from Chinese-foreign joint ventures nationwide or jointly by these departments and the local people's government at a ratio they have agreed upon. Balances of payment of foreign exchange for Chinese-foreign joint ventures established with the approval of local people's governments authorized by the State Council or entrusted by the competent departments of the State or with the approval of the competent departments of the State Council, will be adjusted by the local people's governments or departments with foreign currency revenues from the Chinese-foreign joint ventures established with their approval.

Article 4 Sophisticated products manufactured with advanced or key technology provided by foreign partners or internationally competitive quality products, if they are urgently needed domestically, may receive favourable terms in domestic sales ratios and time limits after they have been appraised by the competent departments and approved in accordance with the authority and the procedures for examination and approval stipulated by the State. For the domestic sales, the producers and the buyers should sign contracts as a confirmation.

Plans for achieving balance of payment of foreign exchange in enterprises defined above will be prepared by the approving departments according to Article 3, second paragraph, of these Provisions. The plans should be delivered, through the administrative channel, to the Ministry of Foreign Economic Relations and Trade or the local department of foreign economic relations and trade for examination and comment and then to the State Planning Commission or the local planning commission for approval and execution by including them in the long-term or annual foreign-exchange allocation plans.

Article 5 If the products manufactured by a Chinese-foreign joint venture are in long-term or urgent domestic demand, they may be used as import substitutes with the approval of the competent department of the State Council or the competent local department on the basis of the quality and specifications of the products and import situation. This import substitution plan should be made clear in the contract or the production and purchase contract signed by the partners of the joint venture.

The departments of foreign economic relations and trade should actively assist domestic users to sign supply and purchasing contracts at international market prices with the joint ventures defined above. Their foreign-exchange consumption plans should be prepared according to Article 3, second paragraph, of these Provisions and should be delivered, through the administrative channel, to the Ministry of Foreign Economic Relations and Trade or the local department of foreign economic relations and trade for examination and comment and then to the State Planning Commission or the local planning commission for approval and execution by including them in the long-term or annual foreign-exchange allocation plans.

Article 6 To achieve balance of payment of foreign exchange, a Chinese-foreign joint venture may, with the approval of a department of foreign economic relations and trade, make up its foreign exchange deficits by marketing domestic products abroad through the foreign partner's overseas sales contacts. Special permits, however, must be obtained from the Ministry of Foreign Economic Relations and Trade for products that are marketed solely by the State, have export quotas or require export permits. A joint venture cannot export such products without a permit.

Article 7 The competent departments are not responsible for adjustment of imbalances of payment of foreign exchange resulting from unfulfilment of export contracts for earning foreign exchange by joint ventures.

Article 8 Sales of products by joint ventures to enterprises capable of paying in foreign exchange in areas other than the Special Economic Zones and the Economic and Technological Development Zones of the open coastal cities can be settled in foreign exchange after approval by State foreign-exchange control departments.

Article 9 If a foreign partner has joined two or more joint ventures in China (including those in different localities and in different businesses) and his lawful foreign exchange incomes are in part excessive and in part insufficient, he can adjust the balance among the ventures upon approval by State foreign-exchange control departments.

The adjustments must be agreed upon by all participating parties.

Article 10 With approval by the departments of foreign economic relations and trade and foreign exchange control, the foreign partners of joint ventures who cannot strike a balance in the payment of foreign exchange may, in accordance with Article 7 of the Law on Chinese-Foreign Joint Ventures, reinvest their RMB share of profits from the joint ventures in domestic enterprises to generate or increase the foreign exchange earnings of these enterprises. In addition to receiving preferential treatment in refunding part of the income tax they have paid, the foreign partners can obtain foreign exchange from the newly increased foreign exchange revenues of the enterprises they have invested in and remit their lawful profits out of China.

Article 11. These Provisions apply to Chinese-foreign joint ventures established in China, to joint ventures and cooperative enterprises established in China's interior by companies, enterprises and other economic organizations from the regions of Hong Kong, Macao and Taiwan, and to joint ventures ad cooperative eterprises invested in by overseas Chinese.

These Provisions do not apply to financial and insurance institutions established by foreign partners in China and those established by partners from Hong Kong, Macao and Taiwan in China's interior.

Article 12   If previous provisions on balance of payment of foreign exchange in Chinese-foreign joint ventures contradict these Provisions, these Provisions shall prevail.

Article 13   The Ministry of Foreign Economic Relations and Trade shall be responsible for interpreting these Provisions.

Article 14   These Provisions shall go into effect as of February 1, 1986.

国务院关于中外合资经营企业外汇收支平衡问题的规定

（一九八六年一月十五日国务院发布）

第一条 为鼓励外国合营者在中国境内兴办中外合资经营企业，促进其外汇收支平衡，以利于生产经营和外国合营者将所得合法利润汇往国外，特制定本规定。

第二条 中外合资经营企业生产的产品应多出口，多创汇，做到外汇收支平衡。

第三条 依法批准兴办的中外合资经营企业，其外汇收支需要调剂的，应按照审批权限，分级管理解决。

经国家主管机关批准兴办的中外合资经营企业，由国家主管机关负责在全国范围内的中外合资经营企业的外汇收入中调剂解决，也可由国家主管机关同地方人民政府按商定的比例调剂解决。经由国务院授权的或国家主管机关委托的地方人民政府或国务院有关部门批准兴办的中外合资经营企业，由各该地方人民政府或部门负责在所批准兴办的中外合资经营企业的外汇收入中调剂解决。

第四条　对于外国合营者提供先进技术、关键技术生产的尖端产品，或在国际上有竞争能力的优质产品，如国内急需，经主管部门鉴定合格，按国家规定的审批权限和审批程序，经过批准，可在内销比例和内销期限上给予优惠。此项内销，应由产需双方签订合同加以明确。

前款企业的外汇平衡方案，按本规定第三条第二款规定由批准机关制订。批准机关制订的外汇平衡方案，应分别按行政序列，送对外经济贸易部或地方经贸部门审查提出意见，报国家计划委员会或地方计划委员会批准后纳入长期或年度用汇计划，予以解决。

第五条　中外合资经营企业生产国内需要长期进口或急需进口的产品，可根据对该项产品的质量、规格要求和进口情况，经国务院主管部门或地方主管部门批准实行进口替代。此项替代，应在双方签订的中外合资经营企业合同或产需合同中加以明确。

经贸部门应积极支持国内用货单位同前款中外合资经营企业按国际价格订立购销合同；其用汇方案按本规定第三条第二款规定制订，并分别按行政序列，送对外经济贸易部或地方经贸部门审查提出意见，报国家计划委员会或地方计划委员会批准后纳入长期或年度进口用汇计划，予以解决。

第六条　中外合资经营企业为求得外汇收支平衡，经对外经济贸易部门批准，可利用外国合营者的销售关系，推销国内产品出口，实行综合补偿。但属于国家统一经营的、有出口配额的和应申报领取出口许可证的产品，须报对外经济贸易部特许批准；未经批准，中外合资经营企业不得经营此类产品的出口业务。

第七条　中外合资经营企业未按合同规定完成其所承担的出口和创汇任务，因而造成外汇收支不平衡的，有关机关不承担调剂解决的责任。

第八条　中外合资经营企业销售给经济特区和沿海开放城市的经济技术开发区以外的其他地区有外汇支付能力的企业的产品，经国家外汇管理部门批准，允许以外币计价结算。

第九条　同一外国合营者在中国境内（包括不同地方、不同部门）兴办两个或两个以上的中外合资经营企业，其合法所得的外汇份额有的有余、有的不足时，经国家外汇管理部门批准，可在其所办的各个企业之间调剂解决。

前款调剂，应取得合营各方同意。

第十条　经对外经济贸易部门和外汇管理部门批准，外汇收支不能平衡的中外合资经营企业的外国合营者，可将其从中外合资经营企业分得的人民币利润，按《中外合资经营企业法》第七条的规定再投资于国内能够新创外汇或新增加外汇收入的企业，除依法享受退还已缴纳的部分所得税的优惠外，并可从接受该项投资企业新增加的外汇收入中获得外汇，以汇出其合法利润。

第十一条　本规定适用于在中国境内兴办的中外合作经营企业，以及香港、澳门、台湾地区的公司、企业和其他经济组织在内地兴办的合资经营企业、合作经营企业，也适用于华侨投资兴办的合资经营企业、合作经营企业。

外国的合营者在中国境内兴办的金融、保险类企业，以及香港、澳门、台湾地区的合营者在内地兴办的此类企业，不适用本规定。

第十二条　本规定发布前的有关中外合资经营企业外汇收支平衡的规定，凡与本规定相抵触的，以本规定为准。

第十三条　本规定由对外经济贸易部负责解释。

第十四条　本规定自1986年2月1日起施行。

REGULATIONS OF THE GENERAL ADMINISTRATION OF CUSTOMS OF THE PEOPLE'S REPUBLIC OF CHINA ON COMMODITIES, TRANSPORTATION VEHICLES, LUGGAGE, PERSONAL BELONGINGS, AND POSTAL PARCELS GOING INTO AND OUT OF SPECIAL ECONOMIC ZONES

(Approved by the State Council on March 21, 1986 and promulgated by the General Administration of Customs on March 25, 1986)

CHAPTER I GENERAL RULES

Article 1 The following Regulations have been made to promote development in the Special Economic Zones, safeguard the interests of the country, and ensure successful progress of socialist economic construction.

Article 2 These Regulations are applicable in the four Special Economic Zones (hereinafter abbreviated to SEZ) of Shenzhen, Zhuhai, Shantou, and Xiamen.

Article 3 The commodities, transportation vehicles, luggage, personal belongings, and mail going into or out of SEZ should pass railway stations, road checkpoints, ports, airports, or post offices where Customs are represented and be declared to and supervised by Customs.

Article 4 Foreign-trade and manufacturing enterprises in SEZ that are engaged in imports and exports should register with Customs with documents showing approval by the foreign-trade administration office at provincial level or higher or the people's government in the SEZ.

If deemed necessary, customs officers will be stationed at the manufacturing enterprises described above to supervise and handle customs procedures. Necessary office space and housing should be provided free of charge by the enterprises.

For Customs inspection, enterprises defined in the first paragraph of this Article should periodically deliver written reports on the use, sale, and inventory of imported goods.

Article 5 Taking advantage of the favourable terms and conveniences the State grants the SEZ to engage in smuggling and other violations of the regulations is strictly prohibited. Customs is authorized by the Provisional Customs Law of the People's Republic of China to inspect any location in the SEZ suspected of storing smuggled goods.

Article 6 State regulations on imports and exports will apply to commodities, transportation vehicles, luggage, personal belongings and mail shipped to the interior of the country from foreign countries and the Hong Kong and Macao regions (hereinafter regarded as beyond the borders) by way of an SEZ or shipped from inland to beyond the borders by way of an SEZ.

Article 7 On the incoming and outgoing commodities, transportation vehicles, luggage, personal belongings and mail, Customs will prepare statistics in categories of imports, exports, SEZ to inland, and inland to SEZ.

CHAPTER II ADMINISTRATION OF COMMODITIES GOING INTO AND OUT OF SEZ

Article 8 Imports and exports of SEZ should be declared to Customs by the consigners, consignees, or their agents with completed declaration forms, import or export permits and other relevent certificates as required by the regulations.

Article 9 The following regulations apply to the handling of customs duties and consolidated industrial and commercial tax (product tax or appreciation tax) on commodities imported for use in an SEZ in its administration offices, enterprises, institutions and other types of units after approval by authorized departments.

(1) Imports of machinery, equipment, parts, components, raw materials, semi-finished materials, fuel and transportation vehicles needed for construction and production in the SEZ, foodstuffs imported for the tourist industry and restaurants in the SEZ, and office equipment and transportation vehicles in reasonable quantity to be used by administration offices, enterprises, and institutions in the SEZ will be exempt from duty.

(2) Commodities and parts and components under State import restrictions will be dutiable at regular rates unless imported solely for the enterprise's own production and operation or for administration offices and institutions' own use, in which case they will be exempt from duty.

(3) Commodities other than those previously specified will be taxed at a 50-percent reduction of imported within the annual quotas examined and approved by State-authorized departments. Any proportion exceeding the quotas will be taxed according to regulations.

Article 10 Products manufactured by enterprises in SEZ will be exempt from export duties.

Article 11 If finished products from enterprises in SEZ are approved for shipping inland, in accordance with State regulations, the consigners or their agents must fill out a Customs Declaration on Commodities Shipped from SEZ to Inland and submit permits and other required certificates for examination according to relevent rules. The products will be permitted to be shipped after inspection by Customs.

Commodities imported by SEZ are prohibited from sale to inland areas unless authorized by the State.

Article 12 Finished products processed or assembled out of raw materials, semi-finished materials, parts, and components (hereinafter shortened to material and parts) imported duty-free by enterprises in SEZ should be exported.

If the finished products defined above are approved for shipping inland, Customs will impose import duties on the materials and parts.   If they are sold in SEZ, Customs will, as specified in Article 9, exempt them from or impose import duties. The finished products will be dutiable at tariff rates for finished products if their imported materials and parts have not been clearly specified as to name, quantity and value by the shippers or their agents.

Article 13 The consignees or their agents must declare to the Customs for Commodities to be shipped from inland to SEZ before they are permitted to be shipped after inspection.

CHAPTER III   ADMINISTRATION OF TRANSPORTA-
TION VEHICLES GOING INTO AND OUT OF SEZ

Article 14 Vessels, trains, motor vehicles and air-borne vehicles going in or out of SEZ must be declared to Customs by the persons in charge, the owners or their agents for Customs inspection.

Article 15 Motor vehicles and vessels used in SEZ by enterprises for passenger or cargo transport service as well as transportation vehicles and vessels owned by individuals and other enterprises and going into and out of SEZ must be registered with Customs by the owners with certificates of approval issued by authorized departments in the SEZ.

The number of vehicles, their licence numbers and models and lists of drivers or crew members must be registered.

CHAPTER IV   ADMINISTRATION OF LUGGAGE,
PERSONAL BELONGINGS AND POSTAL PAR-
CELS GOING INTO AND OUT OF SEZ

Article 16 Luggage and personal belongings shipped into SEZ from beyond the border, or vice versa, and private mail coming into SEZ from beyond the border, or vice versa, should be handled according to Customs regulations on supervision and administration of incoming and outgoing luggage, personal belongings and mail.

Article 17 Household necessities imported by persons who purchase housing or seek permanent residence in SEZ will be granted a duty-free pass if application is made to Customs with certificates issued by authorized departments in the SEZ for approval and if they are for household use only and in reasonable quantity.

Article 18   Luggage and personal belongings of persons travelling between the SEZ and inland will be permitted to pass after Customs inspection if they are within the limit.

Article 19   Private postal parcels from the SEZ to inland or from inland to the SEZ should not exceed a reasonable number.

CHAPTER V   APPENDIX

Article 20   Smuggling and other violations of Regulations will be penalized according to the Provisional Customs Law of the People's Republic of China and related laws. Responsibility for crimes committed will be investigated and affixed by judicial organs according to the law.

Article 21   These Regulations are interpreted by the General Administration of Customs. The Customs in SEZ can make detailed regulations based on these Regulations, which will become effective after being approved by the General Administration of Customs.

Article 22   These Regulations become effective on April 1, 1986.

中华人民共和国海关总署对进出经济特区的货物、运输工具、行李物品和邮递物品的管理规定

（一九八六年三月二十一日国务院批准，
一九八六年三月二十五日海关总署发布）

第一章　总　　则

第一条　为了促进经济特区的发展，维护国家利益，保障社会主义经济建设的顺利进行，制定本规定。

第二条　本规定适用于深圳、珠海、汕头、厦门四个经济特区（以下简称特区）。

第三条　进出特区的货物、运输工具、行李物品、邮递物品，必须经由设有海关机构的铁路车站、公路道口、港口码头、机场、邮局通过，并向海关申报，接受海关监管。

第四条　特区内从事进出口业务的外贸企业、生产企业，应当持省级以上对外经济贸易管理部门或特区人民政府批准的证件，向海关办理

登记手续。

　　海关认为确有必要，可以在前款的生产企业中派驻海关人员进行监管，办理海关手续；各该企业应当免费提供必需的办公场所和用房。

　　本条第一款所列企业应当定期向海关书面报告进口货物的使用、销售、库存等有关情况，由海关进行核查。

　　第五条　严禁利用国家给予特区的优惠和便利条件进行走私违法活动。海关对特区内有藏匿走私物品嫌疑的场所，有权依照《中华人民共和国暂行海关法》的规定进行检查。

　　第六条　由外国和香港、澳门等地区（以下简称境外）通过特区运进内地或者由内地通过特区运出境外的货物、运输工具、行李物品、邮递物品，按照国家对进出口的有关管理规定办理。

　　第七条　特区海关对进出特区的货物、运输工具、行李物品、邮递物品，应当按进口、出口和来往特区与内地等情况分别作出统计。

第二章　对进出特区的货物的管理

　　第八条　特区进出口货物，应当由收货人、发货人或他们的代理人填写进出口货物报关单向海关申报，并按照有关规定交验许可证件和其他有关单证。

第九条　特区内的行政机关、企业、事业等单位，经国家规定的主管机构批准，进口供特区内使用的货物，其关税和工商统一税（产品税或增值税），按以下规定办理：

一、用于特区建设和生产所需的机器、设备、零件、部件、原料、材料、燃料及货运车辆，旅游、饮食业营业用的餐料，行政机关、企业、事业等单位自用的、数量合理的办公用品和交通工具，予以免税。

二、国家规定限制进口的货物及其零件、部件，除供本企业生产或营业自用的，以及供行政机关、事业单位自用的予以免税外，均按规定税率照章征税。

三、本条第一、二项所列物品以外的其它货物，每年由国家授权的部门审定进口额度，在进口额度以内的货物，按规定税率减半计征；对超出额度部分的货物照章征税。

第十条　特区企业出口特区产品，免征出口关税。

第十一条　特区企业生产的制成品，按照国家有关规定，经批准运往内地，发货人或其代理人应当填写《经济特区运往内地货物报关单》，并

且按照有关规定交验许可证件和其他有关单证，
经海关查验后放行。

特区进口的货物，除国家另有规定者外，严
禁转销内地。

第十二条　特区企业使用免税进口的原料、
材料、零件、部件（以下简称料、件）加工装配
的制成品，应复运出口。

前款制成品，经批准运往内地时，海关对进
口料、件补征税款；在特区内销售的，对其所用
的料、件，由海关按照本规定第九条的规定，免
征或补征税款；需补征税款的制成品，发货人或
其代理人对所含进口料、件的品名、数量、价值
申报不清的，海关按制成品补征税款。

第十三条　从内地运进特区的货物，收货人
或其代理人应当向海关申报，经海关查验后放
行。

第三章　对进出特区的运输工具的管理

第十四条　进出特区的船舶、火车、汽车和
航空器，应当由运输工具的负责人、所有人或他
们的代理人向海关申报，接受海关检查。

第十五条　特区内经营客货运输企业的汽
车、船舶和其他企业所有或者个人自有进出特区

的运输汽车、船舶，应当由所属单位或所有人，持特区有关主管部门批准的证件，向海关登记、备案。

登记内容包括：车、船数量，车、船牌照号码、名称及驾驶员（或船员）名单等。

第四章　对进出特区的行李物品和邮递物品的管理

第十六条　由境外运进特区或者由特区运出境外的个人行李物品以及从境外寄入特区或者从特区寄往境外的个人邮递物品，分别按照海关对进出境旅客行李物品和运进运出邮递物品监管办法办理。

第十七条　境外人员在特区购置住宅或者在特区长期居住，需要运进安家物品，应当持特区有关主管部门出具的证明文件向海关申请，经海关核准，在自用、合理数量范围内的，予以查验免税放行。

第十八条　来往于特区与内地的人员携带的行李物品，以合理数量为限，海关查验放行。

第十九条　从特区寄往内地或者从内地寄进特区的个人邮递物品，以合理数量为限。

第五章 附 则

第二十条 对违反本规定的走私、违章行为，应当由海关按照《中华人民共和国暂行海关法》和其他有关法规的规定处理。对触犯刑律的人员，由司法机关依法追究刑事责任。

第二十一条 本规定由海关总署负责解释；各特区海关可根据本规定制定实施细则，报海关总署批准后施行。

第二十二条 本规定自1986年4月1日起施行。

LAW OF THE PEOPLE'S REPUBLIC OF CHINA ON FOREIGN ENTERPRISES

(Adopted at the Fourth Session of the Sixth National People's Congress on April 12, 1986)

Article 1   With a view to expanding economic co-operation and technical exchange with foreign countries and promoting the development of China's national economy, the People's Republic of China permits foreign enterprises, other foreign economic organizations and individuals (hereinafter collectively referred to as "foreign investors") to set up foreign enterprises in China and protects the lawful rights and interests of such enterprises.

Article 2   As mentioned in this Law, "foreign enterprises" refer to enterprises established in China by foreign investors with their own capital exclusively in accordance with relevant Chinese laws.   The term does not include branches set up in China by foreign enterprises and other foreign economic organizations.

Article 3   Foreign enterprises shall be established in such a manner as to help the development of China's national economy; they shall use advanced technology and equipment or market all or most of their products outside China.

Provisions shall be made by the State Council regarding the lines of business the State forbids foreign enterprises to engage in or on which it places certain restrictions.

Article 4 The investments of a foreign investor in China, the profits earned and other lawful rights and interests are protected by Chinese law.

Foreign enterprises must abide by Chinese laws and regulations and must not engage in any activities detrimental to China's public interest.

Article 5 The state shall not nationalize or requisition any foreign enterprise. Under special circumstances, when public interest requires, foreign enterprises may be requisitioned through legal procedures and appropriate compensation shall be made.

Article 6 The application to establish a foreign enterprise shall be submitted for examination and approval to the department under the State Council that is in charge of foreign economic relations and trade or to another agency authorized by the State Council. The authorities in charge of examination and approval shall, within ninety days of receipt of such application, decide whether or not to grant approval.

Article 7 After an application for the establishment of a foreign enterprise has been approved, the foreign investor shall, within thirty days of receipt of the certificate of approval, apply to industry and commerce administration authorities for registration and a business licence. The date of issue of the business licence shall be the date of establishment of the enterprise.

Article 8 A foreign enterprise that meets the conditions for being considered a legal person under Chinese law shall acquire the status of a Chinese legal person, in accordance with the law.

Article 9 A foreign enterprise with foreign capital shall make investments in China within the period approved by the authorities in charge of examination and approval. If it fails to do so, industry and commerce administration authorities may cancel its business licence.

Industry and commerce administration authorities shall inspect and supervise the investment situation of a foreign enterprise.

Article 10 In the event of a separation, merger or other major change, a foreign enterprise shall report to and seek approval from the authorities in charge of examination and approval and register the change with industry and commerce administration authorities.

Article 11 The production and operating plans of foreign enterprises shall be reported to the competent authorities for the record.

Foreign enterprises shall conduct their operations and management in accordance with the approved articles of association and shall be free from any interference.

Article 12 When employing Chinese workers and staff, a foreign enterprise shall conclude contracts with them according to law; matters concerning employment, dismissal, remuneration, welfare benefits, labour protection and labour insurance shall be clearly prescribed.

Article 13 Workers and staff of foreign enterprises may organize trade unions, in accordance with the law, in order to conduct trade union activities and protect their lawful rights and interests.

The enterprises shall provide the necessary conditions for the activities of the trade unions in their respective enterprises.

Article 14 A foreign enterprise must set up account books in China, conduct independent accounting, submit fiscal reports and statements as required and accept supervision by financial and tax authorities.

If a foreign enterprise refuses to maintain account books in China, financial and tax authorities may impose a fine on it, and industry and commerce administration authorities may order it to suspend operations or may revoke its business licence.

Article 15   Within the scope of approved operations foreign enterprises may purchase, either in China or on the world market, raw and semi-processed materials, fuels and other materials they need. When these materials are available from both sources on similar terms, first priority should be given to purchases in China.

Article 16   Foreign enterprises shall apply to insurance companies in China for types of insurance coverage as needed.

Article 17   Foreign enterprises shall pay taxes in accordance with relevant state provisions for tax payment and may enjoy preferential treatment for reduction of or exemption from taxes.

An enterprise that reinvests its profits in China after paying income tax may, in accordance with relevent state provisions, apply for a refund of part of the income tax already paid on the reinvested amount.

Article 18   Foreign enterprises shall handle their foreign exchange transactions in accordance with the state provisions for foreign exchange control.

Foreign enterprises shall open an account with the Bank of China or with a bank designated by the state agency exercising foreign exchange control.

Foreign enterprises shall balance their own foreign

exchange receipts and payments. If, with the approval
of the competent authorities, the enterprises market their
products in China and consequently experience an imbalance in foreign exchange, the said authorities shall help
them correct the imbalance.

Article 19   The foreign investor may remit abroad
profits that are lawfully earned from a foreign enterprise,
as well as other lawful earnings and any funds remaining
after the enterprise is liquidated.

Wages, salaries and other legitimate income earned
by foreign employees in a foreign enterprise may be remitted abroad after the payment of individual income tax
in accordance with the law.

Article 20   With respect to the period of operations of a foreign enterprise, the foreign investor shall report to and secure approval from the authorities in charge
of examination and approval.   For an extension of the
period of operations, an application shall be submitted
to the said authorities 180 days before expiration of the
period.   The authorities in charge of examination and
approval shall, within thirty days of receipt of the application, decide whether or not to grant the extension.

Article 21   When terminating its operations, a foreign enterprise shall promptly issue a public notice and
proceed with liquidation in accordance with legal procedure.

Pending the completion of liquidation, a foreign investor may not dispose of the assets of the enterprise except for the purpose of liquidation.

Article 22   At termination of operations the foreign
enterprise shall nullify its registration with industry and
commerce administration authorities and hand in its

business licence for cancellation.

Article 23   The department under the State Council in charge of foreign economic relations and trade shall, in accordance with this Law, formulate rules for its im plementation, which shall go into effect after being submitted to and approved by the State Council.

Article 24   This Law shall go into effect on the day of its promulgation.

中华人民共和国外资企业法

（一九八六年四月十二日第六届全国人民
代表大会第四次会议通过）

第一条 为了扩大对外经济合作和技术交流，促进中国国民经济的发展，中华人民共和国允许外国的企业和其他经济组织或者个人（以下简称外国投资者）在中国境内举办外资企业，保护外资企业的合法权益。

第二条 本法所称的外资企业是指依照中国有关法律在中国境内设立的全部资本由外国投资者投资的企业，不包括外国的企业和其他经济组织在中国境内的分支机构。

第三条 设立外资企业，必须有利于中国国民经济的发展，并且采用先进的技术和设备，或者产品全部出口或者大部分出口。

国家禁止或者限制设立外资企业的行业由国务院规定。

第四条 外国投资者在中国境内的投资、获得的利润和其他合法权益，受中国法律保护。

外资企业必须遵守中国的法律、法规，不得损害中国的社会公共利益。

第五条 国家对外资企业不实行国有化和征收；在特殊情况下，根据社会公共利益的需要，对外资企业可以依照法律程序实行征收，并给予相应的补偿。

第六条 设立外资企业的申请，由国务院对外经济贸易主管部门或者国务院授权的机关审查批准。审查批准机关应当在接到申请之日起九十天内决定批准或者不批准。

第七条 设立外资企业的申请经批准后，外国投资者应当在接到批准证书之日起三十天内向工商行政管理机关申请登记，领取营业执照。外资企业的营业执照签发日期，为该企业成立日期。

第八条 外资企业符合中国法律关于法人条件的规定的，依法取得中国法人资格。

第九条 外资企业应当在审查批准机关核准的期限内在中国境内投资；逾期不投资的，工商行政管理机关有权吊销营业执照。

工商行政管理机关对外资企业的投资情况进行检查和监督。

第十条 外资企业分立、合并或者其他重要事项变更，应当报审查批准机关批准，并向工商行政管理机关办理变更登记手续。

第十一条　外资企业的生产经营计划应当报其主管部门备案。

外资企业依照经批准的章程进行经营管理活动，不受干涉。

第十二条　外资企业雇用中国职工应当依法签定合同，并在合同中订明雇用、解雇、报酬、福利、劳动保护、劳动保险等事项。

第十三条　外资企业的职工依法建立工会组织，开展工会活动，维护职工的合法权益。

外资企业应当为本企业工会提供必要的活动条件。

第十四条　外资企业必须在中国境内设置会计帐簿，进行独立核算，按照规定报送会计报表，并接受财政税务机关的监督。

外资企业拒绝在中国境内设置会计帐簿的，财政税务机关可以处以罚款，工商行政管理机关可以责令停止营业或者吊销营业执照。

第十五条　外资企业在批准的经营范围内需要的原材料、燃料等物资，可以在中国购买，也可以在国际市场购买；在同等条件下，应当尽先在中国购买。

第十六条 外资企业的各项保险应当向中国境内的保险公司投保。

第十七条 外资企业依照国家有关税收的规定纳税并可以享受减税、免税的优惠待遇。

外资企业将缴纳所得税后的利润在中国境内再投资的，可以依照国家规定申请退还再投资部分已缴纳的部分所得税税款。

第十八条 外资企业的外汇事宜，依照国家外汇管理规定办理。

外资企业应当在中国银行或者国家外汇管理机关指定的银行开户。

外资企业应当自行解决外汇收支平衡。外资企业的产品经有关主管机关批准在中国市场销售，因而造成企业外汇收支不平衡的，由批准其在中国市场销售的机关负责解决。

第十九条 外国投资者从外资企业获得的合法利润、其他合法收入和清算后的资金，可以汇往国外。

外资企业的外籍职工的工资收入和其他正当收入，依法纳缴个人所得税后，可以汇往国外。

第二十条 外资企业的经营期限由外国投资者申报，由审查批准机关批准。期满需要延长的，应当在期满一百八十天以前向审查批准机关提出申请。审查批准机关应当在接到申请之日起三十天内决定批准或者不批准。

第二十一条 外资企业终止，应当及时公告，按照法定程序进行清算。

在清算完结前，除为了执行清算外，外国投资者对企业财产不得处理。

第二十二条 外资企业终止，应当向工商行政管理机关办理注销登记手续，缴销营业执照。

第二十三条 国务院对外经济贸易主管部门根据本法制定实施细则，报国务院批准后施行。

第二十四条 本法自公布之日起施行。

PROVISIONS OF THE STATE COUNCIL FOR ENCOURAGEMENT OF FOREIGN INVESTMENT

(October 11, 1986)

Article 1 These provisions are formulated to improve the investment environment, facilitate the absorption of foreign investment, introduce advanced technology, improve product quality, and expand exports in order to generate foreign exchange in the interest of developing the national economy.

Article 2 The State encourages foreign companies, enterprises and other economic organizations or individuals (hereinafter referred to as "foreign investors") to establish Chinese-foreign joint ventures, Chinese-foreign cooperative enterprises and foreign-owned enterprises (hereinafter referred to as "enterprises with foreign investment") within the territory of China.

The State grants special preferences to enterprises with foreign investment as listed below:

(1) Enterprises that produce goods mainly for export and have a foreign exchange surplus after the annual foreign exchange expenditures incurred in production and operation and the foreign exchange needed for remittance abroad of profits earned by foreign investors are deducted from the total annual foreign exchange revenues (hereinafter referred to as "export enterprises");

(2) Enterprises possessing advanced technology

supplied by foreign investors and engaged in developing new products and upgrading and replacing products for increasing foreign exchange generated by exports or for import substitution (hereinafter referred to as "technologically advanced enterprises").

Article 3   Export enterprises and technologically advanced enterprises shall be exempt from payment to the State of all subsidies to staff and workers, except for the payment of or allocation of funds for labour insurance, welfare costs and housing subsidies for the Chinese staff and workers in accordance with the provisions of the State.

Article 4   Fees for the use of sites by export enterprises and technologically advanced enterprises, except for sites located in busy urban sectors of large cities, shall be computed and charged according to the following standards:

(1)   Five to twenty RMB yuan per square metre per year in areas where the development fee and the site-use fee are computed and charged together;

(2)   Not more than three RMB yuan per square metre per year in areas where the development fee is computed and charged on a one-time basis or in areas in which the sites are developed by the above-mentioned enterprises themselves.

Exemptions for specified periods of time from the fees stipulated in the foregoing provisions may be granted at the discretion of local people's governments.

Article 5   Export enterprises and technologically advanced enterprises shall be given priority in obtaining water, electricity, transportation service and communication facilities needed for their production and distribution of goods. Fees shall be computed and charged at rates for local state enterprises.

Article 6   Export enterprises and technologically advanced enterprises, after examination by the Bank of China, shall be given priority in receiving loans for short-term working capital needed for the production and dis-tribution of their goods, as well as for other credit they need.

Article 7   When foreign investors in export enter-prises and technologically advanced enterprises remit abroad profits distributed to them by such enterprises, the amount remitted shall be exempt from income tax.

Article 8   After expiration of the period for a re-duction in or exemption from enterprise income tax in accordance wth the provisions of the State, export enter-prises in which the value of export products in a parti-cular year amounts to 70 percent or more of the value of their products for the same year may pay enterprise income tax of one half the prevailing tax rate.

Export enterprises in Special Economic Zones and in Economic and Technological Development Zones and other export enterprises that are already paying enterprise income tax at a reduced rate of 15 percent and fulfil the foregoing conditions shall pay enterprise income tax at a reduced rate of 10 percent.

Article 9   After expiration of the period of reduc-tion in or exemption from enterprise income tax in ac-cordance with the provisions of the State, technologically advanced enterprises may be granted a three-year exten-sion of the period at one half the prevailing tax rate.

Article 10   Foreign investors who reinvest the pro-fits distributed to them by their enterprises in the establishment or expansion of export enterprises or technologically advanced enterprises in China for a period of operation of not less than five years shall, after application to and approval by the tax authorities, be refunded the total enterprise income tax already paid on the reinvested portion. If the investment is withdrawn before the expiration of five years of operation, the refunded income tax shall be repaid.

Article 11   Export products of enterprises with foreign investment, except for crude oil, refined oil and other products subject to special State provisions, shall be exempt from consolidated industrial and commercial tax.

Article 12   Enterprises with foreign investment may arrange for the export of their products directly or through agents, in accordance with State provisions. For products that require an export licence, in accordance with the annual export plan of such enterprises, an application for an export licence may be made every six months.

Article 13   Machinery and equipment, vehicles used in production, raw and processed materials, fuel, parts, spare parts, components and fittings (including imports restricted by the State) that enterprises with foreign investment need to import in order to carry out their export contracts do not require further application for examination and approval and do not require import licences. Customs shall exercise supervisions and control and inspect and release such imports on the basis of the enterprise or export contract.

The imported material and parts mentioned above are restricted to the use of the enterprise importing them and may not be sold on the domestic market. If they are used for products to be sold domestically, import procedures shall comply with relevant provisions and taxes shall accord with pertinent regulations.

Article 14   Under the supervision of foreign exchange control departments, enterprises with foreign investment may trade foreign exchange surpluses and deficiencies among themselves.

The Bank of China and other banks designated by the People's Bank of China may grant loans in Renminbi to enterprises with foreign investment against foreign exchange cash deposits.

Article 15   People's governments at all levels and relevant departments in charge shall guarantee the right of autonomy of enterprises with foreign investment and shall support the management of enterprises with foreign investment in accordance with internationally advanced scientific methods.

Within the scope of their approved contracts, enterprises with foreign investment have the right to determine their own production and operation plans, raise and use funds, purchase production materials, sell products, and establish levels and forms of wages and bonus and allowance systems.

Enterprises with foreign investment may, in accordance with their production and operation requirements, devise their own organizational structure and personnel system, employ or dismiss senior managerial personnel, and increase or dismiss their staff and workers. They may recruit and employ technical personnel, managerial personnel and workers in their localities. The units to which such personnel belong shall support and permit

their transfer. Staff members and workers who violate
rules and regulations and thereby bring about bad consequences may, depending on the seriousness of the case,
be penalized or even discharged. Enterprises with foreign
investment that recruit, employ, dismiss or discharge staff
members and workers shall file a report with the local
labour and personnel department for the record.

Article 16 All districts and departments must implement the Circular of the State Council for Firmly Curb-
ing the Indiscriminate Levy of Charges on Enterprises.
People's governments at provincial level shall formulate
specific measures to strengthen supervision and administration.

Enterprises with foreign investment that encounter
unreasonable charges of fees may refuse to pay such fees
and may also appeal to local economic commissions or to
the State Economic Commission.

Article 17 People's governments at all levels and
relevant departments in charge shall strengthen the coor-
dination of their work, improve efficiency in handling
matters and promptly examine and approve matters submitted by enterprises with foreign investment that require
response and resolution. In case of an agreement, contract and articles of association of an enterprise with foreign investment that are to be examined and approved by
the departments in charge under the State Council, the
examining and approving authority must, within three
months from the date of receipt of all documents, decide
whether to approve or not.

Article 18 The export enterprises and technologically advanced enterprises mentioned in these Provisions
shall be recognized as such jointly by the foreign econo-

mic relations and trade departments where they are located and relevant departments, in accordance with the contracts of such enterprises, and certificates shall be issued for the purpose.

If the annual exports of an export enterprise fall short of creating a surplus in the foreign exchange balance, as stipulated in the enterprise contract, the taxes and fees already reduced or exempted in the previous year shall be made up in the following year.

Artirle 19 Except for articles in these Provisions expressly applicable to export enterprises or technologically advanced enterprises, articles shall apply to all enterprises with foreign investment.

These Provisions shall, from the date of implementation, apply to enterprises with foreign investment that obtained approval for establishment before the date of implementation of these Provisions and qualify for the preferential terms of these Provisions.

Article 20 Matters pertaining to enterprises with investment from and established by companies, enterprises and other economic organizations or individuals of Hong Kong, Macao or Taiwan shall be handled with reference to these Provisions.

Article 21 The Ministry of Foreign Economic Relations and Trade shall be responsible for interpreting these Provisions.

Article 22 These Provisions shall go into effect on the date of promulgation.

国务院关于鼓励外商投资的规定

（一九八六年十月十一日）

第一条 为了改善投资环境，更好地吸收外商投资，引进先进技术，提高产品质量，扩大出口创汇，发展国民经济，特制定本规定。

第二条 国家鼓励外国的公司、企业和其他经济组织或者个人（以下简称外国投资者），在中国境内举办中外合资经营企业、中外合作经营企业和外资企业（以下简称外商投资企业）。

国家对下列外商投资企业给予特别优惠：

一、产品主要用于出口，年度外汇总收入额减除年度生产经营外汇支出额和外国投资者汇出分得利润所需外汇额以后，外汇有结余的生产型企业（以下简称产品出口企业）；

二、外国投资者提供先进技术，从事新产品开发，实现产品升级换代，以增加出口创汇或者替代进口的生产型企业（以下简称先进技术企业）。

第三条 产品出口企业和先进技术企业，除按照国家规定支付或者提取中方职工劳动保险、福利费用和住房补助基金外，免缴国家对职工的各项补贴。

第四条　产品出口企业和先进技术企业的场地使用费，除大城市市区繁华地段外，按下列标准计收：

一、开发费和使用费综合计收的地区，为每年每平方米五元至二十元；

二、开发费一次性计收或者上述企业自行开发场地的地区，使用费最高为每年每平方米三元。

前款规定的费用，地方人民政府可以酌情在一定期限内免收。

第五条　对产品出口企业和先进技术企业优先提供生产经营所需的水、电、运输条件和通信设施，按照当地国营企业收费标准计收费用。

第六条　产品出口企业和先进技术企业在生产和流通过程中需要借贷的短期周转资金，以及其他必需的信贷资金，经中国银行审核后，优先贷放。

第七条　产品出口企业和先进技术企业的外国投资者，将其从企业分得的利润汇出境外时，免缴汇出额的所得税。

第八条 产品出口企业按照国家规定减免企业所得税期满后，凡当年企业出口产品产值达到当年企业产品产值70％以上的，可以按照现行税率减半缴纳企业所得税。

经济特区和经济技术开发区的以及其他已经按15％的税率缴纳企业所得税的产品出口企业，符合前款条件的，减按10％的税率缴纳企业所得税。

第九条 先进技术企业按照国家规定减免企业所得税期满后，可以延长三年减半缴纳企业所得税。

第十条 外国投资者将其从企业分得的利润，在中国境内再投资举办、扩建产品出口企业或者先进技术企业，经营期不少于五年的，经申请税务机关核准，全部退还其再投资部分已缴纳的企业所得税税款。经营期不足五年撤出该项投资的，应当缴回已退的企业所得税税款。

第十一条 对外商投资企业的出口产品，除原油、成品油和国家另有规定的产品外，免征工商统一税。

第十二条 外商投资企业可以自行组织其产品出口，也可以按照国家规定委托代理出口。属于需要申领出口许可证的产品，按照企业年度出口计划，每半年申领一次许可证。

第十三条　外商投资企业为履行其产品出口合同，需要进口（包括国家限制进口）的机械设备、生产用的车辆、原材料、燃料、散件、零部件、元器件、配套件，不再报请审批，免领进口许可证，由海关实行监管，凭企业合同或者进出口合同验放。

前款所述进口料、件、只限于本企业自用，不得在国内市场出售；如用于内销产品，应当按照规定补办进口手续，并照章补税。

第十四条　外商投资企业之间，在外汇管理部门监管下，可以相互调剂外汇余缺。

中国银行以及经中国人民银行指定的其他银行，可以对外商投资企业开办现汇抵押业务，贷放人民币资金。

第十五条　各级人民政府和有关主管部门应当保障外商投资企业的自主权，支持外商投资企业按照国际上先进的科学方法管理企业。

外商投资企业有权在批准的合同范围内，自行制定生产经营计划，筹措、运用资金，采购生产资料，销售产品；自行确定工资标准、工资形式和奖励、津贴制度。

外商投资企业可以根据生产经营需要，自行

确定其机构设置和人员编制，聘用或者辞退高级经营管理人员，增加或者辞退职工；可以在当地招聘和招收技术人员、管理人员和工人，被录用人员所在单位应当给予支持，允许流动；对违反规章制度，造成一定后果的职工，可以根据情节轻重，给予不同处分，直至开除。外商投资企业招聘、招收、辞退或者开除职工，应当向当地劳动人事部门备案。

第十六条　各地区、各部门必须执行《国务院关于坚决制止向企业乱摊派的通知》，由省级人民政府制定具体办法，加强监督管理。

外商投资企业遇有不合理收费的情况可以拒交；也可以向当地经济委员会直到国家经济委员会申诉。

第十七条　各级人民政府和有关主管部门，应当加强协调工作，提高办事效率，及时审批外商投资企业申报的需要批复和解决的事宜。由国务院主管部门审批的外商投资企业的协议、合同、章程，审批机关必须在收到全部文件之日起三个月以内决定批准或者不批准。

第十八条　本规定所指产品出口企业和先进技术企业，由该企业所在地的对外经济贸易部门会同有关部门根据企业合同确认，并出具证明。

产品出口企业的年度出口实绩，如果未能实现企业合同规定的外汇平衡有结余的目标，应当在下一年度内补缴上一年度已经减免的税、费。

第十九条　本规定除明确规定适用于产品出口企业或者先进技术企业的条款外，其他条款适用于所有外商投资企业。

本规定施行之日前获准举办的外商投资企业，几符合本规定的优惠条件的，自施行之日起适用本规定。

第二十条　香港、澳门、台湾的公司、企业和其他经济组织或者个人投资举办的企业，参照本规定执行。

第二十一条　本规定由对外经济贸易部负责解释。

第二十二条　本规定自发布之日起施行。

PROVISIONS FOR ENTERPRISES WITH FOREIGN INVESTMENT ON THE AUTONOMY IN THE EMPLOYMENT OF PERSONNEL AND IN FIXING WAGES AND INSURANCE AND WELFARE FUNDS

(November 10, 1986)

In order to implement the Provisions of the State Council for Encouragement of Foreign Investment, guarantee the autonomy of enterprises with foreign investment in the employment of personnel, and appropriately fix the wages and insurance and welfare funds of Chinese workers and staff, the following provisions have been specially formulated:

1. Autonomy of enterprises with foreign investment in the employment of personnel.

(1) In line with production and management needs enterprises with foreign investment can make their own decisions on organizational structure and personnel employment. Assisted by the local labour and personnel department, they can recruit workers and staff by themselves and choose the best through examinations.

If the locality cannot provide the needed technical and managerial personnel, the enterprise can recruit them in other parts of the country after obtaining approval from the labour and personnel department of the province, autonomous region or municipality where the enterprise is located.

(2) The units where the technical and managerial personnel and technical workers who have been chosen through examinations to be employed by an enterprise with foreign investment should actively support and permit their transfer. If a dispute arises, it will be adjudicated by the local labour and personnel department.

(3) Senior managerial personnel appointed by the Chinese side to work at enterprises with foreign investment should have a good grasp of policy, understand techniques and be competent in management, bold in developing new business possibilities and able to cooperate and get along with foreign businessmen. The departments concerned should support their work and, in general, not transfer them during their term. If a transfer is imperative, it must be approved by the board of directors.

(4) Persons who prove unqualified after a probationary or training period and persons who become surplus through changes in production techniques may be dismissed by enterprises with foreign investment. Workers and staff who violate enterprise regulations and cause losses may be punished or expelled, depending on the seriousness of the case.

2. Wages and insurance and welfare funds for workers and staff.

(1) Wages of the workers and staff of enterprises with foreign investment are decided by the board of directors on the principle of their being no lower than 120 percent of the wages of workers and staff in state-owned enterprises of the same kind in the same area and their being adjusted according to the economic efficiency of

the enterprises.   Wages and salaries may be raised if the enterprises' economic efficiency is high or they may be raised only slightly or not at all if economic efficiency is low.

(2) In line with regulations of local people's governments, enterprises with foreign investment should pay old-age pensions and unemployment compensation. Insurance and welfare funds for workers and staff should accord with regulations of the Chinese government for state-owned enterprises; the expenses are to be defrayed from the enterprise's cost of operation.

(3) Enterprises with foreign investment should pay housing subsidies in accord with regulations of local people's government, and the Chinese side should use the money to build or buy houses for the workers and staff.

关于外商投资企业用人自主权和职工工资、保险福利费用的规定

（一九八六年十一月十日）

为了贯彻《国务院关于鼓励外商投资的规定》，保障外商投资企业的用人自主权，适当确定中方职工的工资、保险福利费用，特作如下规定：

一、关于外商投资企业用人自主权

（一）外商投资企业可根据生产经营的需要，自行确定机构设置和人员编制，在所在地区劳动人事部门的协助下，自行招收、招聘职工，通过考核，择优录用。

外商投资企业所需要的工程技术人员和经营管理人员，在当地无法解决的，经所在省、自治区、直辖市劳动人事部门商得有关地区劳动人事部门同意，可到外地招聘。

（二）外商投资企业经过考核，决定录用的在职工程技术人员、经营管理人员和技术工人，原单位应积极支持，允许流动，如有争议，由所

在地区劳动人事部门裁决。

（三）中方委派到外商投资企业工作的高级管理人员，应当是能够掌握政策、懂技术、会管理、勇于开拓，并能与外商合作共事的人员。有关部门对他们的工作应给予支持，在任期内，一般不得调动他们的工作；必须调动的，应征得董事会的同意。

（四）外商投资企业对于经过试用或者培训而不合格的人员，因企业生产技术条件发生变化而富余的人员，可以辞退；对于违反企业规章制度，造成一定后果的职工，可以根据情节轻重，给予不同的处分，直至开除。

二、关于职工工资、保险福利费用

（一）外商投资企业职工的工资水平，由董事会按照不低于所在地区同行业条件相近的国营企业平均工资的 120% 的原则加以确定，并根据企业经济效益好坏逐步加以调整。经济效益好的，工资可以多增；经济效益差的，可以少增或不增。

（二）外商投资企业按照所在地区人民政府的规定，缴纳中方职工退休养老基金和待业保险基金。职工在职期间的保险福利待遇，按照中国政府对国营企业的有关规定执行；所需费用，从企业成本费用中如实列支。

（三）外商投资企业按照所在地区人民政府的规定，支付住房补助基金，由企业中方用于补贴建造、购置职工住房费用。

CUSTOMS REGULATIONS OF THE PEOPLE'S RE-PUBLIC OF CHINA ON THE IMPORT OF MATERIALS AND PARTS NEEDED BY FOREIGN-INVESTED ENTERPRISES TO FULFIL CONTRACTS FOR PRODUCT EXPORTATION

(November 24, 1986)

Article 1   To encourage foreign-invested enterprises to fulfil contracts for product exportation, thus increasing exports and earning more foreign exchange, the following regulations for the import of materials and parts to be processed are made according to the Provisional Customs Law of the People's Republic of China and other decisions by the State Council for encouraging foreign investments.

Article 2   Foreign-invested enterprises are to enjoy preferential treatment and take responsibility for Customs declarations and payment of duties according to these Regulations. They should honestly declare imports and exports to Customs materials needed to fulfil a product-exportation contract, such as machinery, motor vehicles for use in production, raw materials, fuel, parts, assemblies, subsidiary materials and packaging materials (hereinafter shortened to "materials and parts"), are classified as duty-pending goods in customs bond and to be supervised by Customs.

Article 3   The imported machinery, motor vehicles, materials and parts referred to in Article 2 can be inspected and passed by Customs without an import permit but with the enterprises' contracts or product-exportation contracts.

Products processed from imported materials and parts by a foreign-invested enterprise will be inspected and passed for export according to regulations for foreign-invested enterprises' import or export permits set by the Ministry of Foreign Economic Relations and Trade.

If the imported materials and parts are used to produce goods for domestic sale, the foreign-invested enterprise should follow the relevant regulations of the State and complete the required import procedures. For imports requiring a permit, an import permit should be presented to Customs for inspection.

Article 4   The imported materials and parts discussed in Article 2 shall be exempt from import duties and the consolidated industrial and commercial tax according to the quantity actually consumed in processing export-oriented products.

The above duty-free materials and parts include reasonable quantities of catalysts, abrasives, and fuels imported directly for processing products for export and consumed in the production process.

The imported materials and parts are limited to the use of the enterprise in processing export products and cannot be sold on the domestic market.   If the processed products are permitted to be sold domestically, duty will have to be paid on the imported materials and parts as required by regulations.   Duty will be reduced depending on use value for substandard products and leftovers from the production process.

Article 5   When importing materials and parts needed for producing import substitutes, as listed in the catalogues approved by State departments in charge, foreign-invested enterprises may complete the procedures for paying import duties at a later date and the imports will be regarded as duty-free goods by Customs, following these Regulations. If the finished products are provided to domestic customers, import duties and the consolidated industrial and commercial tax will be imposed on the imported materials and parts already used and import procedures will have to be completed as required.

If domestic customers can import a certain item without or with reduced duty, foreign-invested enterprises can enjoy the same benefits, but certificates for duty reduction or exemption, approved by authorized departments will have to be examined as required by State regulations.

Article 6 When purchases are made by foreign-invested enterprises from duty-pending stockpiles of the administrations concerned and when materials and parts are imported by other enterprises entrusted by the foreign-invested enterprises, the goods are considered the same as imports by the foreign-invested enterprises and should be handled in line with the relevant regulations.

Article 7 Foreign-invested enterprises whose business is processing imported materials should register with the local Customs or the Customs administrative division and receive the Registration Manual of the Customs of the People's Republic of China for Foreign-Invested Enterprises Importing Materials and Parts for Processing Export Products in Fulfilment of Product Exportation Contracts (hereinafter shortened to Registration Manual). These enterprises, when possible, should request examination and approval by local Customs and will be handled according to Customs administrative regulations on factories processing duty-pending imported materials.

Upon the import of materials and parts or the export of finished products, foreign-invested enterprises should declare them to Customs at the port of entry or exit with the Registration Manual, three copies of the import or export declarations, receipts of the products, shipping invoices and other relevant certificates. The notes and seals by Customs on the Registration Manual will be used for ratification or cancellation at local Customs or the Customs administrative divisions.

Article 8 Within two months after the fulfilment of each contract specifying the import of materials and parts, ratification and cancellation procedures should be completed at Customs by foreign-invested enterprises with the Registration Manual, import and export declarations and other required certificates.

For inspection by Customs, special account books should be kept and quarterly reports issued by foreign-invested enterprises on the import, storage and withdrawal for production of materials and parts and their transfer to other manufacturers for processing, and on the inventory, exportation and domestic sales of the finished products. Semiannual reports are acceptable for products with long production cycles, upon examination and approval by Customs.

Article 9 If finished products processed with duty-free materials and parts are approved for domestic sale, customs duty for import of the materials and parts and the consolidated industrial and commercial tax shall be paid by the foreign-invested enterprises within one month of the day of approval.

Article 10   The materials and parts imported duty-free by foreign-invested enterprises, unless examined and approved by Customs for special reasons, should be processed into finished products in fulfilment of contracts within one year from the day of import.

Article 11   If the imported materials and parts are processed into products that are then sent to another enterprise to be reprocessed or assembled into export products, the importing enterprise and the reprocessing enterprise should go through procedures at Customs for the transfer and cancellation, with the sales contract or processing contract they have signed and other relevant certificates.   The reprocessing enterprise should follow these Regulations for applying for a new Registration Manual, observe the regulations, and accept Customs' supervision.

Article 12   If after the importation of the materials and parts, there should be any alteration, transfer, cessation or cancellation of the contract, corresponding procedures should be completed promptly by the foreign-invested enterprises at Customs.

Article 13   For the convenience of foreign-invested enterprises and reprocessing enterprises processing materials for export, Customs officers may be stationed at the enterprises, depending on the actual situation, to supervise and inspect related account books.   Offices and necessary conveniences are to be provided by the enterprises.

Article 14   Foreign-invested enterprises must not at will transfer or sell domestically the duty-pending imported materials and parts or the resultant finished products.

Should transfers, domestic sales or other violations of these Regulations occur, penalties will be enforced by Customs according to the Customs law and other pertinent laws and regulations of the State.

Article 15   These Regulations become effective on December 1, 1986.

中华人民共和国海关对外商投资企业履行产品出口合同所需进口料件管理办法

（一九八六年十一月二十四日）

第一条　为鼓励外商投资企业履行其产品出口合同所需进口料、件加工复出口，扩大出口创汇，根据《中华人民共和国暂行海关法》和国务院关于鼓励外商投资的有关规定，特制定本办法。

第二条　外商投资企业应按本办法规定享受其优惠并承担报关、纳税义务，其进出口货物应如实向海关申报。为履行产品出口合同所需进口的机械设备、生产用的车辆，以及原材料、燃料、散件、零部件、元器件、配套件、辅料和包装物料（以下简称料、件）属保税货物，由海关实行监管。

第三条　本办法第二条所述进口机械设备、生产用车辆和料、件，免领进口许可证，海关凭企业合同或者进出口合同验放。

对外商投资企业用进口料、件加工复出口的

产品，复出口时，海关根据对外经济贸易部关于外商投资企业申领进出口许可证办法的规定办理验放。

进口料、件，如用于内销产品，有关外商投资企业应当按照国家有关规定补办进口手续。其中属于实行进口许可证管理的商品还应向海关交验进口货物许可证。

第四条　本办法第二条所述进口的料、件，按实际加工出口产品所耗用的进口料、件免征进口关税和工商统一税。

上述免税料、件包括进口直接用于加工出口产品而在生产过程中消耗掉的、数量合理的触媒剂、催化剂、磨料、燃料等。

进口的料、件，只限本企业加工出口产品使用，不得在国内市场出售；加工的产品因故经批准转为内销处理，对其所耗用的进口料、件应照章补税。对于生产过程中产生的副次品、边角余料，根据其使用价值酌情减免税。

第五条　外商投资企业生产由国家规定的主管部门批准的以产顶进目录内产品所需进口料、件，可比照本办法由海关作为保税货物进行监管，进口时缓办纳税手续。上述产品供应给国内用户时，再向海关补纳所用进口料、件的进口关税和工商统一税，并按照规定补办进口手续。

　　如国内用户从国外进口同类产品可以享受减免税优惠的，外商投资企业供应给该用户的上述产品，也可给予减免税优惠，但应按照国家有关规定交验经主管部门批准的减免税证件。

　　第六条　外商投资企业从有关部门的保税仓库中购进或委托其他企业代理进口的料、件，视同外商投资企业自行进口并按本办法的有关规定办理。

　　第七条　经营进料加工业务的外商投资企业，应持有关合同向所在地海关（或分工管理海关）办理备案登记手续，并由海关核发《中华人民共和国海关对外商投资企业履行产品出口合同所需进口料件加工复出口登记手册》（以下简称登记手册）。有条件的企业经所在地海关核准，可以按海关对进料加工保税工厂的管理规定办理。

　　上述料、件进口和加工成品出口时，外商投资企业应持《登记手册》、进出口货物报关单一式三份、货物发票、装箱单等有关单证向进出境地海关申报。有关海关在《登记手册》上批注、签章后退回外商投资企业，凭以向所在地海关（或分工管理海关）办理核销手续。

第八条　外商投资企业对每个进口合同项下进口的料、件，在有关合同执行完毕后的两个月内，持《登记手册》和进出口货物报关单等有关单据向海关办理核销手续。

外商投资企业对料、件的进口、储存保管、提取使用和转厂加工，以及对加工制成品的库存、出口和内销等情况，应建立专门帐册并按季列表报送海关核查。对生产周期长的产品，经海关核准，可每半年报送一次。

第九条　用免税进口的料、件加工的产品，如经批准转为内销，外商投资企业应从批准之日起一个月内向有关海关补缴原免税进口料、件的关税和工商统一税。

第十条　外商投资企业免税进口的料、件，除因特殊原因经海关核准的以外，应从进口之日起一年内加工成成品并履行有关合同。

第十一条　进口的料、件于加工成品后如不直接出口而是转让给另一承接进料加工复出口的生产企业进行再加工、装配时，进口料、件的企业应会同该生产企业持凭双方签订的购销或生产加工合同等有关单据向海关办理结转和核销手续。该承接进料加工复出口业务的生产企业应按本办法的规定，申领新的《登记手册》，并遵守本办法的有关规定，接受海关监管。

第十二条　料、件进口后，如发生更改、转让、中止、撤销合同等情事，有关外商投资企业应及时向海关办理更改、转让、撤销登记等手续。

第十三条　为了便利外商投资企业以及承接进料加工复出口业务的再生产企业进行加工、出口业务活动，海关根据实际情况可以派出关员驻厂进行实际监管并可查阅有关账册。上述企业应当提供办公场所和必要的方便条件。

第十四条　外商投资企业不得将作为保税货物进口的料、件及其加工的产品擅自转让、内销。如发现有关企业有擅自转让、内销以及其他违反本办法规定的违法行为，由海关依据海关法和国家有关法令、规定进行处理。

第十五条　本办法自 1986 年 12 月 1 日起实行。

FRONTIER HEALTH AND QUARANTINE LAW OF THE PEOPLE'S REPUBLIC OF CHINA

(Adopted at the Eighteenth Session of the Standing Committee of the Sixth National People's Congress on December 2, 1986)

CHAPTER I   GENERAL PROVISIONS

Article 1   This Law is formulated in order to prevent infectious diseases from spreading into or out of the country, to carry out frontier health and quarantine inspection and to protect human health.

Article 2   Frontier health and quarantine offices shall be set up at international seaports, airports and ports of entry at land frontiers and boundary rivers (hereinafter referred to as "frontier ports") of the People's Republic of China.   These offices shall carry out the quarantining and monitoring of infectious diseases and health inspection in accordance with the provisions of this Law.

Health administration departments under the State Council shall be in charge of frontier health and quarantine work throughout the country.

Article 3   Infectious diseases specified in this Law shall include quarantinable infectious diseases and infectious diseases to be monitored.

Quarantinable infectious diseases include plague, cholera, yellow fever and other infectious diseases determined and announced by the State Council.

Infectious diseases to be monitored shall be determined and announced by health administration departments under the State Council.

Article 4   Persons, conveyances and transport equipment, as well as articles such as luggage, goods and postal parcels that may transmit quarantinable infectious diseases, shall undergo quarantine inspection upon entering or exiting the country.   No entry or exit shall be allowed without the permission of a frontier health and quarantine office.   Specific measures for implementation of this Law shall be stipulated in detailed regulations.

Article 5   On discovering a quarantinable infectious disease or a disease suspected to be quarantinable, a frontier health and quarantine office shall, in addition to taking necessary measures, immediatedly notify the local health administration department; at the same time it shall report to the health administration department under the State Council by the most expeditious means possible, within twenty-four hours at the latest.   Post and telecommunications departments shall give priority to transmission of reports of epidemic diseases.

Messages exchanged between the People's Republic of China and foreign countries on the epidemic situation of infectious diseases shall be handled by the health administration department under the State Council in conjunction with other departments concerned.

Article 6   When a quarantinable infectious disease is prevalent abroad or within China, the State Council may order relevant sections of the border to be closed or adopt other emergency measures.

CHAPTER II   QUARANTINE INSPECTION

Article 7   Persons and conveyances entering the country shall be subject to quarantine inspection at designated places at their first frontier port. Except for harbour pilots, no person shall be allowed to embark or disembark and no articles, such as luggage, goods or postal parcels, shall be loaded or unloaded without the health and quarantine inspector's permission. Specific measures for the implementation of this Law shall be stipulated in detailed regulations.

Article 8   Persons and conveyances exiting the country shall be subject to quarantine inspection at the last frontier port.

Article 9   When foreign ships or airborne vehicles anchor or land at places other than frontier ports in China, the persons in charge of the ships or airborne vehicle must report immediately to the nearest frontier health and quarantine office or to the local health administration department. Except in cases of emergency, no person shall be allowed to embark or disembark and no articles, such as baggage, goods and postal parcels, shall be loaded or unloaded without the permission of a frontier health and quarantine office or the local health administration department.

Article 10   When a quarantinable infectious disease, a disease suspected to be quarantinable or a death due to an unidentified cause other than accidental harm is discovered at a frontier port, the relevant department at the frontier port and the person in charge of the conveyance must report immediately to the frontier health and quarantine office and apply for provisional quarantine inspection.

Article 11 Following inspection by quarantine doctors, the frontier health and quarantine office shall sign and issue a quarantine certificate for entry or exit to conveyances uncontaminated by any quarantinable infectious disease or treated for decontamination.

Article 12 Anyone having a quarantinable infectious disease shall be placed in isolation by the frontier health and quarantine office for a period determined by the results of the medical examination, while anyone suspected of having a quarantinable infectious disease shall be kept for observation for a period determined by the incubation period of such disease.

The corpse of anyone who died from a quarantinable infectious disease must be cremated at a nearby place.

Article 13 Any conveyance subject to entry quarantine inspection shall be disinfected, deratted, trated with insecticides or given other sanitation measures if it meets any of the following conditions:

(1) From an area where a quarantinable infectious disease is epidemic;

(2) Contaminated by a quarantinable infectious disease;

(3) Containings rodents that affect human health or insects that are disease carriers.

Apart from exceptional cases, when the person in charge of the foreign conveyance refuses to allow sanitation measures to be taken, the conveyance shall be allowed to leave the frontier of the People's Republic of China without delay under the supervision of the frontier health and quarantine office.

Article 14 A frontier health and quarantine office

shall conduct sanitation inspections and disinfect, derat, treat with insecticides or apply other sanitation measures to articles, such as luggage, goods and postal parcels, that come from an epidemic area and are contaminated by a quarantinable infectious disease or may act as a vehicle of a quarantinable infectious disease.

A consigner or an agent for the transportation of a corpse or human remains into or out of the country must declare the matter to a frontier health and quarantine office; transport thereof, in either direction across the border, shall not be allowed until sanitary inspection proves satisfactory and an entry or exit permit is given.

CHAPTER III   MONITORING OF INFECTIOUS DISEASES

Article 15   Frontier health and quarantine offices shall monitor persons on entry or exit for quarantinable infectious diseases and shall take necessary preventive and control measures.

Article 16   Frontier health and quarantine offices shall be authorized to require persons on entry or exit to complete a health declaration for and produce certificates of vaccination against certain infectious diseases, a health certificate or other relevant documents.

Article 17   Persons suffering from infectious diseases to be monitored, coming from areas in foreign countries where infectious diseases to be monitored are epidemic, or in close contact with patients suffering from infectious diseases to be monitored shall, depending on the case, be issued medical convenience cards, be held for inspection, or be subjected to other preventive or control measures by frontier health and quanrantine offices, which shall promptly notify local health administration departments about such cases. Medical services at all places shall give priority in consultation and treatment to persons possessing medical convenience cards.

CHAPTER IV HEALTH SUPERVISION

Article 18 Frontier health and quarantine offices shall, in accordance with state health standards, supervise sanitary conditions at frontier ports and the sanitary conditions of conveyances on entry or exit at frontier ports. They shall:

(1) Supervise and direct concerned personnel on the prevention and elimination of rodents and insects that are carriers of diseases;

(2) Inspect and test food and drinking water and facilities for their storage, supply and delivery;

(3) Supervise the health of employees engaged in the supply of food and drinking water and check their health certificates;

(4) Supervise and inspect the disposal of garbage, waste matter, sewage, excrement and ballast water.

Article 19 Frontier health and quarantine offices shall have frontier port health supervisor, who shall carry out the tasks assigned by the frontier health and quarantine offices.

In performing their duties, frontier port health supervisors shall be authorized to conduct health supervision and give technical guidance regarding frontier ports and conveyances on entry or exit, to give advice for improvement wherever sanitary conditions are unsatisfactory and factors exist that may spread infectious diseases, and to coordinate departments concerned to take necessary measures and apply sanitary treatment.

CHAPTER V   LEGAL LIABILITY

Article 20   A frontier health and quarantine office may warn or fine, according to the circumstances, any unit or individual that has violated the provisions of this Law by committing any of the following acts:

(1) Evading quarantine inspection or withholding the truth in reports to the frontier health and quarantine office;

(2) Embarking on or disembarking from conveyances upon entry or loading or unloading articles, such as luggage, foods or postal parcels, without the permission of a frontier health and quarantine office and refusing to listen to the office's advice against such acts.

All fines thus collected shall be turned over to the state treasure.

Article 21   If a concerned party refuses to obey a decision on a fine made by a frontier health and quarantine office, he may, within fifteen days after receiving notice of the fine, file a lawsuit in a local people's court. The frontier health and quarantine office may apply to the people's court for mandatory enforcement of a decision if the concerned party neither files a lawsuit nor obeys the decision within the fifteen days term.

Article 22   If a quarantinable infectious disease spreads or is in great danger of being spread as a result of a violation of the provisions of this Law, criminal responsibility shall be investigated in accordance with

Article 178 of the Criminal Law of the People's Republic of China.

Article 23 The personnel of frontier health and quarantine offices must enforce this Law impartially, perform duties faithfully, and promptly conduct quarantine inspection of conveyances and persons upon entry or exit. Those who violate the law or are derelict in their duties shall be given disciplinary sanctions; where circumstances are serious enough to constitute a crime, criminal responsibility shall be investigated in accordance with the law.

CHAPTER VI SUPPLEMENTARY PROVISIONS

Article 24 Where the provisions of this Law differ from those of international treaties on health and quarantine that China has concluded or joined, the provisions of such international treaties shall prevail, with the exception of treaty clauses on which the People's Republic of China has declared reservations.

Article 25 In cases of temporary contact between frontier defence units of the People's Republic of China and those of a neighbouring country, of a temporary visit at a designated place on the frontier by residents of the border areas of the two countries and of entry or exit of conveyances and persons of the two sides, quarantine inspection shall be conducted in line with the agreements between China and the other country or, in the absence of such an agreement, in accordance with the relevant regulations of the Chinese Government.

Article 26 Frontier health and quarantine offices shall charge for health and quarantine services according to state regulations.

Article 27   The health administration department under the State Council shall, in accordance with this Law, formulate rules for its implementation, which shall go into effect after being submitted to and approved by the State Council.

Article 28   This Law shall go into effect on May 1, 1987. On the same day the Frontier Health and Quarantine Regulations of the People's Republic of China, promulgated on December 23, 1957, shall be invalidated.

Appendix:

Article 178 of the Criminal Law:

Article 178   Whoever violates the national border health and quarantine regulations and causes the spread of quarantinable infectious diseases or cause a serious danger of such diseases spreading shall be sentenced to fixed term imprisonment of not more than three years or criminal detention, or he may concurrently or exclusively be sentenced to a fine.

中华人民共和国国境卫生检疫法

（一九八六年十二月二日第六届全国人民代表大会
常务委员会第十八次会议通过）

第一章 总   则

第一条 为了防止传染病由国外传入或者由
国内传出，实施国境卫生检疫，保护人体健康，
制定本法。

第二条 在中华人民共和国国际通航的港
口、机场以及陆地边境和国界江河的口岸（以下
简称国境口岸），设立国境卫生检疫机关，依照
本法规定实施传染病检疫、监测和卫生监督。

国务院卫生行政部门主管全国国境卫生检疫
工作。

第三条 本法规定的传染病是指检疫传染病
和监测传染病。

检疫传染病，是指鼠疫、霍乱、黄热病以及
国务院确定和公布的其他传染病。

监测传染病，由国务院卫生行政部门确定和
公布。

第四条　入境、出境的人员、交通工具、运输设备以及可能传播检疫传染病的行李、货物、邮包等物品，都应当接受检疫，经国境卫生检疫机关许可，方准入境或者出境。具体办法由本法实施细则规定。

第五条　国境卫生检疫机关发现检疫传染病或者疑似检疫传染病时，除采取必要措施外，必须立即通知当地卫生行政部门，同时用最快的方法报告国务院卫生行政部门，最迟不得超过二十四小时。邮电部门对疫情报告应当优先传送。

中华人民共和国与外国之间的传染病疫情通报，由国务院卫生行政部门会同有关部门办理。

第六条　在国外或者国内有检疫传染病大流行的时候，国务院可以下令封锁有关的国境或者采取其他紧急措施。

第二章　检　　疫

第七条　入境的交通工具和人员，必须在最先到达的国境口岸的指定地点接受检疫。除引航员外，未经国境卫生检疫机关许可，任何人不准上下交通工具，不准装卸行李、货物、邮包等物品。具体办法由本法实施细则规定。

第八条　出境的交通工具和人员，必须在最

后离开的国境口岸接受检疫。

第九条　来自国外的船舶、航空器因故停泊、降落在中国境内非口岸地点的时候，船舶、航空器的负责人应当立即向就近的国境卫生检疫机关或者当地卫生行政部门报告。除紧急情况外，未经国境卫生检疫机关或者当地卫生行政部门许可，任何人不准上下船舶、航空器，不准装卸行李、货物、邮包等物品。

第十条　在国境口岸发现检疫传染病、疑似检疫传染病，或者有人非因意外伤害而死亡并死因不明的，国境口岸有关单位和交通工具的负责人，应当立即向国境卫生检疫机关报告，并申请临时检疫。

第十一条　国境卫生检疫机关依据检疫医师提供的检疫结果，对未染有检疫传染病或者已实施卫生处理的交通工具，签发入境检疫证或者出境检疫证。

第十二条　国境卫生检疫机关对检疫传染病染疫人必须立即将其隔离，隔离期限根据医学检查结果确定；对检疫传染病染疫嫌疑人应当将其留验，留验期限根据该传染病的潜伏期确定。

因患检疫传染病而死亡的尸体、必须就近火化。

第十三条 接受入境检疫的交通工具有下列情形之一的，应当实施消毒、除鼠、除虫或者其他卫生处理：

（一）来自检疫传染病疫区的；

（二）被检疫传染病污染的；

（三）发现有与人类健康有关的啮齿动物或者病媒昆虫的。

如果外国交通工具的负责人拒绝接受卫生处理，除有特殊情况外，准许该交通工具在国境卫生检疫机关的监督下，立即离开中华人民共和国国境。

第十四条 国境卫生检疫机关对来自疫区的、被检疫传染病污染的或者可能成为检疫传染病传播媒介的行李、货物、邮包等物品，应当进行卫生检查，实施消毒、除鼠、除虫或者其他卫生处理。

入境、出境的尸体、骸骨的托运人或者其代理人，必须向国境卫生检疫机关申报，经卫生检查合格后发给入境、出境许可证，方准运进或者运出。

第三章 传染病监测

第十五条 国境卫生检疫机关对入境、出境的人员实施传染病监测，并且采取必要的预防、控制措施。

第十六条　国境卫生检疫机关有权要求入境、出境的人员填写健康申明卡，出示某种传染病的预防接种证书、健康证明或者其他有关证件。

第十七条　对患有监测传染病的人、来自国外监测传染病流行区的人或者与监测传染病人密切接触的人，国境卫生检疫机关应当区别情况，发给就诊方便卡，实施留验或者采取其他预防、控制措施，并及时通知当地卫生行政部门。各地医疗单位对持有就诊方便卡的人员，应当优先诊治。

第四章　卫生监督

第十八条　国境卫生检疫机关根据国家规定的卫生标准，对国境口岸的卫生状况和停留在国境口岸的入境、出境的交通工具的卫生状况实施卫生监督：

（一）监督和指导有关人员对啮齿动物、病媒昆虫的防除；

（二）检查和检验食品、饮用水及其储存、供应、运输设施；

（三）监督从事食品、饮用水供应的从业人员的健康状况，检查其健康证明书；

（四）监督和检查垃圾、废物、污水、粪便、压舱水的处理。

第十九条　国境卫生检疫机关设立国境口岸卫生监督员，执行国境卫生检疫机关交给的任务。

国境口岸卫生监督员在执行任务时，有权对国境口岸和入境、出境的交通工具进行卫生监督和技术指导，对卫生状况不良和可能引起传染病传播的因素提出改进意见，协同有关部门采取必要的措施、进行卫生处理。

第五章　法律责任

第二十条　对违反本法规定，有下列行为之一的单位或者个人，国境卫生检疫机关可以根据情节轻重，给予警告或者罚款：

（一）逃避检疫，向国境卫生检疫机关隐瞒真实情况的；

（二）入境的人员未经国境卫生检疫机关许可，擅自上下交通工具，或者装卸行李、货物、邮包等物品，不听劝阻的。

罚款全部上缴国库。

第二十一条　当事人对国境卫生检疫机关给予的罚款决定不服的，可以在接到通知之日起十五日内，向当地人民法院起诉。逾期不起诉又不履行的，国境卫生检疫机关可以申请人民法院强制执行。

第二十二条　违反本法规定，引起检疫传染病传播或者有引起检疫传染病传播严重危险的，依照《中华人民共和国刑法》第一百七十八条的规定追究刑事责任。

第二十三条　国境卫生检疫机关工作人员，应当秉公执法，忠于职守，对入境、出境的交通工具和人员，及时进行检疫；违法失职的，给予行政处分，情节严重构成犯罪的，依法追究刑事责任。

第六章　附　　则

第二十四条　中华人民共和国缔结或者参加的有关卫生检疫的国际条约同本法有不同规定的，适用该国际条约的规定。但是，中华人民共和国声明保留的条款除外。

第二十五条　中华人民共和国边防机关与邻国边防机关之间在边境地区的往来，居住在两国边境接壤地区的居民在边境指定地区的临时往来，双方的交通工具和人员的入境、出境检疫，依照双方协议办理，没有协议的，依照中国政府的有关规定办理。

第二十六条　国境卫生检疫机关实施卫生检疫，按照国家规定收取费用。

第二十七条　国务院卫生行政部门根据本法制定实施细则，报国务院批准后施行。

第二十八条　本法自1987年5月1日起施行。1957年12月23日公布的《中华人民共和国国境卫生检疫条例》同时废止。

附：

刑法有关条文：

第一百七十八条　违反国境卫生检疫规定，引起检疫传染病的传播，或者有引起检疫传染病传播严重危险的，处三年以下有期徒刑或者拘役，可以并处或者单处罚金。

PROVISIONAL RULES OF THE PEOPLE'S BANK OF CHINA GOVERNING THE MORTGAGE OF FOREIGN-INVESTED ENTERPRISES WITH FOREIGN EXCHANGE FOR RENMINBI LOANS

(November 26, 1986)

These Rules are formulated to help develop the business of mortgaging with foreign exchange for Renminbi loans in accordance with the Provisions of the State Council for Encouragement of Foreign Investment.

Article 1 The mortgagors. Any registered Chinese-foreign joint venture, Chinese-foreign cooperative enterprise and foreign enterprise within Chinese territory has the right to apply for Renminbi loans with their own foreign exchange (including that borrowed from abroad) as mortgage.

Article 2 Uses of mortgaged loans. The mortgaged loans can be used as circulating capital or be invested in fixed assets.

Article 3 Variety and time limit of mortgaged loans. Two kinds of mortgaged loans are available: short-term loans and medium- and long-term loans. The time limit for short-term loans is three months, six months, or one year. The time limit for medium- and long-term loans is over one year with a maximum of five years.

Article 4 Variety of mortgaged foreign exchanges.

Only five foreign exchanges can be used as a mortgage at present: U.S. dollar, Japanese yen, Hong Kong dollar, West German mark, and English pound sterling.

Article 5   Mandated by the People's Bank of China, the Bank of China and other financial units handle loan mortgages, except in the Special Economic Zones.

Article 6   Application for loans. Units applying for loans shall first declare the sources and amounts of their foreign exchange to the State Foreign Exchange Administration or its branches and, after verification and approval, go through application formalities, including filling out an application form, in a bank designated by the People's Bank of China.

Article 7   Granting of loans. Mortgagors shall apply for credit to the proper banks and, after being checked and approved, sign the Contract on Loans with the banks authorized to handle the business.

Article 8   Recalling of loans. Mortgagors must not return loans before they are due. On the due date, mortgagors shall return the original amount of the loan in Renminbi and the banks concerned shall give back the original amount of mortgaged foreign exchange. The exchange is not influenced by exchange rates. If the mortgagors fail to return the loans in Renminbi at maturity, the mortgaged foreign exchange will be turned over to the People's Bank of China.   Units that have borrowed foreign exchange for mortgage from abroad bear the responsibility of paying back their creditors the foreign exchange capital and interest.

Article 9   Calculation of the amount of the loan in Renminbi.   The amount of Renminbi as a loan extended by banks to mortgagors must not exceed the value of the mortgaged properties calculated in Renminbi at the exchange (buying price) promulgated by the State Foreign Exchange Administration on the day of mortgage.

Article 10 The Renminbi loans provided by the banks and the mortgaged foreign exchanges paid by the mortgagors shall both be interest-free.

Article 11 The right of interpreting these Procedures belongs to the People's Bank of China.

Article 12 These Rules shall go into effect as of the day of promulgation.

中国人民银行关于外商投资企业外汇抵押人民币贷款的暂行办法

（一九八六年十一月二十六日）

根据《国务院关于鼓励外商投资的规定》，为开展外汇抵押人民币贷款业务，特制定本办法。

第一条　抵押贷款的对象。凡在中华人民共和国境内注册的中外合资经营企业、中外合作经营企业和外资企业，均可以其自有外汇（包括从境外借入外汇）作抵押，申请办理人民币贷款。

第二条　抵押贷款的用途。可以用于流动资金，也可以用于固定资产投资。

第三条　抵押贷款的种类和期限。抵押贷款分短期和中长期两种。短期抵押贷款的期限分三个月、六个月、一年。中长期抵押贷款为一年以上，最长不超过五年。

第四条　抵押外币的种类。用于抵押的外汇，目前限于美元、日元、港元、联邦德国马克和英镑五种。

第五条　抵押贷款业务除经济特区外，由中国人民银行委托中国银行和其它金融机构办理。

第六条　抵押贷款的申请。申请抵押单位应先到国家外汇管理局或其分局申报外汇、资金来源和数额，经核准后到中国人民银行指定的受托行办理贷款申请手续，填写借款申请书。

第七条　抵押贷款的发放。抵押单位提出的申请，经银行审查同意后，应与受托行签定《借款合同》。

第八条　抵押贷款的收回。贷款未到期，抵押单位不能提前归还。贷款到期后，抵押单位应归还原数额人民币贷款，受托银行退回原数额抵押外汇，不受汇率变动的影响。到期不能归还人民币贷款的，抵押外汇归中国人民银行所有。凡以境外借入外汇做抵押的，仍由抵押单位对原债务关系中的债权人履行偿还外债本息的义务。

第九条　人民币贷款数额的计算。银行对抵押单位发放的人民币贷款，最高不得超过抵押品按抵押日国家外汇管理局公布的人民币汇价（买入价）所计算的数额。

第十条　银行发放的人民币贷款与抵押单位付的抵押外汇，相互不计利息。

第十一条　本办法解释权属于中国人民银行。

第十二条　本办法自公布之日起实行。

PROCEDURES OF THE MINISTRY OF FOREIGN ECONOMIC RELATIONS AND TRADE CONCERNING THE PURCHASE AND EXPORT OF DOMESTIC PRODUCTS BY FOREIGN-INVESTED ENTERPRISES TO BALANCE THE REVENUE AND EXPENDITURE OF FOREIGN EXCHANGE

(Promulgated on January 20, 1987)

Article 1 These Procedures on the purchase and export of domestic products by foreign-invested enterprises are formulated in accordance with relevant provisions of the State Council to help those enterprises balance revenue and expenditure of foreign exchange.

Article 2 A foreign-invested enterprise should in principle achieve a balance of foreign-exchange revenue and expenditure by exporting its own products, but if it has temporary difficulties doing so, it may apply to purchase and export domestic products (except those under centralized state management) for a certain period of time to solve the difficulties.

Article 3 A foreign-invested enterprise wishing to purchase and export domestic products in order to make up its foreign-exchange deficit, as described in the preceding Article, shall first submit an application to the authority in charge of foreign economic relations and trade in the province or an equivalent administrative division where it is located, indicating the foreign-exchange quotas and corresponding amount of Renminbi it needs to purchase and export domestic products for deficit compensation, the names, specifications and quantities of the domestic products to be purchased, and the exporting channels.

Article 4 The quantity of domestic products that a foreign-invested enterprise is permitted to purchase is limited to the amount of foreign exchange the enterprise needs to make up the deficits in foreign exchange needed for production and management in the current year, the foreign venturer's share of the profits to be remitted abroad, or the foreign exchange for liquidation of the enterprise.

Article 5 A foreign-invested enterprise should purchase domestic products to balance its foreign-exchange revenue and expenditure mainly in the province, autonomous region, and centrally administered municipality where it is located. If the purchase is transregional, the enterprise shall first obtain approval from the department of foreign economic relations and trade of the province where the products are manufactured.

Article 6 The domestic products purchased by a foreign-invested enterprise for its balance of foreign-exchange revenue and expenditure shall be transported abroad and sold outside China; they must not be resold at a profit in China.

Article 7 A foreign-invested enterprise may itself export the domestic products it has purchased for its balance of foreign-exchange revenue and expenditure or may entrust a Chinese-foreign trade corporation to handle the export business on its behalf.

Article 8 In addition to the export of domestic pro-

ducts by foreign-invested enterprises the people's governments of provinces, autonomous regions, centrally administered municipalities and cities (or regions) with independent budget planning may organize the export of
their local products through their foreign trade companies
with the right of business operation if they guarantee fulfilment of the state plan for export. The foreign exchange
from the export shall be distributed to the product-sup-
plying units according to the foreign-exchange quotas set
by the State, and the remaining foreign exchange may
be earmarked by the local people's governments to balance
the foreign-exchange revenue and expenditure of foreign-
invested enterprises under the supervision of the local administrations of foreign exchange.

Article 9 If the products that a foreign-invested
enterprise wishes to purchase, as indicated in Article 3,
and the products that the people's governments of provinces, autonomous regions, centrally administered
municipalities and cities with independent budget planning
export on their own, as indicated in Article 8, must have an
export licence issued by the State or must be exported according to State exporting quotas, the export plans must
be submitted to the Ministry of Foreign Economic Relations and Trade for approval. The export of other commodities shall be approved by provincial authorities in
charge of foreign economic relations and trade and then reported to the Ministry of Foreign Economic Relations and
Trade for the record.

The above-mentioned examining and approving
authorities shall give an official reply within one month
from the date of receipt of application. The export of
any product that must have an export licence shall go

through the formalities for an export licence in accordance with the Procedures of the Ministry of Foreign Economic Relations and Trade Concerning Application for Import and Export Licences by Foreign-Invested Enterprises.

Article 10   These Procedures shall go into effect as of the date of promulgation.

对外经济贸易部关于外商投资企业购买国内产品出口解决外汇收支平衡办法

（一九八七年一月二十日公布）

第一条 根据国务院有关规定，为帮助外商投资企业求得外汇收支平衡，经申请批准，允许购买国内产品出口以弥补本企业的外汇缺额，特制订本办法。

第二条 外商投资企业原则上应通过出口本企业的产品，达到外汇收支平衡。对于暂时存在困难的外商投资的生产性企业，可以在一定期限内申请购买国内产品（国家规定统一经营的商品除外）出口，以解决本企业的外汇收支平衡。

第三条 凡符合本办法第二条规定的外商投资企业，如需要购买国内产品出口解决外汇收支平衡的，应事先向企业所在地的省级对外经济贸易部门提出申请，说明当年需要购买国内产品出口弥补所需的外汇额度和相应的人民币金额、申请购买国内产品的名称、规格和数量、出口渠道等。

第四条　外商投资企业经批准购买国内产品出口的数量，仅限于弥补企业当年生产经营所需要的外汇和外方投资者汇出分得的利润，或企业结业清算所需汇出的外汇。

第五条　外商投资企业经批准购买国内产品出口解决外汇收支平衡，主要应在企业所在的省、自治区、直辖市购买产品；如需跨省采购，应事前征得产地省级对外经济贸易部门同意。

第六条　外商投资企业经批准购买用于解决外汇收支平衡的国内产品，必须运往中国境外销售，不准在中国境内倒卖。

第七条　外商投资企业经批准购买用于解决外汇收支平衡的国内产品，本企业可以自行出口，也可以委托中国外贸公司代理出口。

第八条　除经批准由外商投资企业购买国内产品出口外，各省、自治区、直辖市、计划单列市（区）人民政府，在保证完成国家出口计划的前提下，可以通过有经营权的外贸公司组织本地区的产品出口，由此按照国家外汇留成规定所得的外汇额度，以规定比例给供货单位外，其余额，可以在当地外汇管理部门监管下，由地方人民政府专项用于调剂解决外商投资企业的外汇收支平衡。

第九条　本办法第三条规定的外商投资企业申请购买国内产品出口和第八条规定由省、自治区、直辖市、计划单列市（区）人民政府组织出口的产品，凡属于国家实行出口许可证管理的商品和国内有出口配额的商品，应报对外经济贸易部批准。其他商品由省级对外经济贸易部门批准，报对外经济贸易部备案。

上述审批部门应在收到申请之日起一个月内给予批复。经批准出口的产品，凡属于实行许可证的商品，应按照《对外经济贸易部关于外商投资企业申领进出口许可证办法》办理出口许可证手续。

第十条　本办法自公布之日起施行。

PROCEDURES OF THE MINISTRY OF FOREIGN ECONOMIC RELATIONS AND TRADE CONCERNING APPLICATION FOR IMPORT AND EXPORT LICENCES BY FOREIGN-INVESTED ENTERPRISES

(Promulgated on January 24, 1987)

Article 1 With a view to simplifying procedures for import and export licences and facilitating business for foreign-invested enterprises, these Procedures are formulated in accordance with the Regulations for the Implementation of the Law of the People's Republic of China on Chinese-Foreign Joint Venturers and the Provisions of the State Council for Encouragement of Foreign Investment.

Article 2 For machinery, equipment and other materials for which import licences are required and which a foreign participant has contributed as investment, foreign-invested enterprises shall apply for import licences in accordance with the list of imported equipment and materials approved by relevant authorities. For goods not requiring import licences, Customs clearance shall be based on inspection of enterprise's list of approved imports.

Article 3 For their production of exports, foreign-invested enterprises may import machinery, equipment, vehicle (trucks, vehicles for special use and vans), raw

materials, fuel, parts, assemblies, components and accessories (including those requiring import licences) without
an import licence. Importation shall be supervised by
Customs, and clearance, based on the documents and contract approving the establishment of the enterprise and
the import and export contract. The imported articles
must be for the enterprise's own use in production and
must not be sold or transferred to others. If for some
special reason the imported articles mentioned above or
products made from them are to be sold on the domestic
market, the foreign-invested enterprises must go through
import formalities in accordance with the following Article
4.

Article 4   For sales of products on the domestic
market and for domestic business operations within the
scope of operations stipulated in the approved contract,
foreign-invested enterprises wishing to import for production machinery, equipment, vehicles, raw material, fuel,
parts, assemblies, components and accessories for which
import licences are required may apply directly for import
licences every six months in accordance with a plan approved by relevant authorities. For goods requiring no
import licence, Customs clearance shall be based on inspection of the documents and contract approving the
establishment of the enterprise.

Article 5   To import a reasonable quantity of
articles for a foreign-invested enterprise's own non-produc-
tive use for which import licences are required, the enterprise shall apply for import licences at provincial-level
departments of foreign economic relations and trade.

Article 6   To export products for which export
licences are required, foreign-invested enterprises shall

apply for export licences every six months in accordance with the enterprises' annual export plans.

Article 7 To export products within the scope of their operations for which export licences are not required, foreign-invested enterprises may export them without export licences, and Customs clearance shall be based on inspection of the export contract and other related documents.

Article 8 If in order to ensure a balance of foreign exchange foreign-invested enterprises wish to export products that they themselves have not produced and that require export licences, the enterprises shall apply for export licences in accordance with approved documents. For goods requiring no export licence, Customs clearance shall be based on inspection of the export contract and other related documents.

Article 9 Foreign-invested enterprises shall apply for import and export licences to the relevant authority in charge of issuing licences for various categories of products, as administered and promulgated by the Ministry of Foreign Economic Relations and Trade.

Article 10 These Procedures shall go into effect on the day they are promulgated.

对外经济贸易部关于外商投资企业申领进出口许可证的实施办法

（一九八七年一月二十四日公布）

第一条 为了简化办理进出口许可证手续，便于外商投资企业开展业务，根据《中华人民共和国中外合资经营企业法实施条例》和《国务院关于鼓励外商投资的规定》，特制定本办法。

第二条 外商投资企业外国投资者作为投资而进口的设备和物料，属于实行进口许可证管理的商品，凭批准的该企业的进口设备和物料清单，领取进口许可证；不属于实行进口许可证管理的商品，海关凭原批准该企业的进口设备、物料清单验放。

第三条 外商投资企业为生产出口产品所需进口（包括实行进口许可证管理的）机械设备、生产用车辆（指运输用货车、特种车和客货两用车）、原材料、燃料、散件、零部件、元器件、配套件，免领进口许可证，由海关实行监管，凭批准成立企业的文件、合同或进出口合同验放。

上述进口机械设备、生产用车辆、料、件，只限本企业生产自用，不得在国内转让出售；其进口料、件或用进口料、件所生产的产品，因特殊情况转为内销，应按本办法第四条规定补办进口手续。

第四条　外商投资企业在批准的经营范围内，为生产内销产品和国内经营业务所需进口的机械设备、生产用车辆、原材料、燃料、散件、零部件、元器件、配套件，其中属于实行进口许可证管理的商品，凭确认的企业进口计划，每半年申领一次进口许可证；不属于实行进口许可证管理的商品，海关凭批准成立企业的文件、合同验放。

第五条　外商投资企业进口本企业自用的、数量合理的非生产物品，其中属于实行进口许可证管理的商品，由省级对外经济贸易部门核发进口许可证。

第六条　外商投资企业出口本企业生产的产品，其中属于实行出口许可证管理的商品，凭企业年度出口计划每半年申领一次出口许可证。

第七条　外商投资企业在本企业经营范围内出口本企业生产的、不属于出口许可证管理的商品，海关凭出口合同等有关证件验放。

第八条　外商投资企业经批准为解决外汇收支平衡，出口非本企业生产的产品，凡属于实行出口许可证的商品，凭批准文件申领出口许可证，不属于出口许可证管理的商品，海关凭出口合同等有关证件验放。

第九条　外商投资企业申领进出口许可证，均按对外经济贸易部公布的分级管理发证的品种，分别向有关发证机关申请办理。

第十条　本办法自公布之日起施行。

PROCEDURES OF THE MINISTRY OF FOREIGN ECONOMIC RELATIONS AND TRADE FOR APPROVAL AND ASSESSMENT OF EXPORT-ORIENTED ENTERPRISES AND TECHNO-LOGICALLY ADVANCED ENTERPRISES WITH FOREIGN INVESTMENT

(Promulgated on January 27, 1987)

In accordance with the Provisions of the State Council for Encouragement of Foreign Investment (hereinafter referred to as the Provisions), these Procedures are formulated to approve and assess export-oriented enterprises and technologically advanced enterprises with foreign investment.

Article 1 All Chinese-foreign joint ventures, Chinese-foreign cooperative enterprises and foreign enterprises approved and established within the territory of China in accordance with the law that conform with the export-oriented or technologically advanced enterprises referred to in Article 2 of the Provisions can, after receiving certificates of examination and approval, enjoy the relevant preferential treatment stipulated in the Provisions.

Article 2 A foreign-invested enterprise that meets all three of the following requirements can be acknowledged as an export-oriented enterprise:

(1) The enterprise must produce products for export;

(2) Its products are mainly for export (whether the

enterprise exports its products itself, entrusts some foreign trade company with its products, or uses other means of exportation), and the annual value of products for export accounts for more than 50 percent of the total annual output value of its products;

(3) The enterprise has achieved a balance between revenue and expenditure in operational foreign exchange or has realized a surplus at the end of the year. (The formula for calculation is: The year-end remainder of foreign-exchange income and expenditure equals the previous year's remainder plus the current year's foreign-exchange business income minus the current year's foreign-exchange operational expenditure.)

Article 3   An export-oriented enterprise that meets the requirements specified in Article 2 can enjoy preferential treatment in accordance with Article 8 of the Provisions if the annual value of its products for export is over 70 percent of the total output value of all its products and it has passed the annual review.

Article 4   An enterprise that meets the following requirements can be acknowledged as a technologically advanced enterprise:

The technology, technological process and principal equipment employed by the foreign-invested enterprise are on the list of items for investment encouragement promulgated by the State and are characterized as advanced and applicable; its products are in short supply on the domestic market or are newly developed, or they can replace less-advanced domestic products of the same kind, expand exports, or substitute for imports.

Article 5   An enterprise that is qualified to be both an export-oriented enterprise and a technologically advanced enterprise can choose between the two to enjoy corresponding preferential treatment.

Article 6 The examining and approving agency of export-oriented enterprises and technologically advanced enterprises should be the department of foreign economic relations and trade of the province, autonomous region, municipality directly under the Central Government or city with independent planning where the enterprises are located or the people's government (administrative committee) of a Special Economic Zone. However, export-oriented enterprises and technologically advanced enterprises run by ministries and organizations directly under the State Council shall be examined and approved by the Ministry of Foreign Economic Relations and Trade.

Any foreign-invested enterprise that conforms with Articles 2, 3 and 4 of these Procedures should submit the following documents to the proper examining and approving agency:

(1) A written application for export-oriented or technologically advanced enterprise status;

(2) A copy of the contract and the instrument of ratification;

(3) A project feasibility study report and the instrument of ratification.

Article 7 Within thirty days of the date of receipt of all the documents specified in Article 6 the examining and approving agency shall decide whether or not to approve the enterprise. A technologically advanced enterprise shall be examined and approved jointly with the relevant departments in charge.

Article 8 The form of the written application for an export-oriented enterprise or a technologically advanced enterprise and the certificate of approval shall be prepared by the Ministry of the Foreign Economic Relations and Trade. The certificate of approval shall be signed and sealed by examining and approving agencies at different levels as specified in Article 7; the original shall be kept by the applicant and copies sent to other departments concerned at the same level for the record. The certificate of approval issued by the examining and approving agency and the enterprise's written application must be reported to the Ministry of Foreign Economic Relations and Trade and the State Economic Commission for the record.

Article 9 In accordance with State regulations, a foreign-invested enterprise shall submit its annual export plan and regularly report statistical data on actual exports to the original examining and approving agency, which shall use them as the basis for its assessment of the enterprise.

Article 10 The original examining and approving agency should have the departments concerned make annual checks of export-oriented and technologically advanced enterprises. On the basis of requirement specified and contracts approved in Articles 2, 3 and 4 of these Procedures, the enterprise's export plan, annual report of actual exports, technical index, quality of products and percentage of domestically produced parts in the products shall be checked and assessed.

Article 11 Examining and approving agencies should send lists of the export-oriented and technologically advanced enterprises that have passed the annual check to departments concerned. These enterprises can continue to enjoy preferential treatment in the coming year. Enterprises that fail the year-end assessment should pay the annual taxes from which they were originally exempted in preferential treatment for export-oriented or technologically advanced enterprises.

If an approved export-oriented or technologically advanced enterprise fails the review of its production and business for three successive years, the examining and approving agency shall, jointly with relevant departments in charge, revoke the certificate of approval of the enterprise.

Article 12 The methods to approve and check the foreign-invested enterprises established in the Special Economic Zones of Shenzhen, Zhuhai, Xiamen and Shantou should be worked out by the people's governments (administrative committees) of the zones in accordance with these Procedures and in light of actual conditions and be reported to the Ministry of Foreign Economic Relations and Trade for the record.

Article 13 From the day of issue of these Procedures, approval and assessment of export-oriented and technologically advanced enterprises with foreign investment must be carried out in accordance with these Procedures.

对外经济贸易部关于确认和考核外商投资的产品出口企业和先进技术企业的实施办法

（一九八七年一月二十七日公布）

根据《国务院关于鼓励外商投资的规定》（以下简称《规定》），为确认和考核外商投资的产品出口企业和先进技术企业，特制定本办法。

第一条　在中国境内依法批准设立的中外合资经营企业、中外合作经营企业和外资企业，凡符合《规定》第二条的产品出口企业和先进技术企业，经确认和考核领取证明后，都可享受《规定》中的有关优惠待遇。

第二条　凡同时具备下列三个条件的外商投资企业，可确认为产品出口企业：

一、外商投资企业必须是生产出口产品的企业；

二、产品主要用于出口（包括企业自行出口，委托外贸公司代理出口及其它方式出口），年出口产品的产值达到当年全部产品的产值总额

50％以上；

　　三、当年实现营业外汇收支平衡或有余（计算公式为：年末外汇收支余额＝上年结转余额＋本年实现营业外汇收入－本年营业外汇支出）。

　　第三条　符合第二条规定的产品出口企业，凡当年出口产品的产值达到企业全部产品的产值总额70％以上的，经年度考核合格后，可按《规定》的第八条享受优惠待遇。

　　第四条　凡符合下列条件的，可确认为先进技术企业：

　　外商投资企业采用的技术、工艺和主要设备，属于国家公布的鼓励投资的项目，具有先进性和适用性；是国内短缺的，或其产品是新开发的，或对国内同类产品能更新换代的，能增加出口或替代进口的。

　　第五条　一个企业同时具备产品出口企业和先进技术企业条件的，可择其一享受相应的优惠待遇。

　　第六条　产品出口企业和先进技术企业的审核确认机关是该企业所在的省、自治区、直辖市或计划单列市的对外经济贸易部门或经济特区的人民政府（管理委员会）。但国务院各部门、直属机构举办的产品出口企业和先进技术企业，则统一由对外经济贸易部审核确认。

凡符合本办法第二、三、四条规定的外商投资企业，可分别向上述审核确认机关，提交下列文件，申请审核确认。

一、产品出口企业申请书或先进技术企业申请书；

二、合同副本及批准文件；

三、项目可行性研究报告及批准文件。

第七条　各级审核确认机关收到第六条所列文件后，应在三十天内完成审核事宜，予以确认或不予确认。对于先进技术企业的审核确认，应会同有关主管部门办理。

第八条　《产品出口企业申请书》、《先进技术企业申请书》和确认证书格式，由对外经济贸易部统一制定。确认证书分别由前款各级审核确认机关签署盖章。正本交申请企业留存，副本分送同级有关部门备案。各级审核确认机关出具的确认证书及企业申请书应报对外经济贸易部、国家经济委员会备案。

第九条　外商投资企业应按国家有关规定，自主编制企业年度出口计划，并定期编报出口实绩统计报表，报原审核确认机关，作为考核出口企业的依据。

第十条　对产品出口企业和先进技术企业，原审核确认机关要组织有关部门逐年进行考核。依据本办法第二、三、四条规定的条件和批准的合同，对企业出口计划、年度出口实绩以及技术指标、产品质量、国产化程度等方面检查考核。

第十一条　审核确认机关每年要将考核合格的产品出口企业和先进技术企业的名单汇编成册，通报有关部门。这些企业可继续在新的年度享受各项优惠待遇。如年终考核不合格的企业应补交本年度已享受产品出口企业或先进技术企业优惠待遇而减免的税费。

经确认的产品出口企业和先进技术企业在生产经营中连续三年考核不合格的，原审核确认机关应会同有关主管部门研究吊销产品出口企业和先进技术企业确认证明。

第十二条　深圳、珠海、汕头、厦门经济特区内的外商投资企业的确认考核办法，由经济特区的人民政府（管理委员会）根据本办法，结合经济特区的实际制订，报对外经济贸易部备案。

第十三条　自本办法公布之日起，对外商投资的产品出口企业和先进技术企业的确认和考核，一律照此实施。

PROCEDURES OF THE MINISTRY OF FINANCE FOR IMPLEMENTATION OF THE PREFERENTIAL TAX TREATMENT ARTICLES OF THE PROVISIONS OF THE STATE COUNCIL FOR ENCOURAGEMENT OF FOREIGN INVESTMENT

(January 31, 1987)

These Procedures are formulated to implement the relevant articles concerning preferential tax treatment of the Provisions of the State Council for Encouragement of Foreign Investment (hereinafter referred to as the Provisions).

1. Article 7 of the Provisions ("when foreign investors in export enterprises and technologically advanced enterprises remit abroad profits distributed to them by such enterprises, the amount remitted shall be exempt from income tax") means that when foreign investors remit abroad profit distributed to them by Chinese-foreign jointly operated export enterprises or technologically advanced enterprises for the year 1986 and later years, income tax, 10 percent of the remitted amount, shall be exempted. For profit distributed in advance for the year 1986 and remitted before promulgation of the Provisions, income tax paid for the remitted amount shall be refunded. When foreign partners remit abroad profit distributed to them for years prior to 1986, income tax shall be imposed on remittance in accordance with the original rules.

2. Article 8 of the Provisions ("After expiration of the period for a reduction in or exemption from enterprises income tax in accordance with the provisions of the State, export enterprises in which the value of export products in a particular year amounts to 70 percent or more of the value of their products for the same year may pay enterprise income tax of one half the prevailing tax rate"), shall be applied to export-oriented enterprises with or without a period for exemption from and reduction in enterprise income tax, in accordance with the present tax law and other relevant regulations.

(1) For above-mentioned export enterprises, in condition of that their annual export value makes up 70 percent or more of their total annual output value, after the ratification issued by the examining and approving agency have been checked and approved by the local tax authority, such enterprises can then enjoy preferential treatment of a 50 percent reduction in enterprise income tax, based on the prevailing tax rate.

(2) Export enterprises that received their certificates of approval in 1986 will have their prepaid quarterly enterprise income taxes for 1986 reconciled at the end of the year, with a refund for any overpayment or a supplement for any underpayment.

(3) If income tax rate for the above-mentioned export enterprises, after a 50 percent reduction, is lower than 10 percent, the enterprise shall be subject to enterprise income tax at the rate of 10 percent.

3. Article 9 of the Provisions ("After expiration of the period of reduction in or exemption from enterprise income tax in accordance with the provisions of the State, technologically advanced enterprises may be granted a

three-year extension of the period at one half the prevailing tax rate"), shall be applied to technologically advanced enterprises with or without a period for exemption from or reduction in enterprise income tax, in accordance with the present tax law and relevant rules.

(1) The above-mentioned technologically advanced enterprises whose period for exemption from or reduction in enterprise income tax, in accordance with the present tax law and relevant regulations, has not yet expired shall pay 50 percent of their enterprise income tax in the first three years following expiration of the period. The technologically advanced enterprises whose period for exemption from or reduction in enterprise income tax has already expired or ones that have no such period, shall pay 50 percent of their enterprise income tax the year they are approved as technologically advanced enterprises and the following two years. For those enterprises established after 1986 that do not have a period for exemption from and reduction in enterprise income tax, in accordance with the present tax law and relevant regulations, enterprise income tax shall be imposed at a 50 percent reduction rate in three years from the first profit-making year.

(2) The quarterly enterprise income tax paid in advance by technologically advanced enterprises in 1986 shall be reconciled at the end of the year, with a refund for any overpayment or a supplement for any underpayment.

(3) If the enterprise income tax rate for above-mentioned technologically advanced enterprises, after the 50 percent reduction, is lower than 10 percent, the enterprise shall be subject to enterprise income tax at the rate of 10 percent.

4. Article 10 of the Provisions ("foreign investors who reinvest the profits distributed to them by their enterprises in the establishment or expansion of export enterprises or technologically advanced enterprises in China for a period of operation of not less than five years shall, after application to and approval by the tax authorities, be refunded the total enterprise income tax already paid on the reinvested portion"), applies only to foreign investors who reinvest their share of profit distributed to them by the enterprise, for establishing or extension of export enterprises or technologically advanced enterprises, but the profit must be distributed for the year of 1986 and later years; foreign investors' reinvestment of profit distributed prior to 1986 shall be treated in accordance with the original regulations.

5. A foreign-invested enterprise approved as an export enterprise and a technologically advanced enterprise by the examining and approving agency in the same year shall be allowed to enjoy one or the other of two preferential treatments specified in Articles 8 and 9 of the Provisions, but not both. A technologically advanced enterprise that conforms to Article 8 of the Provisions shall enjoy the preferential treatment specified following expiration of the three-year period for 50 percent reduction in enterprise income tax.

6. A Chinese-foreign venture for cooperative exploration and development of petroleum and precious metal resources shall not be eligible for the preferential taxes cited in the Provisions.

7. In implementing the preferential tax policy specified in the Provisions, all departments and areas must follow these Procedures.

财政部贯彻国务院《关于鼓励外商投资的规定》中税收优惠条款的实施办法

（一九八七年一月三十一日）

为了贯彻执行国务院《关于鼓励外商投资的规定》（以下简称《规定》）中有关的税收优惠条款，特制定本实施办法。

一、关于《规定》第七条"产品出口企业和先进技术企业的外国投资者，将其从企业分得的利润汇出境外时，免缴汇出额的所得税"，是指外国投资者从中外合资经营的产品出口企业和先进技术企业分得的1986年度及以后年度的利润汇出境外时，免征汇出额10%的所得税，对其在《规定》发布之日前汇出的1986年度预分利润，汇出时已缴纳的汇出额的所得税税款，应给予退税。外国合营者将1986年以前年度分得的利润汇出境外时，其汇出额的所得税仍按原规定执行。

二、关于《规定》第八条"产品出口企业按照国家规定减免企业所得税期满后，凡当年企业出

口产品产值达到当年企业产品产值70%以上的,
可以按照现行税率减半缴纳企业所得税",适用
于按照现行税法及有关规定,有减免企业所得税
期限的产品出口企业和没有减免企业所得税期限
的产品出口企业。

(一)上列产品出口企业,凡当年出口产品
产值达到当年企业产品产值70%以上(含70%)
的,须持凭审核确认机关出具的证明文件,经当
地主管税务机关审查确认后,方可享受当年按现
行税率减半缴纳企业所得税的优惠。

(二)对于1986年度被确认为产品出口企
业,其1986年预缴的季度企业所得税税款,可在
办理年度所得税汇算清缴时,多退少补。

(三)上列产品出口企业减半后的企业所得
税税率低于10%的,按10%的税率缴纳企业所
得税。

三、关于《规定》第九条"先进技术企业按照
国家规定减免企业所得税期满后,可以延长三年
减半缴纳企业所得税",适用于按照现行税法及
有关规定,有减免企业所得税期限的先进技术企
业和没有减免企业所得税期限的先进技术企业。

(一)上列先进技术企业,按现行税法及有
关规定减免企业所得税期限未满的,可在该企业

减免企业所得税期满后的第一年至第三年减半缴纳企业所得税；按现行税法及有关规定减免企业所得税期限已满的，或没有减免企业所得税期限的，可从被确认为先进技术企业的当年至第三年减半缴纳企业所得税；对1986年以后新办的，凡是按现行税法及有关规定没有减免企业所得税期限的，可从该企业获利年度起的第一年至第三年减半缴纳企业所得税。

（二）上列先进技术企业1986年预缴的季度企业所得税税款，可在办理年度所得税汇算清缴时，多退少补。

（三）上列先进技术企业减半后的企业所得税税率低于10%的，按10%税率缴纳企业所得税。

四、关于《规定》第十条"外国投资者将其从企业分得的利润，在中国境内再投资举办、扩建产品出口企业或者先进技术企业，经营期不少于五年的，经申请税务机关核准，全部退还其再投资部分已缴纳的企业所得税税款"，是指外国投资者将其从企业分得的利润，在中国境内再投资举办、扩建产品出口企业和先进技术企业时，必须是1986年及其以后年度分得的利润；外国投资者用1986年以前年度的利润再投资的，仍按原规定执行。

　　五、对于一个外商投资企业在同一个年度内经审核确认机关批准其为产品出口企业和先进技术企业时，可允许该企业选择享受《规定》第八、九两条中的任何一条优惠，不能同时享受两种优惠待遇。对于先进技术企业三年减半征收企业所得税期满后，如符合《规定》第八条的，可享受该条的优惠。

　　六、中外合作勘探开发石油、贵重金属资源的企业的税收，不适用《规定》中的税收优惠条款。

　　七、各地区、各部门贯彻执行《规定》中的税收优惠政策，一律以本实施办法为准。

PROVISIONAL RULES GOVERNING THE ISSUE OF FOREIGN-EXCHANGE GUARANTEES BY RESIDENT INSTITUTIONS IN CHINA

(Promulgated by the People's Bank of China on February 20, 1987)

1. These Provisional Rules are formulated to promote foreign economic and technical cooperation, ensure the smooth expansion of financial activities and strengthen the regulation of foreign-exchange guarantees.

2. The foreign exchange guarantee mentioned herein refers to the promise by a guarantor to repay the creditor with his own funds in foreign exchange if a debtor defaults on his contracted debt.

3. The regulators of foreign-exchange guarantees are the State Foreign Exchange Administration and its branch offices (hereinafter referred to as exchange control authorities).

4. The issuance of foreign-exchange guarantees is restricted to the following institutions:

(1) Financial institutions with legal authority to deal in foreign-exchange guarantees;

(2) Nonfinancial enterprises which qualify as legal persons and have foreign-exchange sources.

The cumulative sum total of foreign-exchange guarantees issued by a financial institution and its total foreign liabilities shall not exceed twenty times its foreign-exchange equity funds.

The total amount of foreign exchange guarantees issued by a nonfinancial institution shall not exceed its foreign-exchange equity funds.

5. The scope of foreign-exchange guarantees:

(1) A foreign-exchange guarantee may be provided for a resident enterprise registered according to Chinese law, but the guarantee must not be provided to cover the registered capital of the enterprise.

(2) Foreign-exchange guarantees shall not be provided for Chinese enterprises abroad, unless approved by the exchange control authorities.

(3) Foreign-exchange guarantees shall not be provided for foreign organizations or foreign-invested enterprises, unless they put up foreign-exchange assets of equal value as collateral.

6. The guarantor shall complete the following before issuing a foreign-exchange guarantee:

(1) A feasibility study of the project under guarantee;

(2) A thorough investigation of the credit standing of the debtor;

(3) Adoption of necessary measures for counter-guarantee.

7. In providing a foreign-exchange guarantee the guarantor shall sign written contracts with both the debtor and the creditor, clearly defining the respective rights and obligations of the guarantor, creditor and debtor.

8. The creditor has the right to demand from the guarantor, when deemed necessary, his financial report, statement of foreign-exchange revenue and expenditure and other related documents.

9. The contract between the creditor and debtor,

guaranteed by the guarantor, can be amended only with the consent of the guarantor. Without his consent the guarantor shall automatically be relieved from all his obligations under the guarantee.

10. After a guarantee is provided, the guarantor shall perform his obligations thereunder in case the debtor fails to fulfil his contractual obligations within the term of the contract. The guarantor then has the right to claim reimbursement from the debtor.

11. If the creditor fails to fulfil his contractual obligations after a guarantee is provided, the guarantor shall automatically be relieved of his obligations. The guarantor has the right to claim compensation from the creditor.

12. After a guarantee is issued, the guarantor has the right to supervise the funds and financial conditions of the debtor. The specific method of supervision is to be defined clearly in mutual consultation between the guarantor and the debtor.

13. As required by exposure to actual risks, the guarantor has the right to demand that the debtor put up appropriate collateral and pay guarantee fee.

14. A resident institution must, within ten days of issuance of guarantee, present the guaranteed contract and other related documents to local exchange control authorities for the record.

15. Exchange control authorities shall, depending on the seriousness of the offence, take disciplinary action against institutions and units violating these Provisional Rules in the form of warning, fine and/or revocation of licence to handle foreign-exchange guarantees.

16. The power of interpretation of these Provisional Rules is vested in the State Foreign Exchange Administration.

17. These Provisional Rules shall come into force on the date of promulgation.

境内机构提供外汇担保的
暂行管理办法

（中国人民银行一九八七年二月二十日公布）

一、为了促进对外经济技术合作、保证金融活动顺利开展、加强对外汇担保的管理，特制订本办法。

二、本办法所称外汇担保，系指担保人以自有的外汇资金向债权人承诺，当债务人未按合同规定偿付债务时，由担保人履行偿付义务的保证。

三、外汇担保的管理机关为国家外汇管理局及其分局（以下简称"外汇管理部门"）。

四、可以提供外汇担保的机构仅限于：

（一）法定经营外汇担保业务的金融机构；

（二）有外汇收入来源的非金融性质的企业法人。

金融机构提供的外汇担保总额和其对外债务总额累计不超过自有外汇资金的二十倍。

非金融机构提供的外汇担保总额不得超过其

334

自有的外汇资金。

五、外汇担保的范围是：

（一）可为中国境内的按中国法律登记注册的企业提供担保，但不得对企业注册资本提供担保；

（二）未经国家外汇管理部门批准，不得为中国驻外企业提供外汇担保；

（三）除外国机构或外资企业有等值的外汇资产作抵押外，不得为外国机构或外资企业提供外汇担保。

六、担保人提供担保前，应作好以下工作：

（一）对担保项目的可行性分析研究；

（二）掌握债务人的资信情况；

（三）落实必要的反担保措施。

七、担保人提供外汇担保,应分别与债权人、债务人订立书面合同，订明担保人、债权人、债务人各方面的权利和义务。

八、根据需要，债权人有权要求担保人提供其财务报告和外汇收支情况等有关资料。

九、担保人提供担保后，债权人与债务人如需修改所担保的合同，还须取得担保人的同意。如未经担保人同意修改原合同，担保人的担保义务将自行解除。

十、担保人提供担保后，在其所担保的合同有效期内，一旦债务人未按合同规定履行其义务，担保人应履行担保义务。担保人履行担保义务后，有权向债务人进行追偿。

十一、担保人提供担保后，在担保合同的有效期内，如债权人未按合同履行其义务，担保人的担保义务自行解除。担保人有权要求债权人赔偿相应的损失。

十二、担保人出具担保后，有权对债务人的资金和财务情况进行监督。具体监督方式可由担保人和债务人协商订明。

十三、根据担保的实际风险，担保人有权要求债务人提供相应的抵押物并收取一定的担保费。

十四、境内机构出具担保后，必须在十天内将担保合同等有关资料报当地外汇管理部门备案。

十五、对违反本办法的机构和单位，外汇管理部门将视情节轻重，对其进行警告、罚款、取消经营外汇担保业务的处分。

十六、本办法的解释权属于国家外汇管理局。

十七、本办法自公布之日起实施。

INTERIM PROVISIONS OF STATE ADMINISTRATION FOR INDUSTRY AND COMMERCE CONCERNING THE RATIO BETWEEN THE REGISTERED CAPITAL AND TOTAL INVESTMENT IN CHINESE-FOREIGN JOINT VENTURES

(Promulgated on March 1, 1987)

Article 1 In accordance with the Law of the People's Republic of China on Chinese-Foreign Joint Ventures and Regulations for the Implementation of the Law of the People's Republic of China on Chinese-Foreign Joint Ventures, these Interim Provisions are formulated to determine the ratio between registered capital and total investment in Chinese-foreign joint ventures.

Article 2 The registered capital of a Chinese-foreign joint venture shall be in proportion to its scale and scope of production and business operation. The parties to the joint venture shall share profits and partake risks and losses according to the ratio of their registered capital.

Article 3 The ratio between the registered capital and the total investment in a Chinese-foreign joint venture shall comply with the following regulations:

(1) If a Chinese-foreign joint venture has a total investment of US$ 3 million or less, its registered capital should account for at least seven tenths of the total investment.

(2) If a Chinese-foreign joint venture's total investment is over US$ 3 million and up to US$ 10 million inclu-
sive, its registered capital should make up at least half
the total investment; if the total investment is below
US$ 4.2 million, the registered capital should not be
lower than US$ 2.1 million.

(3) If a Chinese-foreign joint venture's total investment is over US$ 10 million and up to US$ 30 million in-
clusive, its registered capital should account for at least
two fifths of the total investment; if the total investment is
below US$ 12.5 million, the registered capital should not
be lower than US$ 5 million.

(4) If a Chinese-foreign joint venture's total investment exceeds US$ 30 million, its registered capital should
constitute at least one third of the total investment; if the
total investment is below US$ 36 million, the registered
capital should not be less than US$ 12 million.

Article 4   If a Chinese-foreign joint venture, under
special circumstances, cannot meet the above-mentioned
regulations, it has to be approved jointly by the Ministry
of Foreign Economic Relations and Trade and the State
Administration for Industry and Commerce.

Article 5   If a Chinese-foreign joint venture in-
creases its investment, the ratio between the supplemental
registered capital and the increase in investment should
accord with these Interim Provisions.

Article 6   The ratio between registered capital and
total investment in Chinese-foreign cooperative enterprises
shall be determined in accordance with these Interim Provisions.

Article 7   These Interim Provisions also apply for
the determination of ratio between registered capital and

total investment in enterprises invested by Hong Kong, Macao or Taiwan companies, enterprises, other economic entities or individuals.

Article 8   These Interim Provisions shall go into effect from the day of their promulgation.

国家工商行政管理局
关于中外合资经营企业注册资本与
投资总额比例的暂行规定

（一九八七年三月一日公布）

第一条 根据《中华人民共和国中外合资经营企业法》及《中华人民共和国中外合资经营企业法实施条例》，为了明确中外合资经营企业注册资本与投资总额的比例，特制定本规定。

第二条 中外合资经营企业的注册资本，应当与生产经营的规模、范围相适应。合营各方按注册资本的比例分享利润和分担风险及亏损。

第三条 中外合资经营企业的注册资本与投资总额的比例，应当遵守如下规定：

（一）中外合资经营企业的投资总额在300万美元以下（含300万美元）的，其注册资本至少应占投资总额的7/10。

（二）中外合资经营企业的投资总额在300万美元以上至1000万美元（含1000万美元）的，其注册资本至少应占投资总额的1/2，其中投资总额在420万美元以下的，注册资本不得低于210万美元。

（三）中外合资经营企业的投资总额在1000万美元以上至3000万美元（含3000万美元）的，其注册资本至少应占投资总额的2/5，其中投资总额在1250万美元以下的，注册资本不得低于500万美元。

（四）中外合资经营企业的投资总额在3000万美元以上的，其注册资本至少应占投资总额的1/3，其中投资总额在3600万美元以下的，注册资本不得低于1200万美元。

第四条　中外合资经营企业如遇特殊情况，不能执行上述规定，由对外经济贸易部会同国家工商行政管理局批准。

第五条　中外合资经营企业增加投资的，其追加的注册资本与增加的投资额的比例，应按本规定执行。

第六条　中外合作经营企业、外资企业的注册资本与投资总额比例，参照本规定执行。

第七条　香港、澳门及台湾的公司、企业和其他经济组织或者个人投资举办的企业，其注册资本与投资总额的比例适用本规定。

第八条　本规定自公布之日起执行。

BANK OF CHINA REGULATIONS ON PROVIDING LOANS TO FOREIGN-INVESTED ENTERPRISES

(Approved by the State Council on April 7, 1987, and promulgated by the Bank of China on April 24, 1987)

Article 1 These Regulations are formulated with a view to supporting the production and operation of foreign-invested enterprises, expending international economic and technical cooperation, and promoting the development of China's national economy.

Article 2 In line with State policy and under its business principle of safety, benefit and service, the Bank of China grants loans to foreign-invested enterprises to finance their construction and operation, priority being given to those that can generate good economic efficiency with export-oriented products and those that are technologically advanced.

Article 3 Foreign-invested enterprises, which refers to Chinese-foreign joint ventures, Chinese-foreign cooperative enterprises and wholly foreign-owned enterprises registered in China (hereinafter shortened to enterprises), are eligible to apply to the Bank of China for loans provided they meet the conditions specified in Article 7 of these Regulations.

Article 4 In granting loans the Bank of China must sign loan agreements with the borrowing enterprises and strengthen its management of the loans.

Article 5   The Bank of China grants the following kinds of loans to enterprises:

1.   Fixed-assets loan to finance construction, the purchase of technology and equipment and installation in connection with capital construction and technological-transformation projects. It takes the following forms:

(1)   Medium- and short-term loans;

(2)   Buyer's credit;

(3)   Syndicated loan;

(4)   Project financing.

2.   Working-capital loan to meet financial requirement of the enterprises in manufacturing and marketing products and for normal operation.   It takes the following forms:

(1)   Production reserves and revolving funds;

(2)   Temporary credit;

(3)   Overdraft on current account.

3.   Renminbi loan against mortgage, to be handled by the Bank of China according to the Provisional Rules of the Bank of China Governing the Mortgage of Foreign-Invested Enterprises with Foreign Exchange for Renminbi Loans.

4.   Standby credit, to be given by the Bank of China for special purposes after review and approval of the enterprise's application.

Article 6   Loans can be provided in local and foreign currencies.   Local currency refers to Renminbi and foreign currencies to the U.S. dollar, English pound sterling, Japanese yen, Hong Kong dollar, West German mark and other convertible currencies acceptable to the Bank of China.

Article 7   An enterprise is qualified to apply to the Bank of China for a loan provided that:

1. It has obtained a business licence issued by the State industry and commerce administration authorities of the P.R.C. and opened account(s) with the Bank of China;

2. It has fully paid up its registered capital at the specified time, which has been certified according to relevant regulations;

3. It has presented its board of directors' loan resolution and provided for power of attorney;

4. Its capital construction project has been approved by planning authorities;

5. It has the ability to repay the loan and can provide reliable securities for repayment of principal and interest.

Article 8   The term of the loan shall start on the date the loan agreement becomes effective and end on the date specified in the loan agreement, when principal, interest and charges are to be fully repaid.

Article 9   The term of a fixed-assets loan shall not exceed seven years.   However, it can be extended appropriately for some special projects, subject to the approval of the Bank of China and provided such an extension ends one year before expiration of the enterprise's business licence.

Article 10   The term of a working-capital loan shall not exceed twelve months.

Article 11   For Renminbi loans the interest rate for state-owned enterprises regulated by the People's Bank of China shall be applicable.

For foreign-currency loans the interest rate shall be

either the consolidated interest rate set by the Bank of China or the rate agreed upon by lender and borrower in light of international market conditions. In case a foreign buyer's credit or other credit facilities are involved, the interest rate shall be that specified in the related agreement plus a margin.

Article 12 For a Renminbi loan the interest period shall be set and interest calculated according to the regulations of the People's Bank of China. For a foreign-currency loan the same shall accord with relevant provisions of the loan agreement.

Article 13 Loans provided to enterprise by the Bank of China shall undergo the following procedures:

1. The enterprise shall file an application with the Bank of China along with relevant certificates and documents as required;

2. The Bank of China shall review and examine the application, certificates and documents. Upon approval, the Bank of China shall negotiate and sign a loan agreement with the borrower.

Article 14 The enterprise shall use the loan at the time, in the amount and for the purpose stipulated in the loan agreement.

Article 15 In applying for a loan, the enterprise must provide security acceptable to the Bank of China, if so required.

Article 16 The enterprise shall provide the Bank of China with securities in the following forms:

1. Guarantee: The enterprise shall submit to the Bank of China an irrevocable letter of guarantee, issued by a financial institution, enterprise and/or unit with good credit standing and debt-service capability, for repayment

of the principal and interest of the loan.

2.   Mortgage: the enterprise may mortgage its properties, rights and interests to the Bank of China as securities for repayment of the principal and interest of the loan.   The following items are acceptable as collateral:

(1)   House property, machinery and equipment;

(2)   Marketable goods in stock;

(3)   Deposits or certificates of deposit in terms of foreign currencies;

(4)   Negotiable securities and bills;

(5)   Equity shares and other transferable rights and interests.

Article 17   When a loan is made with mortgage on its properties, the enterprise shall sign a mortgage agreement with the Bank of China, to be duly notarized by a Chinese notary public.   Insurance on the full value of the mortgaged properties shall be taken out with the People's Insurance Company of China.

Both a guarantee and a mortgage may be required from the enterprise if the Bank of China deems it necessary.

Article 18   The enterprise must meet its obligations under the loan agreement to repay the principal and pay interest and other relevant monies in good time and full amount.

Article 19   The enterprise's net cash income after tax must be applied first to the repayment of a fixed assets loan.

Article 20   The Bank of China is entitled to resort to the following actions against an enterprise that violates a loan agreement, according to the provisions thereof and depending on the seriousness of the case, in order to protect its own interests:

1. Demand the enterprise rectify the default within a time limit;

2. Suspend disbursement of the loan;

3. Recall the loan before its maturity;

4. Call on the guarantor to meet his obligations.

Article 21 In the event the enterprise fails to repay the principal with interest on a guaranteed loan when due, the guarantor is responsible for full payment of the principal, interest and other relevant monies. In the case of a loan against mortgage, the Bank of China shall be entitled, according to laws and regulations, to have priority in recovering the principal, interest and other monies outstanding by converting collateral in to money or selling it at auction.

Default interest shall be charged on an overdue loan at a rate 20 to 50 percent over the interest rate of the loan agreement as from the due date.

Article 22 The Bank of China has the right to supervise utilization of the loan by the enterprise. Before the loan is fully repaid, the enterprise must periodically submit to the Bank of China reports, statements and other materials on plans for and implementation of construction, production, sales and financial status. If any owner of the enterprise is a separate legal entity, it shall provide annual financial statements to the Bank of China when the bank deems it necessary.

When the Bank of China does its audit, the enterprise must provide correct information and necessary facilities.

Article 23 Before the loan is fully repaid, all operating payments and receipts of the enterprise must be settled through its account(s) maintained with the Bank of China, unless the Bank of China agrees otherwise, and funds must not be transferred to any other bank or financial institution. The Bank of China has the right to require the enterprise to open a retention account if it deems it necessary.

Article 24   The Bank of China shall be notified promptly of any important resolution or decision on financial matters made by the board of directors or the owners of an enterprise and of any personnel change in the board of directors. Any material change, amendment and/or supplement to a joint-venture or cooperative contract as well as to the articles of association of the enterprise must be submitted in advance to the Bank of China for comment if the bank's interests may be affected thereby.

Article 25   Unless the Bank of China agrees otherwise, Chinese shall be the prevailing language used in the loan agreement, its appendices and other legal documents related thereto, and the governing law shall be the law of the People's Republic of China.

Article 26   The detailed rules for implementation of these Regulations shall be formulated by the head office of the Bank of China. Branches of the Bank of China located in Special Economic Zones may devise and execute detailed rules of their own, depending on actual business conditions and subject to the approval of the head office.

Article 27   These Regulations shall become effective on the date of promulgation, and the previous Interim Procedures for the Handling of Loans by the Bank of China to Chinese-Foreign Joint Ventures, approved by the State Council and promulgated by the Bank of China on March 13, 1981, shall be nullified at the same time.

Loan agreements signed between the Bank of China and enterprises before promulgation of these Regulations shall follow their original provisions.

中国银行对外商投资企业贷款办法

（一九八七年四月七日国务院批准，
一九八七年四月二十四日中国银行公布）

第一条 为支持外商投资企业的生产经营活动，扩大对外经济技术合作，有利于促进国民经济的发展，特制定本办法。

第二条 中国银行按照国家政策，本着安全、有利、服务的原则，对外商投资企业的建设工程及生产经营所需的资金提供贷款，优先支持经济效益好的产品出口企业和先进技术企业。

第三条 外商投资企业，即中外合资经营企业、中外合作经营企业和外资企业（以下简称企业），凡符合本办法第七条规定的贷款条件的，均可向中国银行申请贷款。

第四条 中国银行办理贷款，必须与借款企业签订借款合同，并加强贷款管理。

第五条 中国银行对企业办理下列贷款：

一、固定资产贷款。用于基本建设项目和技术改造项目的工程建设费，技术、设备购置费及安装费。贷款方式分为：

（一）中短期贷款；

（二）买方信贷；

（三）银团贷款；

（四）项目贷款。

二、流动资金贷款。用于企业在商品生产、商品流通及正常经营活动过程中所需的资金。贷款方式分为：

（一）生产储备及营运贷款；

（二）临时贷款；

（三）活存透支。

三、现汇抵押贷款。中国银行按中国人民银行《关于外商投资企业外汇抵押人民币贷款的暂行办法》的规定办理。

四、备用贷款。根据企业申请的特定用途，经中国银行审查同意安排待使用的贷款。

第六条　贷款货币分为本币和外币两类。本币即人民币；外币包括美元、英镑、日元、港币、联邦德国马克以及中国银行同意的其他可兑换货币。

第七条　外商投资企业申请贷款应当具备以下条件：

一、企业取得中国工商行政管理机关发给的

营业执照，并在中国银行开立帐户。

二、企业注册资本按期如数缴纳，并经依法验资。

三、企业董事会作出借款的决议和出具授权书。

四、企业固定资产投资项目，已由计划部门批准。

五、企业有偿还贷款能力，并提供可靠的还款、付息保证。

第八条　贷款期限的计算，自借款合同生效之日起，至合同规定的还清全部本息和费用之日止。

第九条　固定资产贷款期限，不超过7年，个别特殊项目经中国银行同意，可适当延长，但不得超过企业营业执照限定的经营期结束前一年。

第十条　流动资金贷款期限，不超过12个月。

第十一条　人民币贷款利率按中国人民银行规定的国营企业贷款利率执行。

外币贷款利率，按中国银行总行制定的综合利率执行；也可以由借贷双方根据国际市场利率协商确定。使用外国买方信贷和其他信贷的利率，以其协议利率为基础加一定利差确定利率。

第十二条　人民币贷款按中国人民银行规定的计息期和计息办法执行；外币贷款按借款合同规定的计息期和计息办法执行。

第十三条　企业向中国银行申请贷款，按以下程序办理：

一、企业提出借款申请书，并根据所需借款的具体情况提供相应的证明和资料；

二、中国银行对企业的借款申请书及提供的证明和资料进行审查评估，经审核同意后，借贷双方协商签订借款合同。

第十四条　企业应当按照借款合同规定的时间、金额和用途使用贷款。

第十五条　企业向中国银行申请贷款，中国银行认为需要担保的，必须提供经中国银行认可的担保。

第十六条　企业向中国银行提供以下担保：

一、信用担保。企业向中国银行提供由资信可靠、有偿付债务能力的金融机构、企业及其他单位出具的保证偿付贷款本息的不可撤销的保函。

二、抵押担保。由企业将其财产和权益抵押给银行，做为偿付中国银行贷款本息的保证。下列各项可以抵押：

（一）房产、机器设备；

（二）库存的适销商品；

（三）外币存款或者存单；

（四）可变现的有价证券及票据；

（五）股权及其他可转让的权益。

第十七条　抵押担保贷款，企业须与中国银行签署抵押文件。抵押文件须经中国公证机关公证。抵押物须向中国人民保险公司投足额保险。

中国银行认为必要时，企业应当提供信用加抵押担保。

第十八条　企业须按照借款合同的规定按期如数偿还贷款，支付利息和费用。

第十九条　企业在纳税之后的净现金收入，应当首先偿还固定资产贷款。

第二十条　对不遵守借款合同规定的企业，中国银行有权根据借款合同，视违约情节，采取以下措施以维护权益：

一、限期纠正违约事件；

二、停止发放贷款；

三、提前收回贷款；

四、通知担保人履行担保责任。

第二十一条　企业如未按期归还贷款本金和

支付利息，信用担保货款，由担保企业（单位）负责偿还所欠贷款本息和费用；抵押担保贷款，中国银行依据法律规定有权以抵押物折价或者以变卖抵押品的价款，优先得到偿付贷款的本息及其他欠款。

企业逾期未还的贷款，中国银行从逾期之日起加收20％至50％的罚息。

第二十二条　中国银行有权对企业使用贷款的情况进行检查。在还清贷款之前，企业应当向中国银行定期报送有关工程建设进度和生产、销售、财务等各项计划以及执行情况的报表、资料。企业业主为另一法人的，中国银行认为必要时，业主的年度财务报表，应当报送中国银行。

中国银行进行信贷检查时，企业应当如实反映情况并提供工作便利。

第二十三条　企业在还清贷款前，经营中的资金往来，除中国银行同意者外，均须通过在中国银行开立的帐户办理，不得擅自将资金转移到其他银行或者金融机构。中国银行认为必要时，有权要求企业开立"保管帐户"。

第二十四条　企业董事会或者业主有关财务方面的重大决议或者决定以及董事会的人事变动等，应当及时通知中国银行；企业的合营合同和合作合同及企业章程的重大修改和补充，如影响到中国银行债权时，应当事先征求中国银行的意见。

第二十五条　除中国银行同意者外，企业与中国银行签订的借款合同及附件等法律文件的有效文字为中文，适用法律为中华人民共和国法律。

第二十六条　本办法的实施细则，由中国银行总行制定。经济特区内的中国银行，可根据其业务的具体情况，拟定细则，报中国银行总行批准后执行。

第二十七条　本办法自公布之日起施行。1981年3月13日国务院批准、中国银行公布的《中国银行办理中外合资经营企业贷款暂行办法》同时废止。

本办法施行以前中国银行与企业签订的借款合同，仍按原订条款执行。

APPENDICES

附　录

ENGLISH-CHINESE GLOSSARY

英汉词汇对照表

A

Accelerated depreciation　加速折旧

Accessories　配套件

Account books　会计帐簿

Accountant　　会计师

Adjudication　裁决

Adjustments　调剂

Administration for Industry and Commerce　工商行政管理局

Administrative regulations　　行政法规

Agent　代理人

Agreement　协议

Airborne vehicles　航空器

Alter　涂改

Amend　修改

Annual　年度

Annual financial statements 年度财务报表

Applicant　申请人

Application form　申请表

Appointment to a post 任命

Approve 批准

Arabic numerals　阿拉伯数字

Arbitrate by default　缺席仲裁

Arbitration 仲裁

Arbitration body　仲裁机构

Article of association　章程／组织章程

Assemblies 散件

Assignable　可转让

Assignment of contract 转让合同

Attorney's office　律师事务所

Authorities in charge of examination and approval　审查
    批准机关

Autonomy　由主权

B

Baggage　行李

Bank of China　中国银行

Bill of lading 提单

Bills　票据

Branches　分支机构

Breach of contract　违约

Breach-of-contract damages　违约金

Brokerage fees　佣金

Budget　预算

Business information　商情资料

Business licence　营业执照

Business office　营业所

Business permit　营业执照

Buyer　买方

Buyer's credit　买方贷款

C

Called-up capital　实收资本

Cancel　注销

Capital goods　生产资料

Cash　现金

Certificate　证书

Certificate of vaccination　预防接种证书

Chemical formula　化学式

China Council for the Promotion of International Trade
中国国际贸易促进委员会

Chinese-foreign cooperative enterprises　中外合作经营企业

Chinese-foreign cooperative exploration and development

of natural resources 中外合作勘探自然资源

Chinese-foreign joint bank 中外合资银行

Chinese-foreign joint ventures 中外合资经营企业

Citizen 公民

City open to the outside 开放城市

Coerce 强迫

Collateral 担保

Commissions 回扣／佣金

Commodity 商品

Commodity inspection 商品检验

Compensation 赔偿

Components 原器件

Compulsory licensing 强制许可

Conceal 隐瞒

Confiscate 没收

Confiscation of property 没收财产

Consign 托运

Consignee 收货人

Consignor 发货人

Consolidated Industrial and Commercial Tax 工商统一
  税

Consolidated interest rate 综合利率

Consult 咨询

Conveyances 交通工具

Contract 合同

Cost of parts and materials 料件费

Cost of reparation 修理费

Counterguarantee 反担保

Credit standing 资信情况

Creditor 债权人

Criminal law 刑法

Criminal responsibility 刑事责任

Current account 活期存款

Customs 海关

(Customs) clearance 放行

Customs Law 海关法

C.I.F. 到岸价格

D

Debtor 债务人

Debt-service capability 偿还能力

Deceive 欺骗

Declare 申报

Dependent (patent) claim 从属权利要求

Deposit reserve funds 存款储备金

Deposits 存款

Depreciation 折旧

Design 设计

Detail 细节

Difference 差额

Disciplinary penalties　行政处罚

Disciplinary sanctions　行政处分

Discounting of bills 票据贴现

Discuss and appraise　评议

Dismissal　解雇

Dock　码头

Documentary bills　押汇

Domicile 住所

Drawings　图纸

Dutiable value 完税价格

Duty free　免税

Duty-pending goods 保税货物

E

Efficiency　效率

Employ　雇佣

Energy consumption 能源消耗

Energy development　能源开发

Enter a bid　投标

Enterprise with foreign investment/foreign-invested enterprise　外资企业

Enterprises with overseas Chinese investments 侨资企业

Environmental protection 环境保护

Equipment　设备

Equivalent academic level 同等学历

Evasion of foreign exchange control   逃汇

Examination as to substance   实质审查

Examine   考核／审查

Examine and approve   核准／审批

Exemption from taxes   免税

Exploitation   开采

Exploration   勘探

Export   出口

Export license   出口许可证

Export-oriented enterprise/export enterprise   产品出口企业

Extension   宽展期／延长

F

Feasibility   可行性

Fees   费用

File an objection   提出异议

File suit   起诉

Finance   金融／财政

Financial authorities   财政机关

Financial institution   金融机构

Financial statements   财务报表

Fiscal reports and statements   会计报表

Fixed assets   固定资产

Forbid   禁止

Force majeure   不可抗力事件

Foreign bank   外资银行

Foreign enterprise   外商投资企业

Foreign exchange   外汇

Foreign exchange equivalent   等值外汇

Foreign exchange control   外汇管理

Foreign-exchange assets   外汇资产

Foreign-owned enterprise 外商投资企业

Forge 伪造

Frontier ports   国际口岸

F.O.B. 离岸价格

G

General Administration of Customs   海关总署

General tariff rates   普通税率

Goods 货物

Guarantee   担保／信用担保

Guarantor   担保人

Guaranty   担保

Guesthouse 宾馆

Guide lines   方针

H

Habitual residence 经常居所

Handling fee 手续费

Health certificate 健康证明
Health declaration form 健康申明卡
Hotel 饭店

I

Illegal procurement of foreign exchange 套汇
Import 进口
Import license 进口许可证
Import of technology 技术引进
In accordance with 按照
In time 按时
Incidental charges 附带费用
Income tax 所得税
Independent accounting 独立核算
Independent (patent) claim 独立权利要求
Individual income tax 个人所得税
Industrial design 外观设计
Industrial property rights 工业产权
Industry and commerce administration authorities 工商
    行政管理机关
Infectious disease 传染病
Infringe 侵犯
Inspect 检验
Install 安装
Insurance 保险

Insurance company 保险公司
Insurance coverage 保险范围
Interest 利息
Interest period 计息期
Interest rate 利率
Interim 暂行
International practice 国际惯例
International treaty 国际条约
Invalid 无效
Invalidation 宣告无效
Inventor 发明人
Invent/invention 发明
Investigate 调查
Investment 投资
Investor 投资者
Invoice 发票
Irrevocable 不可撤销

J

Jointly assess 评议
Judicial authorities 司法机关

L

Labour insurance 劳动保险
Labour management 劳动管理

Labour protection　劳动保护

Law　法律

Lawful rights and interests　合法权益

Laws and regulations　法规

Lawyer's office　律师事务所

Lease　租赁

Legal liability　法律责任

Legal person　法人

Legal representative　法定代表人

Legislation　立法

Letter of confirmation　确认书

Letter of guarantee　保函

Liability guaranty　责任担保书

Liability to pay compensation　赔偿责任

License　执照

License plate　牌照

License　许可证

Liquidate　清算

Loan　贷款／放款

Losses　亏损

Luggage　行李

M

Managerial personnel　经营管理人员

Mandatory enforcement　强制执行

Market 市场

Market price 市场价格

Mathematical formula 数学式

Measures/methods/procedures 办法

Meditate 调解

Method of payment 支付方式

Minerals 矿产

Minimum tariff rates 最低税率

Ministry of Finance 财政部

Ministry of Foreign Economic Relations and Trade
对外经济贸易部

Ministry of Justice 司法部

Misuse 冒用

Modification of contract 变更合同

Mortgage 抵押／抵押担保

N

Negotiable 可变现的

Negotiable securities 有价证券

Negotiation 洽谈

Notary 公证

Notary office 公证处

O

Objection 异议

Objective of a contract   合同标的
Operating capital 营运资金
Original cost 原价
Overdraft   透支
Overseas Chinese enterprise 侨资企业
Ownership by the whole people 全民所有

P

Partial   局部
Parts 零部件
Passport 护照
Patent   专利
Patent administration office   专利管理机关
Patent agent 专利代理人
Patent certificate   专利证书
Patent Office 专利局
Patent relating to national security   保密专利
Patent Re-examination Board   专利复审委员会
Patent right   专利权
Patentee   专利权人
Pay for the losses 赔偿损款
Paying tax 纳税
Payment   缴纳
Penalize/penalty 处罚
People's Bank of China 中国人民银行

People's court 人民法院

People's procuratorate 人民检查院

Perform 履行

Permit 许可证

Personal postal matter 个人邮递物品

Personnel 人员

Personnel department 人事部门

Pilot 引航员

Plagiarize 剽窃

Plaintiff 申诉人

Policy 政策

Port 港口／口岸

Postal matter 邮递物品

Postal parcel 邮包

Power of attorney 委托书

Practise fraud 弄虚做假

Preceding claim 在前权利要求

Preferential treatment 优惠待遇

Prescribed form 规定格式

Principal and interest 本息

Principles 原则

Procedure 程序

Production 生产

Production reserves 生产储备

Profit rate 利润率

Profiteering 投机倒把

Project financing 项目贷款

Provisional 暂行

Public interest 社会公共利益

Q

Qualification of a legal person 法人资格

Quarantine 检疫

R

Raw materials 原料

Record of assets and liabilities 资产负债表

Reduction of taxes 减税

Refund 退还

Register 登记

Registered capital 注册资本

Register with/for the record 备案

Registration form 登记表

Regulations on Customs Duties for Imports and Exports
海关进出口税则

Reimport 复运进口

Reinvest 再投资

Remuneration 报酬

Renminbi (RMB) 人民币

Rental 租金

Representative office 代表机构

Rescission of contract 解除合同

Rescission 解除

Reserve funds 储备金

Residence card 居住证

Residence certificate 居留证件

Resident representative agencies   常驻代表机构

Reveal 泄露

Revoke 撤销

Revolving funds 营运资金

Reward 奖励

Re-examination 复审

Right of priority 优先权

Rights and interests 权益

Rules and regulations 规章制度

S

Safety 安全

Safety in production   安全生产

Sale on the domestic market 内销

Securities 证券

Seller 卖方

Semi-finished materials   材料

Service charges   手续费

Settling bank   结算银行

Shares 股票

Shipper 发货人

Smuggling 走私

Sophisticated products 尖端产品

Special Economic Zone 经济特区

Special preferential treatment 特别优惠待遇

Speculate 投机倒把

Standby credit 备用贷款

State Administrative for Industry and Commerce 国家工商管理局

State Economic Commission 国家经济委员会

State Foreign Exchange Administration (SFEA) 国家外汇管理局

State Planning Commission 国家计划委员会

State-owned enterprise 国营企业

Supervision 监督

Surcharge for delayed payment 滞纳金

Syndicated loan 银行贷款

T

Tariff Regulations Commission 关税税则委员会

Tariff Regulations on Imports and Exports 进出口关税条例

Tariff/customs duty 关税

Tax authorities 税务机关

Tax payer 纳税人

Tax rate 税率

Tax Rates of Consolidated Industrial and Commercial Tax 工商统一税税目表

Technical contents 技术内容

Technical features 技术特征

Technological data 技术资料

Technological field 技术领域

Technological norms 技术规范

Technological process 工艺流程

Technological service 技术服务

Technologically advanced enterprise 技术先进企业

Term of a loan 贷款期限

Termination of contract 终止合同

Terms of contract 合同条款

Time limit 期限

Total investment 降资总额

Trade 贸易

Trade fair 交易会

Trade method 贸易方式

Trade union 工会

Trademark 商标

Transaction price 成交价格

Transfer 转让

Transportation 运输

Transportation vehicles 运输车辆

Travel permit   旅行许可证
Treaty   条约

U

Utility model   实用新型

V

Visa   签证
Void   无效

W

Welfare benefits   福利
Withdraw   撤回
Witness   证人
Workers and staff   职工
Working capital   流动资金
Written authorization   授权书
Written contract   书面合同

汉英词汇对照表

CHINESE-ENGLISH GLOSSARY

（按首字汉语拼音次序排列）

A

阿拉伯数字　Arabic numerals

安装　install

安全生产　safety in production

按时　in time

按照　in accordance with

安全　safety

B

保险　insurance

保密专利　patent relating to national security

保险公司　insurance company

保险范围　insurance coverage

保税货物　duty-pending goods

保函　letter of guarantee

报酬　remuneration

办法　measures/methods/procedures

备案 register with/for the record

备用贷款 standby credit

本息 principal and interest

变更合同 modification of contract

票据贴现 discounting of bills

宾馆 guesthouse

不可撤销 irrevocable

不可抗力事件 force majeure

C

财政机关 financial authorities

财务报表 financial statements

财政部 Ministry of Finance

材料 semi-finished materials

裁决 adjudication

差额 difference

产品出口企业 export-oriented enterprise/export enterprise

偿还能力 debt-service capability

常驻代表机构 resident representative agencies

撤回 withdraw

撤销 revoke

程序 procedure

成交价格 transaction price

储备金 reserve funds

出口　export

出口许可证　export licence

处罚　penalize/penalty

传染病　infectious disease

从属权利要求　dependent (patent) claim

存款　deposits

存款储备金　deposit reserve funds

D

贷款　loan

贷款期限　term of a loan

代表机构　representative office

代理人　agent

担保　guaranty/collateral/guarantee

担保人　guarantor

到岸价格　C.I.F.

等值外汇　foreign exchange equivalent

登记　register

登记表　registration form

抵押　mortgage

调查　investigate

抵押担保　mortgage

独立权利要求　independent (patent) claim

独立核算　independent accounting

对外经济贸易部　Ministry of Foreign Economic Relations and Trade

F

发货人　consigner/shipper
法律责任　legal liability
发明　invent/invention
发明人　inventor
法定代表人　legal representative
法规　laws and regulations
法律　law
法人　legal person
法人资格　qualification of a legal person
发票　invoice
饭店　hotel
反担保　counterguarantee
放行　(customs) clearance
放款　loans
方针　guide lines
费用　fees
分支机构　branches
复审　re-examination
附带费用　incidental charges
福利　welfare benefits
复运进口　reimport

G

港口　port

个人所得税　individual income tax

个人邮递物品　personal postal matter

工艺流程　technological process

工业产权　industrial property rights

工商行政管理局　Administration for Industry and Commerce

工商统一税　Consolidated Industrial and Commercial Tax

工商统一税税目表　Tax Rates of Consolidated Industrial and Commercial Tax

工会　trade union

工商行政管理机关　industry and commerce administration authorities

公民　citizen

公证　notary

公证处　notary office

股票　shares

固定资产　fixed assets

雇佣　employ

关税税则委员会　Tariff Regulations Commission

关税　tariff/customs duty

规章制度　rules and regulations

规定格式　prescribed form

国际惯例   international practice
国际条约   international treaty
国家外汇管理局 State Foreign Exchange Administration (SFEA)
国家经济委员会   State Economic Commission
国际口岸   frontier ports
国家工商管理局   State Administration for Industry and Commerce
国家计划委员会   State Planning Commission
国营企业   state-owned enterprise

H

海关   Customs
海关总署   General Administration of Customs
海关法   Customs Law
海关进出口税则 Regulations on Customs Duties for Imports and Exports
航空器   airborne vehicles
合法权益   lawful rights and interests
合同   contract
合同标的   objective of a contract
合同条款   terms of contract
核准   examine and approve
护照   passport
化学式   chemical formula

环境保护　environmental protection

回扣　commissions

货物　goods

活期存款　current account

J

技术引进　import of technolgy

技术内容　technical contents

技术服务　technological service

技术特征　technical features

技术资料　technological data

技术规范　technological norms

技术领域　technological field

技术先进企业　technologically advanced enterprise

计息期　interest period

加速折旧　accelerated depreciation

健康申明卡　health declaration form

健康证明　health certificate

减税　reduction of taxes

检验　inspect

尖端产品　sophisticated products

监督　supervision

检疫　quarantine

奖励　reward

交易会　trade fair

交通工具　conveyances

缴纳　payment

解除　rescission

解除合同　rescission of contract

解雇　dismissal

结算银行　settling bank

进出口关税条例　Tariff Regulations on Imports and Exports

金融／财政　finance

金融结构　financial institution

进口　import

进口许可证　import licence

禁止　forbid

经营管理人员　managerial personnel

经济特区　Special Economic Zone

经常居所　habitual residence

居住证　residence card

局部　partial

居留证件　residence certificate

K

开采　exploitation

开放城市　city open to the outside

勘探　exploration

考核　examine

可转让　assignable

可行性　feasibility

可变现的　negotiable

口岸　port

会计师　accountant

会计帐簿　account books

会计报表　fiscal reports and statements

宽展期　extension

矿产　minerals

亏损　losses

L

劳动保护　labour protection

劳动保险　labour insurance

劳动管理　labour management

利率　interest rate

利润率　profit rate

利息　interest

离岸价格　F.O.B.

立法　legislation

料件费　cost of parts and materials

零部件　parts

流动资金　working capital

律师事务所　lawyer's office/attorney's office

旅行许可证　travel permit

履行 perform

M

码头 dock
买方 buyer
买方贷款 buyer's credit
卖方 seller
冒用 misuse
贸易 trade
贸易方式 trade method
免税 duty free/exemption from taxes
没收 confiscate
没收财产 confiscation of property

N

纳税 paying tax
纳税人 tax payer
内销 sale on the domestic market
年度 annual
年度财务报表 annual financial statements
弄虚作假 practise fraud
能源开发 energy development
能源消耗 energy consumption

P

牌照 licence plate

赔偿　compensation

赔偿责任　liability to pay compensation

配套件　accessories

赔偿损款　pay for the losses

批准　approve

票据　bills

剽窃　plagiarize

评议　jointly assess/discuss and appraise

普通税率　general tariff rates

Q

起诉　file suit

欺骗　deceive

期限　time limit

洽谈　negotiation

签证　visa

强制许可　compulsory licensing

强制执行　mandatory enforcement

强迫　coerce

侨资企业　enterprise with overseas Chinese investments/overseas Chinese enterprises

侵犯　infringe

清算　liquidate

全民所有　ownership by the whole people

权益　rights and interests

确认书　letter of confirmation
缺席仲裁　arbitrate by default

R

人民币　Renminbi (RMB)
人民法院　people's court
人民检察院　people's procuratorate
人员　personnel
人事部门　personnel department
任命　appointment to a post

S

散件　assemblies
商标　trademark
商品　commodity
商品检验　commodity inspection
商情资料　business information
社会公共利益　public interest
设备　equipment
设计　design
申请人　applicant
申报　declare
申请表　application form
申诉人　plaintiff
审查　examine

审查批准机关　authorities in charge of examination and approval

审批　examine and approve

生产　production

生产储备　production reserves

生产资料　capital goods

实用新型　utility model

实质审查　examination as to substance

实收资本　called-up capital

市场　market

市场价格　market price

授权书　written authorization

收货人　consignee

手续费　service charges/handling fee

书面合同　written contract

数学式　mathematical formula

税务机关　tax authorities

税率　tax rate

所得税　income tax

司法机关　judicial authorities

司法部　Ministry of Justice

T

套汇　illegal procurement of foreign exchange

逃汇　evasion of foreign exchange control

特别优惠待遇　special preferential treatment

提单　bill of lading

提出异议　file an objection

调解　meditate

调剂　adjustments

条约　treaty

统一工商税　consolidated industrial and commercial tax

同等学历　equivalent academic level

透支　overdraft

投标　enter a bid

投资　investment

投资总额　total investment

投机倒把　speculate/profiteering

投资者　investor

涂改　alter

图纸　drawings

退还　refund

托运　consign

W

外观设计　industrial design

外汇　foreign exchange

外汇管理　foreign exchange control

外商投资企业　enterprise with foreign investment/
　　foreign invested enterprise

外资银行　foreign bank

外汇资产　foreign-exchange assets

外资企业　foreign enterprise/foreign-owned enterprise

完税价格　dutiable value

委托书　power of attorny

违反合同　breach of contract

违约　breach of contract

违约金　breach-of-contract damages

伪造　forge

无效　void/invalid

X

细节　detail

现金　cash

效率　efficiency

项目贷款　project financing

协议　agreement

泄露　reveal

信用担保　guarantee

行政法规　administrative regulations

刑事责任　criminal responsibility

行李　luggage/baggage

行政处分　disciplinary sanctions

行政处罚　disciplinary penalities

刑法　criminal law

修改　amend
修理费　cost of reparation
许可证　licence/permit
宣告无效　invalidation

Y

押汇　documentary bills
延长　extension
异议　objection
引航员　pilot
银团贷款　syndicated loan
隐瞒　conceal
营业所　business office
营业执照　business permit/business licence
营运资金　operating capital/revolving funds
佣金　brokerage fees/commission
优先权　right of priority
有价证券　negotiable securities
优惠待遇　preferential treatment
邮包　postal parcel
有价证券　securities
邮递物品　postal matter
预防接种证书　certificate of vaccination
预算　budget
原价　original cost

原则　principles

原料　raw materials

原器件　components

运输　transportation

运输车辆　transportation vehicles

Z

在前权利要求　preceding claim

再投资　reinvest

责任担保书　liability guaranty

资产负债表　record of assets and liabilities

自主权　autonomy

资信情况　credit standing

咨询　consult

债权人　creditor

债务人　debtor

暂行　interim/provisional

章程　articles of associations

折旧　depreciation

证券　securities

证书　certificate

证人　witness

政策　policy

职工　workers and staff

支付方式　method of payment

执照　licence

滞纳金　surcharge for delayed payment

中外合资经营企业　Chinese-foreign joint ventures

中外合作经营企业　Chinese-foreign cooperative enterprises

中外合作勘探自然资源　Chinese-foreign cooperative exploration and development of natural resources

终止合同　termination of contract

中国国际贸易促进委员会　China Council for the
Promotion of International Trade

仲裁　arbitration

仲裁机构　arbitration body

中外合资银行　Chinese-foreign joint bank

中国银行　Bank of China

中国人民银行　People's Bank of China

住所　domicile

注册资本　registered capital

注销　cancel

专利　patent

专利代理人　patent agent

专利管理机关　patent administration office

专利证书　patent certificate

专利局　Patent Office

专利复审委员会　Patent Re-examination Board

专利权　patent right

专利权人　patentee

转让合同　assignment of contract

转让　transfer

综合利率　consolidated interest rate

走私　smuggling

组织章程　articles of association

租金　rental

租赁　lease

最低税率　minimum tariff rates

中国对外经济法规汇编

第四辑

*

外文出版社出版

（中国北京百万庄路24号）

邮政编码100037

北京外文印刷厂印刷

中国国际图书贸易总公司发行

（中国北京车公庄西路21号）

北京邮政信箱第399号　　邮政编码100044

1991年（34开）第一版

（英汉）

ISBN 7-119-01263-0/D·72（外）

01620

6—EC—2511P

2442⌀076